'This volume brings together some of the most significant work on the diverse victimization experiences of queer people by leading researchers in the field. It is an essential resource for academics and students; practitioners, advocates, and policy makers; legal, social service, and health care professionals; and anyone who wishes to understand victimology through an intersectional lens.'

Claire M. Renzetti, *Judi Conway Patton Endowed Chair*
for Studies of Violence Against Women and
Professor of Sociology, University of Kentucky

Queer Victimology

This book provides a much-needed focus on the victimization experiences of those within the lesbian, gay, bisexual, transgender, Queer, intersex, or asexual (LGBTQIA) communities. With original research and scholarly work relating to victimization, supplemented by stories and poems detailing firsthand accounts by people in LGBTQIA communities, the volume editors shine a light on the experiences of those who have been harmed or who have suffered because of who they are.

Allowing the reader to gain a deeper understanding of Queer victimization and LGBTQIA victims, the volume delves into how and why people are victimized, as well as how the criminal justice system and other social services interact with victims and each other. The creative pieces included give a direct voice to those who have most often been silenced in the past.

Queer Victimology is essential reading for scholars and students in the areas of criminology, victimology, sociology, gender studies, education, counseling, and/or psychology as well as anyone engaged with Queer, critical, and feminist criminologies, gender studies, diversity, and criminal justice.

Shelly Clevenger is Chair of the new Department of Victim Studies at Sam Houston State University. She received her Ph.D., M.A., and B.A. in Criminology from Indiana University of Pennsylvania.

Shamika Kelley is a forensic DNA expert who provides reports, technical reviews, and expert testimony in criminal cases, and implements a structured research agenda focusing on the needs of crime victims and criminal justice stakeholders to enhance victim support and case processing.

Kathleen Ratajczak is an assistant professor in the Department of Victim Studies at Sam Houston State University.

Queer Victimology

Understanding the Victim Experience

Edited by Shelly Clevenger,
Shamika Kelley and Kathleen Ratajczak

Routledge
Taylor & Francis Group

NEW YORK AND LONDON

Designed cover image: © Getty Images/arvitalya

First published 2024
by Routledge
605 Third Avenue, New York, NY 10158

and by Routledge
4 Park Square, Milton Park, Abingdon, Oxon, OX14 4RN

Routledge is an imprint of the Taylor & Francis Group, an informa business

© 2024 selection and editorial matter, Shelly Clevenger, Shamika Kelley and Kathleen Ratajczak; individual chapters, the contributors

The right of Shelly Clevenger, Shamika Kelley and Kathleen Ratajczak to be identified as the authors of the editorial material, and of the authors for their individual chapters, has been asserted in accordance with sections 77 and 78 of the Copyright, Designs and Patents Act 1988.

Library of Congress Cataloging-in-Publication Data
Names: Clevenger, Shelly, editor. | Kelley, Shamika, editor. | Ratajczak, Kathleen, editor.
Title: Queer victimology : understanding the victim experience / edited by Shelly Clevenger, Shamika Kelley and Kathleen Ratajczak.
Description: New York, NY : Routledge, 2024. | Includes bibliographical references and index. | Summary: "This book provides a much-needed focus on the victimization experiences of those within the lesbian, gay, bisexual, transgender, queer, intersex, or asexual (LGBTQIA) communities. With original research and scholarly work relating to victimization, supplemented by stories and poems detailing first-hand accounts by people in LGBTQIA communities, the volume editors shine a light on the experiences of those who have been harmed or who have suffered because of who they are. Allowing the reader to gain a deeper understanding of queer victimization and LGBTQIA victims, the volume delves into how and why people are victimized, as well as how the criminal justice system and other social services interact with victims and each other. The creative pieces included give a direct voice to those who have most often been silenced in the past. Queer Victimology is essential reading for scholars and students in the areas of criminology, victimology, sociology, gender studies, education, counseling, and/or psychology as well as anyone engaged with queer, critical, and feminist criminologies, gender studies, diversity, and criminal justice"—Provided by publisher.
Identifiers: LCCN 2023016340 | ISBN 9781032510767 (hardback) | ISBN 9781032505282 (paperback) | ISBN 9781003400981 (ebook)
Subjects: LCSH: Sexual minorities—Crimes against. | Gays—Crimes against. | Victims of crimes.
Classification: LCC HV6250.4.S49 Q44 2024 | DDC 362.88—dc23/eng/20230531
LC record available at https://lccn.loc.gov/2023016340

ISBN: 978-1-032-51076-7 (hbk)
ISBN: 978-1-032-50528-2 (pbk)
ISBN: 978-1-003-40098-1 (ebk)

DOI: 10.4324/9781003400981

Typeset in Sabon
by Apex CoVantage, LLC

I dedicate this book to all Queer victims. I hope that highlighting experiences of victimization in this book will prevent future victimizations.
—Shelly Clevenger

To all those who are excluded and marginalized.
—Shamika Kelley

To those who always push me to consider the needs of all, especially the most vulnerable.
—Kathleen Ratajczak

Contents

Preface

The Need for Queer Victimology: Understanding the Victim Experience

The need for this book arises out of the absence of the Queer voices in victimology. Historically, there has been exploration of victims and victimization that has mainly focused on heterosexual and cisgender victims. This book seeks to remedy this with a focus on victims' experiences and giving voices to those who have previously been silenced. The authors within this volume each provide information and understanding about what a Queer victim experiences. This volume also blends scholarly chapters with creative pieces. We particularly wanted to include creative works as they can often convey meaning or experiences in a different or unique way to help the reader understand the Queer victim experience.

Each author uses different language or different abbreviations within this volume. We gave our contributors the ability to use their own preferred terms when referencing lesbian, gay, transgender, Queer or questing, intersex, or asexual individuals. This means that you will see LGBT, LGBTQ, LGBTQI, LGBTQIA+ or the term Queer used. We will also use the term Queer as an inclusive term for any individuals which fall within any of these groups. The goal of this book is to give power and voice to all.

This book is broken up into three sections for ease of understanding the Queer victim experience and Queer victimology. Section One is *Queer Victimology and Types of Victimization*. This will allow the reader to get an introduction first into where we currently are in terms of Queer victimology with *Chapter 1: Taking Stock of Queer Victimology* written by Emily Lenning and Sara Brightman allows the reader to know where the field of Queer criminology has been and also where it is headed. Chapters within this section also focus on issues such as a hate crime against the Queer community, with *Chapter 3: LGBTQA+ Hate Crime Victimization* by Zachary T. Malcom and Kristin M. Lloyd and *Chapter 4: LGBTIQ Hate, Harassment, and Abuse Online* by Luke Hubbard and Rachel Keighley and giving the reader and in-depth look at these issues. Additional chapters in this section focus on how specific crimes impact those in the Queer community, with and *Chapter 5: The Consequences of Polyvictimization among Transgender and Gender Nonconforming People* by Shanna Felix, Andia M. Azimi, and Dana L. Radatz as well as *Chapter 6: Sexual Consent, Sexual Coercion, and Victimization within the LGBTQA+ Community* by Brooke A de Heer focus on specific victimizations within the Queer community. *Chapter 7: Intimate Partner Violence within the LGBTQ+ Community: Prevalence, Unique Experiences, and Critical Needs* by Danielle C. Slakoff and Stacie Merken as this chapter provides great details about intimate partner violence and the unique circumstances that Queer victims experience in terms of victimization and help seeking. We also have two creative pieces in this section, *Chapter 2: A Cautionary Tale by* Rahul Sinha Roy and *Chapter 7: The Limitations of a Statute* by Jane E. Palmer, which provide insight into the victimization experience.

Section One lays the groundwork for Section Two, which is *Queer Victimology and Queer Identities*. The chapters in this section explore how Queer identities impact victimization. In *Chapter 8: Victimization among Transgender and Gender Diverse Youth: Research Poems on Family, Religion, Identity, and Resilience* by Megan S. Paceley, Rey Flores, Isaac Sanders, Emera Greenwood, Patricia Sattler, and Jacob Goffnett the authors gain insight through poems into how victims experience the world. In *Chapter 9: Indigenous Victimization and the Colonized Rainbow* by Sheena L. Gilbert and Karen Z. Armenta Rojas, the issue of Indigenous cultures, Queer individuals and victimization is explored. In *Chapter 10: Framing Bi+ Experiences of Intimate Partner Violence: The Role of Monosexism and Bi+ Stigmas* by Casey D. Xavier Hall, Jessie Miller, and Lauren Brittany Beach the reader will gain understanding about issues in intimate partner violence for Queer individuals. *Chapter 11: Queer Victims of Violence and Butch, Femme, Bear, and Twink Identities: An Empirical Test of Norm-Centered Stigma Theory* by Meredith G.F. Worthen allows the reader to better understand Norm-Centered Stigma Theory and how this impacts identity. Finally, in *Chapter 12: Police Do Not Protect Us, and Other Lessons I learned As a Queer Victim* written by Allyn Walker, we get a firsthand account about the issues that Queer victims may experience with law enforcement and the system based on their identity.

Our final section of this book, *Section Three: Queer Victimology and Queer Victimization in the System*, the chapters explore specific systems and how this impacts victims and victimization. In *Chapter 13: Queer Invisibility: LGBTQA+ Victimization in Carceral Settings* by Susana Avalos and Breanna Boppre, the reader will gain an understanding how Queer individuals suffer within carceral institutions as result of their sexual orientation or gender identity. In *Chapter 14: What About Us? The Omission of Queer Experiences in Criminology and Criminal Justice Curricula* by Alessandra Early and Brian E. Rainey, the issue of the lack of teaching for Queer issues and Queer criminology in academia is brought to light. In *Chapter 15: Bad Blood: Media's Role in Blaming the Queer Community for HIV/AIDS* by Jack M. Mills, Caroline A. Mooney, and Kyle G. Knapp, we see an illustration of the way the media has portrayed people within the Queer community, often in a negative light. Finally, in *Chapter 16: You Are Entitled to a Strange and Wonderful Queer future*, Vanessa R. Panfil leaves us with inspiration words going forward.

As rights within the Queer community are under attack nationwide within the United States and internationally, shedding light on these issues is more important than ever before. We look at this book as a form of activism and protest those who have been harmed, had a negative experience within a system, or suffered because of who they are. Discrimination and maltreatment based on identity is not acceptable. Queer victims and Queer people, we are with you. We see and hear you, and we demand better! Resist. Persist. Change the culture.

Shelly Clevenger, Shamika Kelley, and Kathleen Ratajczak

Queer Victimology and Types of Victimization

Chapter 1

Taking Stock of Queer Victimology

Emily Lenning and Sara Brightman

Taking stock of Queer victimology is a more perplexing task than one might assume it to be. It is true that victimologists have been studying Queer victims of crime, at least certain types of crimes, for some time. Indeed, Queer victims are far more often the focus of criminological research than Queer offenders. As can be seen in the remaining chapters of this book, which focus on rather specific forms of victimization, Queer victims have not been *completely* ignored by criminologists. Though they have not been completely ignored, Queer victims have been under-investigated and misunderstood, hence the need for a subfield dedicated to centering and privileging the experiences of LGBTQ+ people within victimological work. In many ways this book is an invitation to forge that field, and this chapter serves as an invitation to imagine what a Queer victimology might look like. Thus, rather than take stock of Queer victimology by offering you a detailed overview of the literature that is covered in greater depth in the remaining chapters of this book, we want to take stock of what might make Queer victimology worthy of its own recognition as a subfield within victimology more broadly. Drawing on examples from the existing literature, we want to focus on what the task of Queer victimology should be, what unique issues Queer victimology can help us understand, what unique challenges face our understanding of Queer victimization, and what issues future Queer victimological projects might investigate.

Queer(ing) Victimology

The establishment of a subfield of criminology labeled Queer victimology is an even newer concept than the relatively young field of Queer criminology, which has only been firmly established in the current century. Queer criminology, as a distinct branch of critical criminology, emerged in the early 2010s, sparked by strategic panel organizing at the 2011 American Society of Criminology meeting (Peterson & Panfil, 2014). That spark was quickly followed by the development of a Queer criminology listserv, the publication of several seminal books (e.g., Ball, 2016: Buist & Lenning, 2016; Dwyer et al., 2016; Peterson & Panfil, 2014), an avalanche of peer-reviewed scholarship, and the formal establishment of the American Society of Criminology's Division on Queer Criminology in 2020. We agree with Guadalupe-Diaz' (2019, p. 19) assertion that, "while substantial groundwork has been laid for Queer criminological inquiry, less work has been done to actively Queer victimology."

Though Queer people have been tertiarily included in criminological research since its birth, they were most often included through the lens of sexual deviance (Woods, 2015).

DOI: 10.4324/9781003400981-2

Only in the last thirty or so years have Queer people been included in criminological research in any sincere or meaningful way, and that research, though growing, is still quite limited in size and scope (Woods, 2015). Besides the recent surge of Queer criminological work, Queer identities are still frequently included in criminological research as static variables in an "add Queer and stir" approach, much as women were considered in criminological research prior to the emergence of feminist criminology (Buist & Lenning, 2016). As of this writing, there are no other monographs explicitly dedicated to Queer victimology, and basic web or library searches produce relatively few studies or commentaries that claim to be Queer victimology centered or oriented. This is, no doubt, in part because defining victimology or labeling one a victim is complicated from a Queer perspective.

At a basic level, victimology "is the scientific study of victims of crime; including identifying and defining forms of victimization; studying the physical, emotional, and financial harms that victims suffer; researching and explaining the causes of victimization, as well as the short-term and long-term consequences of victimization, the characteristics of victims, victim and offender relationships, the risks of victimization, the informal and formal responses to victimization, and victim representation in the media" (Wright & Brightman, 2018, p. 12). The problem with simply adding "Queer" in front of "victims" to distinguish a "Queer victimology" is that both victim and crime are subjective terms—particularly when we are talking about a group of people whose bodies, behaviors, and identities have literally been criminalized (Buist & Lenning, 2016; Mogul et al., 2011). Whether they face prison or execution for engaging in same-sex sexual behavior, face prosecution in countries that ban gay propaganda, or live in countries that enforce rigid gender-specific dress codes, "throughout history and across the globe, Queer people have had their bodies regulated, been arrested, and have faced punishment for no other reason than their sexual and gender identities and behaviors" (Buist & Lenning, 2016, p. 25). Further, the term Queer can be both problematic and complicated, and therefore cannot simply be slapped on to victimology as a qualifier without serious consideration and care. Working out these definitional issues, or at least recognizing them and anticipating the debates to come, is the first step to Queering victimology.

Victims of crime have a long history of having to fight for their recognition as victims. This is largely due to the definition of victims being so closely linked with the definitions of crime from a legalistic perspective. As laws began to change, new populations of victims began to emerge, if only by definition, since these victims had always existed. For example, when women were viewed as the property of their husbands, they were not legally considered victims when subjected to physical abuse, echoing the abuse of enslaved people, who were also considered property. As the legal status of women in marriages began to change, so did the recognition of them as victims of physical, financial, emotional, and sexual abuse by their husbands. Over time, the laws began to recognize and protect these victims. New language was created to identify this form of violence against women in the home, specifically the term domestic violence (DV), now often called intimate partner violence (IPV). Although discussed in more detail below, it is important to pause here and recognize the gendered language and relationships discussed in this example of IPV. The historical definitions of relationships and marriage play a role not only in the lack of visibility and recognition of Queer victims in interpersonal relations, but also the harms they have experienced by this failure in the system. Uncovering and highlighting these differences and systemic barriers is one of the ways that a Queer victimology could make unique contributions to our understanding of marginalized victims.

Despite changes in the legal definitions of crime, and therefore recognition of victims, there are still many situations where social definitions, stigmas, stereotypes, and false media portrayals continue to influence how legal actors and the public views some victims (individuals and groups), and thus influences who is or is not viewed as a victim. For example, a child victim of sexual violence might be viewed by those in society as a completely innocent victim- in no way responsible for or contributing in any way to their victimization (Wright & Brightman, 2018). On the other hand, adult women who are victims of sexual violence still face questions about their behavior prior to a sexual assault (as if prior sexual activity or drinking alcohol provoked the assault) or asked what they were wearing (as if their clothing provoked the assault). So, while legal definitions don't include prior behavior or clothing in definitions about what constitutes a sexual assault (in fact rape shield law prevent these excuses from being used by the accused in court), first responders, juries, family, and friends of a victim might very well rely on this sort of prejudicial information as they interact with and even judge sexual assault victims. Once again, it is important to recognize here that rape, sexual assault, and other forms of sexual violence have historically been very narrowly legally and socially defined by gender, sex assigned at birth, and marital status. It wasn't until 2012 that the FBI finally announced it had revised the definition of rape to eliminate the term "forcible" as well as language that limited the label of rape victim only to cisgender women (Wright & Brightman, 2018). Through this change, the language is now gender neutral for both victims and offenders, as well as "reflects a more accurate understanding of sexual violence by including various penetrative violations" (Messinger & Koon-Magnin, 2019, p. 662). This does not mean, unfortunately, that Queer victims of IPV or sexual assault are now treated the same way that cisgender and/or heterosexual victims are treated.

One strategy that criminologists have used to address the problematic nature of defining victimization within a legalistic framework is to measure victimization through harm— not the violation of laws. State and corporate criminologists, for example, often have had to define victimization by the harm caused by an action, rather than through a legalistic framework, due to the power states, and corporations have to help shape, define or resist legal definitions of their harmful behaviors (Canning & Tombs, 2021). Understanding the full range of Queer victimization would certainly benefit from taking a harms approach. For example, Queer teens who are expelled from or choose to leave their homes could be viewed as experiencing multiple harms, from the emotional harms experienced in the home, to the risks and harms they experience on the streets. Since only one in three LGBTQ youth report living in affirming households (The Trevor Project, 2021), it comes as no surprise that LGBTQ youth, especially Queer youth of color, are overrepresented in the homeless youth population (Choi et al., 2015). Though there is no law against being an unsupportive, homophobic, or transphobic parent, the harm that it can cause is surely great enough to be considered a form of victimization in and of itself, let alone the different types of victimization that Queer youth become at risk of as a result.

As a consequence of the struggles related to living on the streets, homeless Queer youth often turn to survival crimes, like selling drugs or sex work, just to get by. A 2011 study conducted by the Urban Institute, for example, found that 68% of Queer youth engaged in survival sex in New York City were living in a shelter, on the streets, or at a friend's home (Dank et al., 2015). While certainly youth who are engaged in sex work are at risk of experiencing violence at the hands of their customers, they are also at risk of experiencing institutional harms, to include discrimination when accessing social services, violent interactions with law enforcement, arrests that permanently tie them to the criminal legal system, and convictions that negatively impact future employment opportunities (Wodda & Panfil, 2021). A legalistic approach to understanding victimization would emphasize the interpersonal violence between the youth and the customer, ignoring the broader harms that force Queer youth to resort to sex work in the first place, the non-criminal harms that they face while engaging in sex work, and the harms that they face after engaging in sex work, all of which have long-lasting impacts on Queer youth. A Queer victimology, then, must embrace a more nuanced definition of victimization, and therefore victims, in order to fully describe, explain, and understand Queer victimization.

Another form of victimization, which would technically fit a legalistic approach but may not immediately be considered criminal in nature is the exclusion of Queer youth from engaging fully public life, to include extracurricular activities that we know to be beneficial when it comes to mental well-being and curbing criminal behavior among teens. Recently, for example, state representatives have feverishly been introducing and enacting bans on transgender athletes participating in (mostly) women's and girls' sports (Burns, 2021). There are currently nine US states that ban trans athletes from playing on sport teams consistent with their gender (Movement Advancement Project, 2021a), and nearly 30 additional states have introduced similar legislation in 2021 (Burns, 2021). Some of these laws go so far as criminalizing non-compliance, such as a ban in Minnesota that would charge trans girls who played on a girls' sports team with a misdemeanor, funneling her through the juvenile justice system (Burns, 2021). One thing that is important to note is that these bans in general do not ban transgender boys from participating in boys and men's sports, so one harm based on differential treatment can be seen there. But the other harm is in the intentional exclusion that these (often teen) athletes face due to these bans. The emotional and psychological harms these laws and policies cause should be viewed within a Queer victimological framework. Imagine the mental anguish experienced by young trans athletes when the US Department of Education, under the Trump Administration, fought against their right to participate in sports. It's no wonder that 42% of Queer youth experience suicidal thoughts (The Trevor Project, 2021), some of which, arguably, are the result of state harm.

In addition to harm within the institutions of education, employment, etc., the state, in the local, state, and federal context most broadly, are responsible for harms against Queer individuals within the criminal legal system. As has already been pointed out, Queer individuals have long been criminalized by state actors, but we can also see many ways they have been victimized by state actors. In fact, the criminalization itself, it could be argued, was and is a harm, a violence, and a form of victimization. Further, research has found that Queer individuals are overrepresented at every stage of the criminal legal system (Jones, 2021). This overrepresentation begins with Queer juveniles but impacts individuals across the Queer spectrum. For example, walking while trans is a term which refers to the profiling and harassment by police that trans women (frequently women of color) often experience. Prisons and jails around the country have a variety of harmful and dangerous policies that impact Queer individuals. Queer inmates are sometimes held in solitary confinement for their "protection," face increased likelihood for being sexually assaulted, are housed in units based on sex assigned at birth, are not provided or have been denied proper medical care (such as hormones), and the list can go on. By taking the harms approach, the definition of Queer victims can and should include the actions by a broad range of state actors and the subsequent harms Queer individuals experience.

To be fair, there are legitimate reasons for some criminologists to take a legalistic approach to research, but doing so raises a second definitional issue, and that is the issue of what constitutes a crime. Crime is subjective and relative, and an act only becomes a crime when it is labeled as such by some governmental entity at the local, state, federal, or international level. Laws that define crimes vary by country, by states within countries, and even by local jurisdictions within states, meaning that what may be considered an act worthy of the label of crime in one place, may not be elsewhere. Laws that criminalize Queer people vary drastically around the world (see Buist & Lenning, 2016), and so too do laws meant to address crimes against members of the Queer community. A poignant example of this is hate crime legislation, which varies by jurisdiction—not only in its implementation, but also in who the law considers to be worthy of protected status. The United States, considered a leader when it comes to recognizing hate crimes, highlights this problem well.

The US is considered to be one of the first countries to recognize the problem of hate crimes, thanks to civil rights groups that were actively confronting white supremacy and racist violence in the 1960s (Chakraborti & Garland, 2015). Though the first federal hate crime legislation in the US was passed in 1968, its scope was limited to crimes committed against people based upon their race, religion, color, and national origin, and only if the crime against them was committed while they were engaged in federally recognized activities (U.S. Department of Justice, 2019). Disability, sexual orientation, gender, and gender identity did not become federally protected statuses until 41 years later, when the Matthew Shepard and James Byrd, Jr. Hate Crimes Prevention Act (HCPA) was passed in 2009, more than a decade after the men the law is named after were brutally murdered. Over the last half century nearly every US state has enacted their own hate crime laws. These state level laws "vary widely across states, leading to a complex-and-inconsistent-patchwork of policies and protections across the country" (Movement Advancement Project, 2021b, p. 1). The laws differ on which groups of people are protected (e.g., 13 states do not protect both sexual orientation and gender identity), whether law enforcement must collect data on hate crimes, whether hate crimes constitute a distinct crime or an enhancement on a different charge, and whether victims of hate crimes are explicitly required to receive resources and certain legal protections, among other differences (Movement Advancement Project, 2021b).

What these differences boil down to is that someone can be considered the victim of a hate crime in one jurisdiction, while in another state they are not, or conversely someone can be considered guilty of a crime in one state and not in another. Thus, victimologists cannot fully understand and explain the magnitude of crimes motivated by bias if they are to rely solely on legalistically defined criminal behavior, because hate-motivated violence occurs whether the state recognizes it (just as women were victims of abuse before the state labeled them victims of a crime). Regardless of state or federal definitions of hate crimes, far too many people are the victims of violent behavior motivated by their perceived or actual identities, and different data sources give us drastically different pictures about just how many people that is, a problem exacerbated by inconsistent state and federal reporting requirements. In 2019, for example, the FBI reported an average of twenty hate crimes per day in the US, while the National Crime Victimization Survey (NCVS) captured an average of 556 per day (Movement Advancement Project, 2021b). In fact, in comparing the FBI's Uniform Crime Reports and the results of the NCVS, the Movement Advancement Project (2021b) estimates that fewer than four of every 100 hate crimes that occur in the US are reported to the FBI. From a victimological perspective, then, data sources matter, and data sources reflect definitions of crime and the reporting of crime, and both of those reflect perceptions (by criminal legal practitioners, researchers, and the public) of who is a victim worthy of our attention and concern.

Yet another definitional issue facing Queer victimology is the use(s) of the term *Queer*, both in terms of it's meaning within criminology and its historical use as a derogatory term. The most common contemporary use of the word Queer, both in general and within criminological circles, is as an umbrella term meant to denote or encompass members of the lesbian, gay, bisexual, and transgender (LGBT) community, as well as to recognize other identities[1] not regularly included in the well-recognized acronym, such as pansexual, demisexual, asexual, and others. Queer criminologists generally embrace the use of the word Queer in this manner but do so with a keen awareness that the term has been used in the past to denigrate members of the Queer community, and that the word continues to be rejected by many, particularly in otherwise marginalized communities, such as the Black community (Buist & Lenning, 2016). A truly Queer victimology must then grapple with the issue of whether a field meant to embrace Queer victims should build itself upon a term that some consider a form of violence and disparagement.

In addition to using Queer as an umbrella term, many Queer criminologists insist that Queering criminology requires invoking the literal definition of the word Queer—something that is strange, odd, or challenging to the norm. It is precisely this understanding of the word that historically lent itself to the term being used as a slur for LGBTQ+ people. By the same logic, a criminology that is Queer, and likewise a Queer victimology, must challenge orthodox approaches to knowledge production and to our understanding of crime and victimization (Buist et al., 2018). Thus, a Queer victimology does not simply "add Queer and stir" by including sexual orientation and gender identity as categorical variables. As we discuss later, doing so does little to elucidate the lived and varied experiences of Queer victims—experiences shaped by a plethora of other identities and social circumstances. Further, a truly Queer victimology, like Queer criminology, moves "beyond the traditional deviance framework and shifts the spotlight from the rule breakers to the rule makers" (Buist & Lenning, 2016, p. 4). A Queer victimology, then, cannot truly understand the victimization of Queer people without thoroughly interrogating the structural conditions, created and codified by those in power, that victimize Queer communities and make Queer people more prone to become victims of interpersonal violence. It is only through the recognition and exploration of these structural conditions that Queer victimology can uncover the unique issues facing Queer victims, confront the challenges of understanding the Queer community, and develop fruitful pathways for future research.

Unique Issues

To have a Queer victimology, research focusing on Queer individuals requires more than "add Queer and stir." Adding Queer as a category might be helpful in capturing basic data and numbers, but fails to identify specific differences in the experiences, causes, and therefore tailored responses to Queer victimization. Delving deeper than quantitative data reveals the ways that forms of victimization may differ for Queer individuals. Reviewing the findings of the Queer IPV victimization literature illustrates the way that an intentionally Queer-centered research agenda drives forward the field of Queer victimology to more effectively identify issues that are unique to Queer victims.

Research has found several causes of IPV in the Queer community which are unique and could not have been identified without a specific focus on Queer people. Messinger (2014) discusses how the relationship between witnessing violence and experiencing child abuse has been linked with what the author describes as opposite-sex IPV (OSIPV) victimization generally. Other research has found that LGBTQ youth are more likely to witness violence and child abuse, which can be related to the higher incidence of LGBTQ IPV (Messinger, 2014).

As with OSIPV, research has found that power differentials play a role in what Messinger (2014) calls same-sex IPV (SSIPV). However, rather than patriarchal gender roles and norms or a lack of egalitarian relationship as the focus of those power differentials, Queer research has found different types of power differentials in Queer relationships. Power differentials which are entirely unique to Queer relationships. For example, Messinger (2014, p. 71) discusses what some researchers call "lesbian fusion" which is described as "isolation from society and dependency on one's intimate partner." The combination of "high levels of fusion and dependency are associated with SSIPV," as well as "greater frequency and severity of SSIPV" (Messinger, 2014, p. 71).

Other power differentials which have been identified, that are unique to Queer relationships, are the "outness" of those in the relationship. Being in the closet or less out can contribute to the isolation of an abused partner who might not be connected to the community, be able to discuss their relationship, or who stay in an abusive relationship due to the threat of outing the victim by the abuser (Messinger, 2014). Conversely, if an abuser is not out, fear of being outed could cause them to isolate their partner even more and use the partner's out "status as a means of control" (Messinger, 2014, p. 71).

Internalized homophobia, considered a form of minority stress, has also been identified as a causal factor in cases of IPV which can be applied to both victims and offenders. Messinger and Roark (2018, p. 280) define minority stress as "stress related to holding views, perceiving others to hold views, or experiencing actions by others tied to anti-LGBTQ discrimination." Messinger (2014) explains that abusers may deal with experiencing minority stress through the violence they impart on their victims, while victims' internalization of heterosexism may cause them to view the abuse as something they deserve for being Queer.

Finally, HIV-positive status can be a predictor for IPV victimization, especially among men who have sex with men (Messinger, 2014). HIV status can be another causal factor for IPV, similar to the power differentials already discussed, but it can also be an abuse tactic as well as a reason victims stay. In these relationships, safe sex practices can be used as a tool of control or retaliation, as a form of abuse, for example, when sex is forced without protection with the intent of causing infection and therefore compelling victims to stay (Messinger, 2014). HIV status can also lead to many other reasons a victim might stay in a relationship. An HIV-positive victim may stay because they rely on their abuser for care or health coverage or because of the fear that they won't find someone else due to their HIV status (Messinger, 2014). If the victim is not the partner who is positive, they might feel such guilt about the abuser's positive status that they are unwilling to leave them (Messinger, 2014).

Research on the IPV abuse of transgender victims has found that the abuse tactics are unique to this population of victims as well. Guadalupe-Diaz's (2019) work on transgender IPV found that many abusers psychologically and emotionally weaponized the victims' trans status, sometimes by questioning or challenging their ability to "pass." As another form of psychological abuse, abusers may "disrespect the victim's gender identity and inhibit their enactment of gender norms" by deadnaming or intentionally misgendering a victim (Messinger & Roark, 2018, p. 280). Other abuse tactics may include blocking the purchase of or destroying gender affirming clothing, as well as inhibiting access to medical resources needed for or to maintain transition (Messinger & Roark, 2018). The physical and sexual assault tactics used against transgender IPV victims also have unique characteristics. For example, an abuser might specifically assault the body parts with strong gender meaning for the victim, based on their personal transition experience (Messinger & Roark, 2018).

Understanding why victims stay in abusive relationships further exemplifies how traditional findings in this area need to be expanded by intentionally centering Queer experiences to broaden understanding and identify unique experiences. Messinger (2014) found that while the reasons Queer victims of IPV stay in abusive relationships had some similarities to prior research on IPV, differences for Queer victims stand out. First, the reasons or causes of isolation for Queer victims is different. Queer victims might have been isolated from their family and friends due to heterosexism and not being accepted by those groups, thus limiting resources which might be available to help victims leave abusive relationships (Messinger, 2014). Further isolation can be caused by the often small Queer communities in many geographic locations, so a small group of friends may be shared by both the victim and abuser (Messinger, 2014). These further isolates victims and provides few places for them to turn for help. Stereotypes and lack of media representation may also limit some victims from leaving an abusive relationship. For example, the media mainly focuses on opposite-sex IPV, while simultaneously failing to have many examples of the diversity of healthy Queer relationships that exist (Messinger, 2014). Additionally, some stereotypes and media representations may portray Queer relationships as being peaceful, especially portraying women as weak and not aggressive (Messinger, 2014).

An important outcome of victimology is being able to help and provide services to victims. While it is important to understand the causes of IPV in Queer relationships, the tactics of abuse, and the reasons that victims stay so that service organizations can provide them with tailored assistance, research is also needed to Queer the victim service providers themselves. According to Messinger and Roark (2018), Queer victims often have perceptions that help is not available or will not be welcoming to them, that it will be dismissive and/or discriminatory. These perceptions are not unfounded, as research has found that agency staff and other responders believe LGBTQ IPV to be less serious (Messinger & Roark, 2018; Messinger, 2014). Other limitations to providing services to Queer IPV victims are the design and heteronormative assumptions which permeate these organizations. For example, IPV has been seen as only a cisgender, heterosexual women's issue, so IPV shelters often lack services for cisgender and transgender male victims and transgender female victims, and in fact may look at male presenting individuals as potential abusers, given the historical focus of IPV (Messinger, 2014). Further, another assumption is that women are not abusers, so IPV shelters often fail to screen women as abusers (Messinger, 2014). By producing Queer-centered research, Queer victimological research can provide the opportunity to more effectively reform victim service organizations.

In addition to the responses to victimization by service providers, such as non-profits, these issues must also be explored by centering the Queer experience to highlight the problems with traditional, even if well-intentioned, official responses to abuse. As previously discussed, IPV went through a process to be identified and taken out of the shadow of the home to be addressed by the criminal legal system. One of the ways the criminal legal system responded to IPV was to implement mandatory arrest or pro-arrest policies, where arrest became the primary response by police toward the abuser. In the time period when these policies began emerging in the 1970s, they applied to cisgender heterosexual married couples, but over time evolved to include dating and cohabitating relations, although often still being narrowly defined within cisgender heterosexual relationships (Hirschel et al., 2007). At the time, researchers and advocates were focused on the violence experienced by cisgender women at the hands of cisgender men. One of the unintended consequences for these policies turned out to be the increase in arrests of women. As the mandatory and pro-arrest policies expanded to more jurisdictions, the 1980s and 1990s found, for a variety of reasons, increasing numbers of women being arrested in IPV situations and in some situations, there were termed "dual arrests," where both the victim and offender were arrested (Hirschel et al., 2007).

Over time, research began to focus on IPV arrests in same-sex relationships. What has been found is that for same-sex couples, arrests are less likely than with opposite-sex couples (Hirschel & McCormack, 2021). However, findings also show that when compared to opposite-sex couples, same-sex couples are far more likely to face a dual arrest. Officers may be relying on stereotypes, both of same-sex couples as well as traditional patriarchal attitudes when making dual arrests, which is evidenced by the data showing male same-sex couples experiencing more dual arrests than female same-sex couples (Hirschel & McCormack, 2021). Unfortunately, a current limitation of the research is the lack of data on transgender individuals in IPV relationships and the police response. Research on officers' perceptions of IPV can help illuminate the decisions for dual arrests and provide context for police responses to Queer IPV. DeJong et al. (2008, p. 688) found that police officers hold several problematic views of IPV, including "simplification of IPV, victim blaming, patriarchal attitudes toward women, and presumption of victim noncooperation." Turning a Queer victimological lens on dual arrests of same-sex couples highlights the need for training for police officers not only on traditional IPV biases, but also about same-sex stereotypes the officers' hold. Additionally, it is important to highlight how dual arrests essentially make an offender out of the victim and funnel Queer individuals unnecessarily into the criminal legal system (Hirschel & McCormack, 2021).

The example of same-sex and trans IPV has been used here to highlight unique issues because, frankly, it is the most developed body of literature that might be considered Queer victimology oriented. That there is so much more we need to understand IPV in the Queer community speaks to the importance of developing a Queer victimological agenda. Focus on other topics and new areas of inquiry are emerging but are far less evolved. This is in large part due to the unique challenges that Queer victimologists face when researching Queer communities.

Unique Challenges

Many of the challenges impeding the development of a Queer victimology are the same issues that the growing area of Queer criminology has been actively grappling with in its formative years. While each individual Queer victimological project will have its own unique challenges, the field in general faces several major obstacles. In our view, the greatest of these obstacles are the dearth of formal data focused exclusively on (or even including) Queer populations, the complicated nature of developing accurate identity categories for Queer research participants, conducting original research with minimal institutional support, and translating research findings into practical and tangible solutions.

Given the role of the state in victimizing Queer people, it should come as no surprise that there are very few governmental data sources focused exclusively on their victimization. In the US, for example, gender identity and sexual orientation categories are included as variables in only a few sets of data, such as the Uniform Crime Reports (UCR) and the National Crime Victimization Survey (NCVS), and the federal government has only expanded their efforts to collect data on LGBTQ people within other agencies in the last decade or so. Even when Queer people are included in these official data sources, it is often in a very limited manner. Again, the process of identifying and defining victims, as described above, often originates from activists, practitioners, and academics prior to legal recognition. As such, research on new and emerging victim populations is challenging when relying on official data sources such as the UCR or NCVS (Woods, 2014). Both organizations only collect data on binary sex categories (male or female) for most of their data collection. While both organizations collect data on bias crimes that have included "sexual orientation bias" (FBI) and "gender" or "sexual orientation" (NCVS), they do so ONLY in the sections on bias crimes (Woods, 2014).

For example, sexual orientation and gender identity are only included in the UCR data related to hate crimes, which only include offenses reported to police departments, who then choose to report their data to the FBI, and even then, the data only tells us which identity category the victim of a hate crime is assumed to have been targeted for. While this information can give us some very skeletal descriptive data, it does nothing to illuminate the causes or consequences of hate crimes. It tells us nothing about the greater context of the crimes themselves, to include any factors besides sexual orientation or gender identity that may have impacted the victim's level of vulnerability, such as their race, age, or socio-economic status. Perhaps even more useful would be understanding characteristics that do not fit into neat nominal categories, like the degree to which a transgender victim of a hate crime passes or is perceived to pass by the offender. If we understand how well a victim passes, meaning the degree to which they present their gender in alignment with socially accepted binary norms, then it could help us understand how these crimes reflect broader societal patterns of toxic masculinity, white supremacy, and cisheteronormativity. Exploring Queer victimization within this deeper context is one of the ways that Queer victimology can make unique contributions.

Official data sources, as well as criminological research historically, has generally used *either* gender or sex as a demographic variable, because they fail to understand the distinction between the two. Ultimately, researchers have used these terms interchangeably and uncritically, which has compromised research results for years. In these instances, researchers are only capturing binary sex or gender categories. Additionally, these data sources fail to provide options for individuals whose sex or gender fall outside of binary social norms, such as intersex, genderQueer, or nonbinary folks (Valcore & Pfeffer, 2018; Crittenden et al., 2020). An additional problem is that official data sources often don't collect data directly from individuals, rather a secondary person is being asked to check one of the limited number of boxes provided, potentially based on their uninformed or biased knowledge of a person's sex or gender (Valcore & Pfeffer, 2018). Furthermore, even if two category options were provided (sex and gender), many individuals who identify along the spectrum in either category would still be excluded when given binary categories. Gender diverse people are miscategorized throughout their lives, in part due to the policies of individual states, where most official forms of identification, such as birth certificates and state IDs, only identify binary sex or binary gender (Valcore & Pfeffer, 2018). Simply looking at an ID, or relying on a police officer to record information, can perpetuate misgendering and lead to the collection of inaccurate data (Lenning et al., 2021).

Though Queer victims may be inaccurately included or completely left out of governmental data sources, there are many nongovernmental organizations (NGOs) that are actively collecting very useful data, some of which is made publicly available for use by other researchers. One example of this is the US Transgender Survey (USTS) designed and implemented by the National Center for Transgender Inequality (James et al., 2016). With over 27,000 participants, the USTS is the largest survey of trans people in the United States, and thus one of our greatest opportunities to understand the trans experience, to include mistreatment and victimization. For example, nearly half (47%) of respondents had been sexually assaulted in their lifetime, and over half (54%) had experienced IPV in some shape or form (James et al., 2016). Trans people who find themselves the victims of these crimes, however, are not guaranteed ideal treatment when they do contact law enforcement. Of respondents who had interacted with police in the previous year, nearly half were misgendered, 20% were verbally harassed, 4% were physically attacked, and 3% were sexually assaulted by officers (James et al., 2016). Though this data is quantitative, and therefore only highlights the scope of these issues, it is far more revealing than any data currently produced by state agencies.

While improving the quantitative data from governmental and nongovernmental sources provides more (in quantity) and accurate (in that data doesn't need to be dropped or collapsed due to low response rates) information, a robust Queer victimology cannot be achieved through quantitative means alone. Strong qualitative research is needed to reach into the depths of lived experience in order to harness the potential contributions of Queer victimology. Qualitative research can be more relational and reveal information that can be hidden from the superficial review of a survey. It can eliminate some of the limitations of binary categories by really talking to, or having open dialogue with, the participants, who can clarify their interpretation and/or meaning of terms, the nuances that can't be captured in a survey. However, qualitative research can be very time intensive. It can be messy, and it can also suffer from low response rates, but the rich findings can be more revealing. Qualitative research often doesn't have the punch that quantitative research can have because quantitative findings can be distilled down, neatly summarized, and easy to locate and cite. Qualitative results, on the other hand, can be as messy as the research itself. The authors of qualitative research take you on a journey through the process, experiences, personal, and social contexts in which they worked with their research participants to achieve the results which can be incredibly powerful and illuminating.

Queer criminologists have begun to offer ways to correct for the historical issue of relying on the use of problematic dichotomous variables. Valcore and Pfeffer (2018) identify strategies used by researchers to address the issue of dichotomous variables, such as a two-step question series to ask about both biological sex and then gender identity, or in reverse order. Another suggestion is to create

> three distinct categories: (1) "man/transman," (2) "woman/transwoman," and (3) "non-binary/different gender identity," . . . to reduce the erasure of people along the spectrum of gender identities while potentially preserving sufficient number of cases in cells to meeting the requirements of many statistical techniques.
>
> (Valcore & Pfeffer, 2018, p. 347)

While some researchers may find it necessary to distinguish between cisgender and transgender individuals, this second option correctly submits that transmen are men and transwomen are women, an idea often ignored within research.

Dank (2015, as cited in Valcore & Pfeffer, 2018) used semi-structured interviews with an open-ended question for gender identification during interviews. They were able to identify seven gender categories from their 300 interviews (Valcore & Pfeffer, 2018). Similarly, participants in an earlier open-ended survey of 249 trans-identified individuals used more than ten unique terms to describe their gender (Lenning, 2009). Innovations such as these might seem daunting, problematic, and methodologically unsustainable at first glance; however, exploratory and qualitative research is necessary for research to move forward. Importantly, language and society are both evolving constantly, so it can not be expected that research will solve this issue without regularly revisiting individual's voices and personal experiences with sex and gender. Further, some studies could benefit from exploring the multiple dimensions of one's gender, to include gender presentation, which may or may not align with a person's perceived or actual gender, thus having an impact on the individual's experiences generally and with victimization more specifically (Lenning, 2009).

Capturing sexual orientation can prove to be even more challenging for researchers than finding ways to separate sex and gender. Research by DeKeseredy et al. (2017, p. 172), for example, report on the results of a survey which had several categories for "sexual orientations and gender identities," including female, male, and other captured within the demographic characteristics, but also gay, lesbian, bisexual, asexual, heterosexual/straight, transwoman, transman, genderQueer/gender-nonconforming, a sexual orientation not listed here, and a gender not listed here. While this research attempted to disaggregate the larger LGBTQ category, it ran into the issue of having such small response numbers from LGBTQ individuals that the researchers resorted to collapsing the data into a single LGBTQ category (DeKeseredy et al., 2017). This research makes an important step in attempting to capture sex, gender, and sexual orientation, but it also highlights the barriers of quantitative data collection and sample size problems in Queer victimological research. Because of the limitations of quantitative data collection described above, and the more significant issue of quantitative data failing to fully capture the Queer experience, it is necessary that Queer victimological research also be qualitative or, ideally, mixed method in design.

All the limitations discussed here cause researchers to miss the nuances of Queer identities, which are far more complicated than binary sex/gender/orientation categories. Even the most thoughtful research designs regularly fail to identify individuals with less common Queer identities, such as nonbinary folks or pansexual people, or individuals who possess multiple Queer identities, such as nonbinary individuals who are also pansexual. The key, and we do not suggest that it is an easy task, is finding a balance between inclusion and exclusion. The more categories we include in our research, the more voices we may capture. The risk, though, is that we may end up with categories so small that we end up excluding people we had hoped to include, as in the example above. There is no quick fix to this problem. It is a challenge that Queer victimologists will need to tackle head on, and continue to grapple with as identities, language, and society evolves.

While developing accurate demographic categories and continuing to adapt our research to reflect the evolving language around Queer identities should be a central task of a Queer victimology, ensuring accurate labels for various sexual orientations and genders does not do enough to capture the Queer experience. These identities are only one slice of a Queer person's whole self, and their experiences are informed by a host of other identities and characteristics that they possess, to include their race, ethnicity, socioeconomic status, abilities, level of education, religion, and so on. Queer people, even those who share the same sexual orientation or gender, are not monolithic. Simply put, not all lesbians, gay men, pansexual folks, trans folks, nonbinary folks, etc., are created equal and, therefore, are not all equally vulnerable to victimization. We can see evidence of this in the crisis of fatal violence facing transgender people in the US. According to data from the Human Rights Campaign (2020), an NGO that has been tracking fatal violence against trans people in the US since 2013, 84% of trans murder victims are trans women, 85% are people of color, and 78% are trans women of color. Thus, a Queer victimology wishing to understand these incidents of fatal violence cannot do so without exploring the multiple dimensions of these victim's identities, all of which impact the opportunities they have in life and consequently, the choices they are forced to make, which may influence their level of vulnerability.

The National Center for Transgender Equality (NCTE), through their USTS (described above) has done some important work in advancing an intersectional understanding of the trans community. With such a large response rate (over 27,000), the organization has been able to capture the experiences of individuals who often comprise such a small subset of responses that findings about them are often considered ungeneralizable—namely, trans people of color. Indeed, the USTS results included enough Black respondents, Latinx respondents, American Indian or Native Alaska respondents, and Asian or Native Hawaiian/Pacific Islander respondents that the NCTE has been able to produce separate reports highlighting the experiences of each group (James et al., 2017; James et al., 2017; James & Magpantay, 2017; James & Salcedo, 2017). Beyond just delineating differences *between* people marked by racial and ethnic categories, the reports demonstrate differences *among* people with shared racial and ethnic identities to explore the impact of other facets of their identities, such as their involvement in faith communities, family life, work-related characteristics, and access to health care, among others. Exploring how these involvements shape the trans experience can tell us much more about an individual's experiences with victimization and the criminal legal system more broadly than when we look at gender or sexual orientation alone. Importantly, for Queer victimologists, the NCTE allows researchers to request access to their data through the Inter-University Consortium for Political and Social Research (ICPSR). Though the USTS data has largely been drawn upon by researchers in health-related fields, the data has great potential for victimologists, and has already been used to understand how experiences with IPV vary within the trans community in relationship to characteristics beyond one's gender identity (King et al., 2021).

In addition to some of the challenges just mentioned, qualitative methods can present additional obstacles for researchers, such as the support for such labor-intensive projects in institutions or finding a publication home for qualitative research. If one finds employment in an academic department that is receptive to Queer victimological research (which is an issue worthy of being unpacked elsewhere), they are sure to find fewer opportunities to support their work with federal grant funds than their peers studying communities that the government is more concerned with. They are then forced to find funding from alternative sources or to conduct research without any financial backing at all, making the research process take much longer than is typical (which is long enough to begin with) unless they are willing to scale back the size of their project, which of course impacts the magnitude and generalizability of the findings. This may be compounded by the subject matter for Queer victimologists, as a result of the issues outlined above.

Assuming one finds the institutional support they need or proceeds successfully without it and produces research worth sharing, they may struggle to get their work published in a peer-reviewed academic journal. Flagship journals in criminology contain few, if any, articles focused on Queer communities (Panfil & Miller, 2014). Queer criminological work has been embraced most often by journals considered to be critical in nature, a trend marked by special issues, such as Volume 22, Issue 1 (2014) of *Critical Criminology*, which focused on the task of Queer/ing Criminology. Though still generally found in the margins, interest in Queer criminological work is growing, as evidenced by more frequent peer-reviewed scholarship and the formation of the American Society of Criminology's Division on Queer Criminology in 2020. Despite the popularity Queer criminology has gained, especially among junior scholars, the reception has not always been warm, and at times it has been unexpectedly chilly. For example, academic journals which might appear to be supportive and affirming of Queer work, may in fact undermine that trust with Queerphobic, biased, or harmful publications. A striking example of this occurred in *Feminist Criminology*, the official journal of the American Society of Criminology's Division of Feminist Criminology, formerly known as the Division on Women and Crime (see Burt, 2020; for a rejoinder see Valcore et al., 2021).

All these multileveled challenges and constraints to harnessing, producing, and disseminating research have the potential to limit the ability of Queer victimologists to translate their research into practical solutions. Thus, ensuring that Queer victimological work makes the impact it is capable of requires ingenuity and a willingness to engage in public victimology. Queer victimologists must be prepared to disseminate their research findings in public forums or less prestigious journals, which could have an impact on one's tenure and promotion prospects. Queer victimologists need to be committed to public service and activism, seeking out and supporting organizations and agencies that are willing to use evidence-based best practices when serving Queer victims. Stigma, stereotypes, homophobia, and transphobia all impact the practitioners who crime victims will come into contact with (i.e., police, victim advocates, etc.), and Queer victimologists must be willing to meet them where they are at with the ultimate goal of moving forward.

Conversely, Queer victimologists need to be prepared to confront the backlash they will likely face as a result of challenging existing and deeply entrenched institutions that have policies baked in that cause discrimination, barriers, or the complete erasure of Queer victims. They also need to be willing to dissect existing and proposed legislation and policies that may be well-intentioned and, on the surface, seem to be in the best interest of Queer victims. One example of this would be hate crime legislation such as the HPCA, discussed above. Though considered a victory for Queer recognition and rights, the law is not without its flaws. As Meyer (2014, p. 114) points out, "hate crime laws have several negative consequences that outweigh the possible benefits," to include increasing the power already held by police and prosecutors (that is often used to victimize Queer people), increased surveillance of a population already subject to over-policing, perpetuating "stranger danger" myths about anti-Queer violence and reinforcing problematic race and class hierarchies. Queer victimologists, then, must be willing to critically examine those victim-centered solutions which they might otherwise be inclined to embrace without question.

Future Directions

Some Queer criminologists argue that the task of Queer criminology is twofold—to center Queer issues and Queer people in research *and* to challenge the criminal legal system as a mechanism of social control and norm policing that uniquely victimizes Queer people (Buist & Lenning, 2016; Buist et al., 2018). Queer victimology should adopt this two-pronged approach, by exploring the ways in which Queer individuals are at greater risk of and experience victimization, as well as exploring the structural conditions that disadvantage and thereby victimize the Queer community, particularly within the branches of the criminal legal system and other institutions that Queer victims come into contact with. For example, the research on IPV has illuminated the unique way that Queer victims interact with police, as well as the problems they can face when accessing victim services in shelters, but there is still much work to do in those areas. Additional areas to explore are victims' interactions with other first responders, such as EMTs, then the nurses, doctors, and staff in hospitals. Services provided to Queer victims by entities even further outside of the criminal legal system also need to be researched, such as counselors, therapists, and non-profit organizations. Interactions with these individuals and agencies can illuminate otherwise hidden aspects of Queer victimization, including secondary victimization and implicit bias among practitioners.

The courtroom is another area where research on the treatment of victims is sorely lacking. Recent cases of violence against transgender people, such as the murder of Ally Lee Steinfeld and the brutal assault against Muhlaysia Booker, have highlighted the need to explore the ways that a victim's Queer identity may be used against them or altogether ignored by both prosecutors and defense attorneys, and how case outcomes relate to how victims are portrayed by these actors in court. In the murder trial for Andrew Vrba, one of four teenagers who were involved in beating, stabbing, maiming, and burning 17-year-old transgender teenager Ally Lee Steinfeld in 2017, both the defense and prosecution misgendered and deadnamed Ally throughout the entire trial. In the trial for one of the men who brutally beat transgender woman Muhlaysia Booker in an incident that was captured on video and went viral, the defense tried to downplay the attack and completely ignore Muhlaysia's gender by claiming that the incident was a mutual altercation between two men (Donaghue, 2019). The impact that misgendering and deadnaming have on courtroom dynamics is only one of many areas that Queer victimologists could expand upon in the area of courts and demonstrates the amount of work that Queer victimologists still have to do to fully understand the myriad issues facing Queer victims throughout the court process.

The victimization of Queer people who are under correctional supervision is an area that has received quite a bit of attention by criminologists, especially their increased risk for physical and sexual assault, but an area that has not been broached is how Queer victims are impacted when the people who offend against them become system involved. Just a few of the questions yet to be answered are, how do Queer victims navigate the correctional system? Are Queer victims given the same attention as other victims when it comes to things like notification for parole hearings or when someone who has victimized them is being released? The correctional system as a whole has rarely been considered from the vantage point of the victimized, thus providing Queer victimologists with multiple opportunities for new lines of inquiry.

Shifting attention from the criminal legal system to the academy, another area that Queer victimologists will need to pay attention to in the future is vicarious trauma, a form of suffering one can experience as a result of conducting research on individuals who have survived brutal violence, as described in this chapter and throughout the other chapters of this book. Vicarious trauma is a hazard for all victimologists, victim advocates, and victim service providers, so Queer victimologists can investigate the toll it takes from multiple perspectives. However, as has been emphasized throughout this chapter, Queer victimology must keep at the forefront of the unique experiences of trauma and victimization of Queer individuals, so in addition to understanding how Queer victimologists deal with vicarious trauma, they will want to explore how that trauma might be confounded when the victimologist themselves is Queer. Queer-identified victimologists in academia, for example, are also having to navigate potentially hostile and unsafe spaces in their employment, be it from other faculty, administrators, staff, or students (Walker et al., 2021). Thus, they are at risk of suffering trauma on multiple levels—both as a firsthand experience and secondarily through their research.

Finally, in keeping with the need to be flexible and to circumvent some research-related challenges, we would urge Queer victimologists to embrace media as a tool for understanding, tracking, and disseminating information about Queer victimization. Future research must focus on the power of mass media and social media to document, cause, perpetuate, and expose Queer victimization. The mass media and social media both exist in a space of tension for Queer people. On the one hand, in recent years the media has been responsible for some forms of Queer representation on TV shows, commercials, and movies. This representation has sometimes been limited, stereotyped, and problematic, while on the other hand, some has been positive, affirming, and inclusive Queer representation not seen before (e.g., Chesney-Lind & Eliason, 2006; Lenning & Buist, 2018). The same tension exists with social media; it can be used as a harmful and hurtful weapon or as a connecting and empowering force. All in all, the media has been both beneficial and detrimental to Queer victims, which Queer victimologists can investigate, creating new avenues of research.

Some media, especially media geared toward young people, has been integral in the recognition of Queer victimization. For example, when MTV ran a movie about the death of Matthew Shepard in 2001 and subsequently shut down programming for 17 hours to run a continuous list of hate crime victims, urging their viewers to contact their legislators in support of the passage of the HCPA. Twenty years later, MTV continues to put the spotlight on Queer victims, most recently featuring LGBTQ victims on three episodes of the second season of *True Life Crime*. Queer victimologists might be especially interested in how these representations, and others like them, have shaped young people's perceptions of Queer victims, and how those perceptions impact their acceptance of myths about victims and subsequently their support of victim-related programs and legislation.

Beyond MTV, the media has brought about attention to the murders of Black trans women across the country. Significantly, recent research has found that the media has made a positive shift in reporting about trans murders by more often humanizing the victims and shining a light on the growing numbers of trans homicides (DeJong et al., 2021). Without the media reporting on these cases, much of the information about the growing number of Black trans women being murdered would never have come to light, because official data sources were just not capturing the scope of these crimes. It was a combination of the media reporting and the scouring of those reports by organizations like the Human Rights Campaign and Transgender Europe that have aided researchers in putting all the pieces together to get a complete picture of the violence facing the trans community. Nevertheless, the media has a lot to learn when it comes to accurately covering these cases, and victimologists can have a hand in promoting thoughtful journalism.

To address gaps in the information provided by the mainstream media, social media, and other media, such as blogs have been tools used by the Queer community to empower and advocate on the behalf of Queer victims of crime. For example, Monica Roberts was a trans activist in the Houston area who created a blog to make sure the media accurately covered (or was corrected) when covering trans-related murders and violence. Others have taken less formal approaches to recognize victimization, such as more privately mourning the loss of Queer friends on social media, in attempts to ensure that they are not erased by the family or friends who didn't accept them. In either instance, the Queer community has used alternative forms of media to tell their stories, and victimologists can use these accounts to better understand the ripple effect that Queer victimization has on the larger community.

On the other hand, social media has also been used to magnify the humiliation experienced by Queer victims, such as Muhlaysia Booker, who's attack by a mob of people was caught on film and posted to social media. In 2016, Witness Media Lab conducted a study which looked at the alarming number of views, shares, and likes received for 329 videos that they identified using the search terms "tranny fight" and "stud fight" (Stevenson & Broadus, 2016). The findings of this research are dually alarming. First, the number of videos they identified for their research, all of which showed physical assaults against transgender and gender nonconforming people, and then the shocking number (nearly 90 million) of people who viewed them. Understanding the impact that these videos have on both the victims portrayed in them and the people who view them can provide unique insight into the ways that the public humiliation of victims confounds their trauma and how exposure to violent acts may lead some people to emulate and further perpetuate violence against Queer people.

Whichever paths Queer victimologists choose to take on their future research journeys, they will no doubt require careful planning, attention to detail and, most importantly, allowing Queer people to have a voice at every step along the way. Thoughtful and sincere Queer victimological research has the potential to shed light on the unique experiences of Queer victims, despite the inevitable challenges. We invite you to learn more about what is already known about Queer victimization in the following chapters and challenge you to apply the lessons learned as you join us in our efforts to initiate, develop, and sustain a uniquely Queer victimology.

Note

1 For a glossary of definitions related to sexual and gender identities, visit https://pflag.org/glossary

References

Ball, M. (2016). *Criminology and queer theory: Dangerous bedfellows?* Brisbane, QLD: Palgrave Macmillan.

Buist, C. L., & Lenning, E. (2016). *Queer criminology*. New York: Routledge.

Buist, C. L., Lenning, E., & Ball, M. (2018). Queer criminology. In W. S. DeKeseredy & M. Dragiewicz (Eds.), *Routledge handbook of critical criminology*, 2nd edition. New York: Routledge.

Burns, K. (2021). The Republican push to ban trans athletes, explained. *Vox*, March 26. Retrieved from www.vox.com/identities/22334014/trans-athletes-bills-explained.

Burt, C. H. (2020). Scrutinizing the U.S. Equality Act 2019: A feminist examination of definitional changes and sociolegal ramifications. *Feminist Criminology*, 15(4), 363–409.

Canning, V., & Tombs, S. (2021). *From social harm to zemiology: A critical introduction*. London: Taylor & Francis.

Chakraborti, N., & Garland, J. (2015). *Hate crime: Impact, causes & responses*, 2nd edition. Thousand Oaks, CA: Sage.

Chesney-Lind, M., & Eliason, M. (2006). From invisible to incorrigible: The demonization of marginalized women. *Crime, Media, Culture*, 2(1), 29–47.

Choi, S. K., Wilson, B. D. M., Shelton, J., & Gates, G. (2015). *Serving our youth 2015: The needs and experiences of lesbian, gay, bisexual, transgender, and questioning youth experiencing homelessness*. Los Angeles: The Williams Institute with True Colors Fund.

Crittenden, C. A., Gateley, H. C., Policastro, C. N., & McGuffee, K. (2020). *Exploring how gender and sex are measured in criminology and victimology: Are we measuring what we say we are measuring?* Women & Criminal Justice, 1–14. https://doi.org/10.1080/08974454.2020.1826388.

Dank, M., Yahner, J., Madden, K., Bañuelos I., Yu, L., Ritchie, A., Mora, M., & Conner, B. (2015). *Surviving the streets of New York: Experiences of LGBTQ youth, YMSM, and YWSW engaged in survival sex*. New York: Urban Institute.

DeJong, C., Burgess-Proctor, A., & Elis, L. (2008). Police officer perceptions of intimate partner violence: An analysis of observational data. *Violence and Victims*, 23(6), 683–696. https://doi.org/10.1891/0886-6708.23.6.683.

DeJong, C., Holt, K., Helm, B., & Morgan, S. J. (2021). "A human being like other victims": The media framing of trans homicide in the United States. *Critical Criminology*, 29, 131–149.

DeKeseredy, W. S., Hall-Sanchez, A., Nolan, J., & Schwartz, M. (2017). A campus LGBTQ community's sexual violence and stalking experiences: The contribution of pro-abuse peer support. *Journal of Gender-Based Violence*, 1(2), 169–185.

Donaghue, E. (2019). Man convicted in videotaped assault of transgender woman who was later found dead. *CBS News*, October 22. Retrieved from www.cbsnews.com/news/muhlaysia-booker-case-man-convicted-in-videotaped-assault-of-transgender-woman-who-was-later-found-slain/.

Dwyer, A., Ball, M., & Crofts, T. (Eds.). (2016). *Queering criminology*. London: Palgrave Macmillan.

Guadalupe-Diaz, X. L. (2019). *Transgressed: Intimate partner violence in transgender lives*. New York: New York University Press.

Hirschel, D., Buzawa, E., Pattavina, A., & Faggiani, D. (2007). Domestic violence and mandatory arrest laws: To what extent do they influence police arrest decisions. *Journal of Criminal Law and Criminology*, 98(1), 255–298.

Hirschel, D., & McCormack, P. D. (2021). Same-sex couples and the police: A 10-year study of arrest and dual arrest rates in responding to incidents of intimate partner violence. *Violence Against Women*, 27(9), 1119–1149. https://doi.org/10.1177/1077801220920378.

Human Rights Campaign. (2020). *An epidemic of violence: Fatal violence against transgender and gender non-conforming people in the United States in 2020*. Retrieved from www.hrc.org/resources/an-epidemic-of-violence-fatal-violence-against-transgender-and-gender-non-conforming-people-in-the-u-s-in-2020.

James, S. E., Brown, C., & Wilson, I. (2017). *2015 U.S. Transgender survey: Report on the experiences of Black respondents*. Washington, DC: National Center for Transgender Equality.

James, S. E., Herman, J. L., Rankin, S., Keisling, M., Mottet, L., & Anafi, M. (2016). *The report of the 2015 U.S. Transgender survey*. Washington, DC: National Center for Transgender Equality.

James, S. E., Jackson, T., & Jim, M. (2017). *2015 U.S. Transgender survey: Report on the experiences of American Indian and native Alaskan respondents*. Washington, DC: National Center for Transgender Equality.

James, S. E., & Magpantay, G. (2017). *2015 U.S. Transgender survey: Report on the experiences of Asian, native Hawaiin, and pacific Islander respondents*. Washington, DC: National Center for Transgender Equality.

James, S. E., & Salcedo, B. (2017). *2015 U.S. Transgender survey: Report on the experiences of Latino/a respondents*. Washington, DC: National Center for Transgender Equality.

Jones, A. (2021). *Visualizing the unequal treatment of LGBTQ people in the criminal justice system: LGBTQ people are overrepresented at every stage of our criminal justice system, from juvenile justice to parole*. Retrieved from www.prisonpolicy.org/blog/2021/03/02/lgbtq/on 8/11/2021.

King, W. M., Restar, A., & Operario, D. (2021). Exploring multiple forms of intimate partner violence in a gender and racially/ethnically diverse sample of transgender adults. *Journal of Interpersonal Violence*, 36(19–20), 10477–10498.

Lenning, E. (2009). Moving beyond the binary: Exploring the dimensions of gender presentation and orientation. *International Journal of Social Inquiry*, 2(2), 39–54.

Lenning, E., Brightman, S., & Buist, C. (2021). The trifecta of violence: A socio-historical comparison of lynching and violence against transgender women. *Critical Criminology*, 29, 151–172.

Lenning, E., & Buist, C. (2018). A crisis behind bars: Transgender inmates, visibility & social justice. In S. Jackson & L. Gordy (Eds.), *Caged women: Incarceration, representation, & media*. New York: Routledge.

Messinger, A. M. (2014). Chapter 4: Marking 35 years of research on same-sex intimate partner violence: Lessons and new directions. In D. Peterson & V. Panfil (Eds.), *Handbook of LGBTQ communities, crime, and justice*. New York: Springer.

Messinger, A. M., & Koon-Magnin, S. (2019). Sexual violence in LGBTQ communities. In W. T. O'Donohue, & P. A. Schewe (Eds.), *Handbook of sexual assault and sexual assault prevention*. Switzerland: Springer Nature.

Messinger, A. M., & Roark, J. (2018). LGBTQ partner violence. In W. S. DeKeseredy, C. M. Rennison, & A. K. Hall-Sanchez (Eds.), *The Routledge international handbook of violence studies* (pp. 277–285). London: Routledge. https://www.taylorfrancis.com/chapters/edit/10.4324/9781315270265-26/lgbtq-partner-violence-adam-messinger-jennifer-roark.

Meyer, D. (2014). Resisting hate crime discourse: Queer and intersectional challenges to neoliberal hate crime laws. *Critical Criminology*, 22(1), 113–125.

Mogul, J. L., Ritchie, A., & Whitlock, K. (2011). *Queer (in)justice: The criminalization of LGBT people in the United States*. Boston, MA: Beacon Press.

Movement Advancement Project. (2021a). Equality maps: Bans on transgender youth participation in sports. Retrieved from www.lgbtmap.org/equality-maps/sports_participation_bans.

Movement Advancement Project. (2021b). *Policy spotlight: Hate crime laws*. Retrieved from www.lgbtmap.org/file/2021-report-hate-crime-laws.pdf.

Panfil, V. R., & Miller, J. (2014). Beyond the straight and narrow: The import of Queer criminology for criminology and criminal justice. *The Criminologist*, July/August, 1–8.

Peterson, D., & Panfil, V. (2014). Introduction: Reducing the invisibility of sexual and gender minorities in criminology and criminal justice. In D. Peterson & V. Panfil (Eds.), *Handbook of LGBTQ communities, crime, and justice*. New York: Springer.

Stevenson, K., & Broadus, K. (2016). *Capturing hate: Eyewitness videos provide new source of data on prevalence of transphobic violence*. New York: Witness Media LAb.

The Trevor Project. (2021). *2021 national survey on LGBTQ youth mental health*. West Hollywood, CA: The Trevor Project.

U.S. Department of Justice. (2019). *Hate crimes laws*. Retrieved from www.justice.gov/crt/hate-crime-laws.

Valcore, J. L., Fradella, H. F., Guadalupe-Diaz, X., Ball, M. J., Dwyer, A., DeJong, C., Walker, A., Wodda, A., & Worthen, M. G. F. (2021). Building an intersectional and trans-inclusive criminology: Responding to the emergence of "gender critical" perspectives in feminist criminology. *Critical Criminology*, 29, 687–706.

Valcore, J. L., & Pfeffer, R. (2018). Systemic error: Measuring gender in criminological research. *Criminal Justice Studies*, 31(4), 333–351.

Walker, A., Valcore, J., Evans, B., & Stephens, A. (2021). Experiences of trans scholars in criminology and criminal justice. *Critical Criminology*, 29, 37–56.

Wodda, A., & Panfil, V. R. (2021). *Sex-positive criminology*. New York: Routledge.

Woods, J. B. (2014). Chapter 2: "Queering criminology": Overview of the state of the field. In D. Peterson & V. Panfil (Eds.), *Handbook of LGBTQ communities, crime, and justice*. New York: Springer.

Woods, J. B. (2015). The birth of modern criminology and gendered constructions of homosexual criminal identity. *Journal of Homosexuality*, 62(2), 131–166.

Wright Quinn, E., & Brightman, S. (2018). *Crime victimization: A comprehensive overview*, 2nd edition. Durham: Carolina Academic Press.

Chapter 2

A Cautionary Tale

Rahul Sinha Roy

I am Aranyak
My Life is simple–
the life I have.

I started exploring this site this year: Grindr
Didn't know much,
Was trying to know (people),
Was exploring my Queer side.

I received a message from an American guy:
"Hi! How are you?"
Perplexed, I asked,
"How did you find me?"
He said he liked my profile.
"Can we get connected on Instagram?" I enquired
Verification is important, I knew . . .

His page seemed okay,
We got talking:
he was polite,
he was gentle,
it was nice.
We shared heart emojis every day.
Things were very, I thought, romantic.
He gave me hope.
As people dream, I dreamt too
of a "happily ever after"
Of course, you can call it a little immature . . .

———

One day he messages me:
he wants to come to India
to meet me.
I was sceptical.
My friend said,

DOI: 10.4324/9781003400981-3

"Let him come,
See where it goes."

He sent me photos-
of his tickets and his luggage
I was shocked:
This cannot be true!
He's really coming?
But I also felt blessed,
I didn't want to overthink.
Just live that moment.
I felt very happy . . .

When I got a message from him
That he had reached India,
I knew I will be meeting him by evening.
I thought I'd take a half-day from office.

But I never meet him.
They "detain" him at the airport.
An "immigration officer" calls me:
"Your friend in a trouble;
he is carrying too much cash,
and he doesn't have a yellow card.
He can't enter the country."
I plead with her:
"Please help him.
He has come to India for the first time."
She asks me to pay for his yellow card.

I think for a second, "What should I do?"
I call my friend: "What should I do?"
My friend warns: "Don't transfer a single penny!"

I call the officer back.
"I can't send any money."
'My guy' calls me:
"I have come to you
And you are behaving like this?"
I was stressed.
I ask him to contact the embassy.
He does not respond.
He deletes my number.

———

I have become more cautious
But I want to share this

So you get cautious too.
What I have faced,
you shouldn't face.

When you look for love,
you think with your heart,
And people take advantage.
They talk to you about love,
give you dreams,
ask for money,
disappear . . .

It hasn't affected me much.
My dreams were definitely shattered.
I used to dream of a life with him.
We both talked about it,
But he was a fraud!
All my feelings were nothing.
If somebody is so bad,
why should I love him anymore?

Chapter 3

LGBTQA+ Hate Crime Victimization

Zachary T. Malcom and Kristin M. Lloyd

Recent sociopolitical movements, such as Black Lives Matter, have ignited a conversation that places hate crime victimization—in all forms—at the forefront of the fight for social justice in the United States. Overall, since the Federal Bureau of Investigation (FBI) began publishing hate crime statistics reports in 1992, members of racial and ethnic minority groups have consistently been the most frequent targets of hate crime offenses. While race and ethnicity are the most prominent motivations for hate crimes, hate crimes motivated by hostility against lesbian, gay, bisexual, transgender, Queer, questioning, asexual and other identities (LGBTQA+) have increased significantly in recent years (Kena & Thompson, 2021; Minter, 2020). Indeed, anti-LGBTQA+ hate crimes have risen so rapidly that they are now the third most common category of hate crimes reported to the FBI, following only race/ethnicity and religion (FBI, 2021). Further, these crimes have garnered greater national attention in the aftermath of the 2016 Pulse nightclub shooting, which killed 49 people and injured 53 others. The Pulse nightclub shooting has become known as the deadliest attack against the LGBTQA+ community in modern US history (Straub et al., 2017).

Importantly, physical violence against LGBTQA+ identifying persons is not unique to contemporary society. As Boswell (1980) explains, research has established anti-LGBTQA+ violence dating back to the Middle Ages. However, the recent increase in the prevalence of anti-LGBTQA+ hate crimes warrant careful discussion in criminological scholarship for two key reasons. First, compared to everyday forms of victimization, hate crimes are often incredibly violent, resulting in severe physical (Comstock, 1991; Dunbar, 2006; Malcom & Lantz, 2021; Stotzer, 2012) and extensive psychological trauma (Herek et al., 1999; Iganski, 2001; Lantz & Kim, 2019). This is especially true with respect to hate crimes committed against transgender individuals, as they are more likely to be fatal (Stotzer, 2009).

Second, individuals who identify as LGBTQA+ often have a strained relationship with the police and are less inclined to disclose their victimization to authorities, resulting in the underestimation—and, therefore, an unclear picture—of anti-LGBTQA+ hate crimes in official data (Pezzella et al., 2019). Additionally, LGBTQA+ identifying individuals may be hesitant to report their victimization to the police due to a fear of being outed, retaliated against, or stigmatized (Lantz, 2020). To this end, the goal of this chapter is threefold. First, we aim to shed light on the prevalence and characteristics of anti-LGBTQA+ hate crimes, including the unique consequences victims suffer and concerns with underreporting. Second, we discuss explanations of anti-LGBTQA+ hate crimes. Finally, we discuss policies that could improve responses to and mitigate the harm associated with hate crimes.

DOI: 10.4324/9781003400981-4

The Prevalence and Characteristics of Anti-LGBTQA+ Hate Crimes

Anti-LGBTQA+ Hate Crimes in UCR and NCVS Data

According to the United States Department of Justice (2021a), the FBI Uniform Crime Reporting (UCR) Program and the National Crime Victimization Survey (NCVS) are the two primary sources of hate crime statistics. As such, the FBI (2021) defines a hate crime as a criminal occurrence "against a person or property motivated in whole or in part by an offender's bias against a race, religion, disability, sexual orientation, ethnicity, gender, or gender identity." Since 2013, on average, 7,500 individuals have been victims of hate crimes annually (Oudekerk, 2019). In the most recent FBI Hate Crime Statistics report published in October 2021, roughly 22.7% of hate crime incidents were motivated by anti-LGBTQA+ prejudice—a six percentage point increase from 2007 (United States Department of Justice, 2021b).

In contrast, the NCVS recorded an estimated average of 235,800 annual hate crime victimizations from 2013 to 2019 (Kena & Thompson, 2021). Most recently, Kena and Thompson (2021) indicated that there were roughly 305,390 total hate crime victimizations in 2019. Importantly, unlike UCR data, which only includes information about hate crimes reported to the police, NCVS data includes hate crimes that are both reported and not reported to the police. According to the NCVS, a criminal incident is recorded as a hate, or bias, crime when: (1) the victim perceives a criminal occurrence to have been motivated by an offender's prejudice toward their actual or perceived characteristics—including their race, ethnicity, gender, disability, sexual orientation, or religion; and (2) the victim reports at least one of following three types of evidence to demonstrate that the act was hate-motivated: the use of hate language by the offender, the presence of hate symbols in the aftermath of the victimization, or police confirmation that the act was a hate crime (Bureau of Justice Statistics, 2019).

The substantial disparity between the number of hate crimes reported in the UCR data and the number reported in the NCVS data suggests that official statistics may be missing up to 150,000 hate crime incidents per year. Regarding anti-LGBTQA+ hate crime specifically, Masucci and Langton (2017) found that approximately 22% of the roughly 204,600 annual hate crime victimizations between 2011 and 2015 were driven by anti-LGBTQA+ bias—a seven percentage point increase from 2007. There are two especially troubling trends in anti-LGBTQA+ bias. First, both major sources of hate crime statistics show an increase in hate crimes against LGBTQA+ populations. Second, official UCR statistics from 2013 to 2017 may have undercounted the number of yearly anti-LGBTQA+ hate crimes by 40,000 or more cases. Taken together, this suggests that victims and law enforcement drastically underreport, misidentify, and misclassify hate crimes (Pezzella et al., 2019).

Underreporting of Anti-LGBTQA+ Hate Crimes

Prior research has documented population-specific challenges faced by LGBTQA+ persons when deciding to report victimization to the police, such as fear that they will be faced with stereotypes or homophobia by the police, fear of potentially outing themselves, and the fear that they will become socially isolated (Briones-Robinson et al., 2016; Dunbar, 2006; Herek et al., 1999; Lantz, 2020). Importantly, Briones-Robinson and colleagues (2016) discovered that around 71% of anti-LGBTQA+ hate crime victims in their sample did not disclose their victimization to the authorities. Given these challenges faced by LGBTQA+ persons, it follows that anti-LGBTQA+ hate crimes are severely underreported. Notably, even when these hate crimes are reported to the police, research finds that even fewer reported hate crimes are successfully prosecuted (Palmer & Kutateladze, 2021).

With this in mind, determining whether a crime occurred and subsequently reporting to police are both complicated and complex decision-making processes. As Lantz and colleagues (2019) explain, victims must make several decisions following a potential hate crime (see also Green et al., 2001; Williams & Tregidga, 2014). First, victims must determine if the act they have just experienced constituted a crime. They must then determine if the crime was motivated by bias.

Importantly, research has found that determining whether a hate crime occurred is especially difficult for LGBTQA+ victims because many are unaware of hate crime laws and are only likely to report hate crime in specific situations, such as those involving White offenders and Black victims, violence, injury, and verbal slurs (see also Lantz et al., 2019; Lyons, 2008).

If one determines that they were a victim of a hate crime, they must then decide whether to report the incident to the police. The problem, however, is that victims of anti-LGBTQA+ hate crimes are especially reluctant to seek formal assistance (i.e., report their victimization to the police) (Briones-Robinson et al., 2016; Palmer & Kutateladze, 2021; Wolff & Cokely, 2007). Notably, there are a variety of reasons why LGBTQA+ victims are frequently reluctant to seek help or report their victimization.

According to Palmer and Kutateladz (2021), one reason anti-LGBTQA+ hate crime victims are often hesitant to disclose their victimization to the police is that they perceive formal help services, including the police, as being ill-equipped for dealing with LGBTQA+ specific problems (see also, Alhusen et al., 2010; Bornstein et al., 2006; Lantz, 2020). More specifically, Palmer and Kutateladze (2021) discovered that victims of anti-LGBTQA+ hate crimes were concerned that they would face homophobia and/or verbal abuse at the hands of law enforcement (see also Herek et al., 1999; Wolff & Cokely, 2007). Another reason victims of anti-LGBTQA+ hate crimes are unwilling to disclose their victimization is fear of stigmatization and the possibility of being outed if they seek help (Ard & Makadon, 2011; Goodmark, 2013; Lantz, 2020). In this context, victims of anti-LGBTQA+ hate crimes frequently lack significant social support and risk being alienated from family and other informal support networks if they choose to disclose their victimization (Dunbar, 2006).

A final aspect of the underreporting of anti-LGBTQA+ hate crimes is that the criminal justice system (e.g., the police and prosecutors) must identify and choose to pursue hate crime charges (Lantz et al., 2019). Hate crimes and prejudice motive, in particular, are difficult to discern among law enforcement agents, and many hate crimes identified by victims do not result in arrests (Boyd et al., 1996; Lantz et al., 2019; Lyons & Roberts, 2014; Walfield et al., 2017). Further, the misclassification of hate crimes by law enforcement officers contributes to the disparities between official data sources and self-report surveys—or the dark figure of hate crimes (Pezzella et al., 2019). Yet, despite issues with underreporting and misclassification of hate in official data, important patterns still emerge concerning the severity of anti-LGBTQA+ hate crimes, as well as to which LGBTQA+ identifying individuals are more likely to be victimized.

The Consequences of Anti-LGBTQA+ Hate Crime

To this point, this chapter has focused on how anti-LGBTQA+ hate crimes are increasing and present unique challenges to victims when navigating the criminal justice system. With this in mind, it is important to point out that hate crimes frequently have more severe consequences than other forms of victimization, particularly those not motivated by bias (Iganski & Lagou, 2015). Research indicates that violent victimization has negative impacts on peoples' lives, but typically, individuals recover within approximately 18 months (Janssen et al., 2021). Victims of hate crimes, however, take much longer to recover from the trauma associated with their victimization (Iganski, 2001). Put simply, hate crimes hurt more than non-bias offenses (Iganski, 2001, p. 626; see also Iganski & Lagou, 2015; Lantz & Kim, 2019).

Hate crime victimization is more traumatizing than other types of victimization in several respects. First, compared to non-bias criminal victimization, hate crimes are frequently associated with more psychological and emotional suffering for victims because they target an individual's personal identity (Herek et al., 1999; Iganski, 2001). Specifically, Iganski (2001) found that hate crime victims generally suffered more profound psychological trauma because the offender was attacking the immutable and fundamental characteristics of the victim (i.e., something that they could not change). Importantly, studies have consistently found that hate crime victims are more likely than victims of non-bias crimes to express elevated levels of anxiety, depression, traumatic stress, rage, insomnia, powerlessness, and fear (Herek et al., 1999; McDevitt et al., 2001). Furthermore, Iganski and Lagou (2015) also noted that being a victim of a hate crime was connected with heightened feelings of vulnerability, irritation, and shock. Taken together, this research suggests that being a direct victim of a hate crime can have several detrimental psychological consequences.

Second, these negative psychological repercussions have been shown to have a detrimental influence not only on the victim, but also on the victim's broader community (i.e., those who share the same characteristics for which the victim was targeted) (Iganski, 2001; Weinstein, 1992). Hate crimes, in this aspect, send a message of inferiority and subordination to a victim group by victimizing one or a few group members (Perry & Alvi, 2012; Rinaldi, 2020), resulting in the indirect victimization of whole communities (Stotzer & Sabagala, 2020). Indeed, research has documented that in the aftermath of a high-profile hate crime victimization, those who shared the victim's characteristics felt increased degrees of fear, anger, shock, inferiority, and vulnerability (Iganski, 2001; Perry & Alvi, 2012; Weinstein, 1992). Iganski (2001), for example, found that following the Matthew Shepard case, LGBTQA+ identifying individuals described intense acute-stress responses to the event. Even though these individuals were not the direct victim of the crime, they reported that because Matthew Shepard was targeted and violently attacked for being gay, the attack sent a message to the entire LGBTQA+ community that it could be them or they could be next (Iganski, 2001).

Third, victims of hate crimes often sustain more severe bodily harm than victims of non-bias crimes (Pezzella & Fetzer, 2017; Malcom & Lantz, 2021; Masucci & Langton, 2017; Messner et al., 2004). For example, Malcom and Lantz (2021) found that hate crime assaults were associated with a 14.6% increase in the likelihood of victims suffering severe physical injury compared to non-bias offenses. Similarly, Pezzella and Fetzer (2017) found that hate crime victims, compared to non-bias crime victims, experience a roughly 23% increase in the odds of suffering serious bodily harm as a result of their victimization. Furthermore,

Kena and Thompson (2021) indicate that violent crime (e.g., simple assault, aggravated assault, sexual assault, and robbery) was involved in 90% of hate crime offenses from 2015 to 2019. Notably, violence is not as common in non-bias offenses. To put this in context, from 2004 to 2015, just 25% of non-bias offenses featured a violent crime (Masucci & Langton, 2017).

While hate crimes are generally associated with harsher consequences for victims, evidence suggests that anti-LGBTQA+ hate crimes hurt more than non-bias crimes and hate crimes against other protected groups (Comstock, 1991; Dunbar, 2006; Stotzer, 2012). Specifically, anti-LGBTQA+ hate crimes are more likely than non-bias crimes and other types of hate crimes to result in physical injury to victims (Dunbar, 2006; Herek et al., 1999; Malcom & Lantz, 2021). Malcom and Lantz (2021), for example, found that anti-LGBTQA+ hate crimes, compared to other types of hate crimes, are associated with a 54.7% increase in the likelihood of victims experiencing serious bodily injury or death. Reflective of this physical violence, the FBI reported that, in 2019, 1,298 of the 1,699 total anti-LGBTQA+ hate crimes were crimes against persons. Breaking this down further, 42% were simple assault, 32% involved intimidation, and 23% involved aggravated assault. In comparison, 401 of the 1,699 total anti-LGBTQA+ hate crimes were crimes against property. These statistics are consistent with research that has found anti-LGBTQA+ hate crimes are likely to be crimes against persons and involve simple assault (Cheng et al., 2013).

Not only are LGBTQA+ identifying individuals more likely than others to be physically victimized, but this violence is often excessively brutal and cruel in nature. Comstock (1991), for example, found that victims of anti-LGBTQA+ hate crimes often suffer painful lacerations and gashes, internal organ damage, head injuries, and multiple fractures of facial bones and ribs.

Importantly, while Malcom and Lantz (2021) found that anti-LGBTQA+ hate crimes were associated with a higher likelihood of victims suffering serious injury or death, these crimes were also much less likely to entail the use of a weapon compared to other types of hate crime. This finding is important because it suggests that perpetrators are willing to inflict severe and brutal injury with their hands and feet in the absence of a weapon. Therefore, we can conclude that extreme prejudice, or bias animus, of the offender toward LGBTQA+ identifying individuals might facilitate the heightened brutality of these crimes (Lantz & Kim, 2019; Levin & McDevitt, 1993; Messner et al., 2004). Taken together, research indicates that victims of anti-LGBTQA+ hate crimes face particularly harsh and violent consequences.

Explanations for Anti-LGBTQA+ Hate Crimes

Hate crimes are often conceptualized as "doing difference," in which hate crime offenders intend to "reinforce hierarchical structures" and subordinate victims they perceive as different and inferior (Perry, 2001, p. 52). As such, hate crimes are intended to mirror power relations in American culture by simultaneously validating the superior group's superiority over a victim's group and penalizing victims for breaching the dominant group's normative standards (i.e., being different) (Perry, 2001). In other words, hate crimes both legitimatize bias toward and mitigate threats from minority groups. In this context, most anti-LGBTQA+ hate crime violence can be understood in terms of heterosexism.

Heterosexism refers to the ideology that stigmatizes LGBTQA+ identifying individuals for not conforming to traditional gender norms (Herek, 1990). As a result, heterosexism is predicated on the belief that heterosexuality is superior to other sexual orientations. In this vein, anti-LGBTQA+ hate crimes are intended to punish victims for defying traditional masculine or feminine norms ingrained in American culture (Berrill, 1990). Indeed, LGBTQA+ identifying individuals are stigmatized and viewed as socially perverse by hate crime perpetrators, which means that offenders perceive LGBTQA+ identifying individuals as threats to heteronormativity in American culture (Berrill, 1990; Bufkin, 1999; Gruenewald & Allison, 2018). In response to this perceived threat, offenders commit hate crimes to reaffirm traditional social hierarchies based on gender and sexuality (Walters, 2011) and to assert their masculinity or femininity (Berrill, 1990).

Research suggests that hate crimes can be classified as thrill-seeking, defensive, retaliatory, or mission (Levin & McDevitt, 1993; McDevitt et al., 2002). In each type of hate crime classification, homophobic and heterosexist views legitimate prejudice and encourage offenders to reduce the threat heterosexuals perceive from LGBTQA+ persons. Levin and McDevitt (1993) and McDevitt et al. (2002) highlighted in their typology of hate crime offenders that most hate crimes are thrill-seeking and spontaneous in nature. In this scenario, perpetrators commit hate crimes for the excitement and elation they experience afterward. Furthermore, perpetrators select victims who they believe are different from them (McDevitt et al., 2002). Relating this back to anti-LGBTQA+ hate crime, it is possible that offenders might be perceiving same-sex behavior as significantly different and offend as a result of the thrill they experience afterwards.

In the case of defensive hate crime, offenders might perceive non-heteronormative behavior as contravening and threatening to the traditional masculine or feminine norms in American society (McDevitt et al., 2002). As a result, the offender views violence as a permissible means of mitigating the threat. The gay panic defense is a common example of a defensive hate crime. In short, this refers to a circumstance in which heterosexuals allege they panicked and murdered or offended against an LGBTQA+ identifying person because the LGBTQA+ identifying person made an unwelcomed sexual advance toward them (Lee, 2008). In essence, the gay panic defense is legitimizing violence against LGBTQA+ identifying individuals for transgressing traditional masculine or feminine norms and making advances toward heterosexuals. Similarly, in mission hate crimes, anti-LGBTQA+ hate crime offenders believe it is their mission to rid the world of LGBTQA+ groups that they view as inferior, different, or threatening to traditional masculine or feminine norms (Levin & McDevitt, 1993).

Retaliatory hate crimes generally occur in response to a hate crime perpetrated against the offender or a member of the offender's group (Levin & McDevitt, 1993). While this may not necessarily be the case in the context of anti-LGBTQA+ hate crimes, research indicates that hate crimes may occur in response to or in revenge for new legislation that expand rights and advantages to historically oppressed groups (King & Sutton, 2013; Manza & Uggen, 2006). Importantly, as hate crime and other forms of legislation move to expand protections toward LGBTQA+ identifying individuals, it is possible that hate crime offenders retaliate against this new legislation. Nonetheless, heterosexism, bias legitimization, and threat appear to be driving factors in anti-LGBTQA+ hate crime.

LGBTQA+-Related Hate Crime Policies

Taken together, the issues raised above highlight a pressing need for inclusive policies related to anti-LGBTQA+ hate crime victimization. As of 2022, basic policies, such as hate crime statutes, have been enacted by the federal government, the District of Columbia, and 47 states (United States Department of Justice, 2021a). Arkansas, South Carolina, and Wyoming are the only states in the union that have not yet passed or enacted hate crime legislation (United States Department of Justice, 2021a), although there are currently attempts to adopt hate crime laws by lawmakers in Arkansas (Associated Press, 2021a) and Wyoming (Associated Press, 2021b). Impressive as it is that many states have adopted hate crime laws, only 31 states include sexual orientation in hate crime statutes, and only 17 states explicitly include gender identity (United States Department of Justice, 2021a). To be sure, a key step in improving policy to prevent and adequately respond to anti-LGBTQA+ hate crime victimization is to expand hate crime laws to protect all LGBTQA+ persons in all 50 states (Palmer & Kutateladze, 2021).

Scholars also emphasize the need to bridge the gap between police and LGBTQA+ communities across the nation to foster trust and respect. To be sure, LGBTQA+ identifying respondents often report having poor interactions and encounters with the police. Specifically, research has found that LGBTQA+ people often fear that police officers are insensitive toward their needs, provide discriminatory treatment, and do not take complaints seriously in situations where LGBTQA+ identity is integral to the victimization (Shields, 2021). As Giannasi (2014) explains, one step in rebuilding trust is providing the opportunity for police officers who identify as LGBTQA+ to join outreach centers where citizens can report victimizations and find other resources while navigating the criminal justice system. To be sure, outreach work significantly improves the relationship between law enforcement agencies and communities that are affected by hate crime victimization (Giannasi, 2014; Giannasi & Hall, 2016).

Additionally, there remains a need to create more inclusive public policies, addressing the culture of anti-LGBTQA+ bias (McKay et al., 2019) and providing accessible means of reporting hate crime victimization (Schweppe et al., 2020). This is especially important within law enforcement agencies and other sources of public support (Palmer & Kutateladze, 2021). Indeed, as the prevalence of hate crime victimization increases—particularly those perpetrated against LGBTQA+ people—policymakers, organizational leadership, and police officers will be tasked with responding to the unique needs of victims. Programs designed to reduce implicit biases and public policies that ensure complete protection of all LGTBQA+ identifying individuals are an important step in creating a culture of inclusiveness.

While society has made strides to protect the most marginalized communities from severe violence and victimization through hate crime statutes by enacting laws, such as the Matthew Shephard and James Byrd Hate Crime Prevention Act, there are other pragmatic steps that have been taken. One such step is the establishment of foundations (such as the Matthew Shepard Foundation) and organizations (such as the Human Rights Campaign) that endlessly advocate for equitable policies and protections for all LGBTQA+ people. For example, the Mathew Shepard Foundation—which was founded by his parents in the wake of his murder—provides training to law enforcement officers on how to identify and prevent hate crimes in their communities. According to the Matthew Shepard Foundation, this training provides law enforcement officers with the skills to not only identify a hate crime when responding, but to also "demonstrate enhanced skills in engaging with victims in a sensitive and respectful manner" (Matthew Shepard Foundation, 2022). Consistent advocacy and partnership with law enforcement agencies are one pragmatic way outside of enacting legislation to attempt to reduce, and even prevent, anti-LGBTQA+ hate crime victimization.

Conclusion

According to official statistics and self-report surveys, anti-LGBTQA+ hate crimes are increasing and are now the third most frequent motivation for hate crime (FBI, 2021; Masucci & Langton, 2017). As the number of hate crimes committed against LGBTQA+ persons continues to rise, it is imperative to continue studying the challenges that victims of anti-LGBTQA+ hate crimes face. Indeed, there are many consequences and challenges of anti-LGBTQA+ hate crime victimization. Victims of such crimes are often faced with acknowledging their victim status, navigating a potentially homophobic criminal justice system, and coping with the extensive physical and psychological trauma associated with victimization (Lantz, 2020; Palmer & Kutateladze, 2021). Importantly, understanding these various challenges and consequences is critical to improving our responses to these crimes. Once we can identify how to address these challenges and consequences, we could then possibly implement policies to help anti-LGBTQA+ hate crime victims genuinely recover and help reduce the widespread and excessively brutal violence against LGBTQA+ persons.

References

Alhusen, J. L., Lucea, M. B., & Glass, N. (2010). Perceptions of and experience with system responses to female same-sex intimate partner violence. *Partner Abuse*, 1(4), 443–462.

Ard, K. L., & Makadon, H. J. (2011). Addressing intimate partner violence in lesbian, gay, bisexual, and transgender patients. *Journal of General Internal Medicine*, 26(8), 930–933.

Associated Press. (2021a). *Arkansas senate OKs alternate, scaled-back hate crimes bill.* Retrieved from https://apnews.com/article/arkansas-legislation-hate-crimes-crime-bills-ec430e679bf14b81567a2be62107a004.

Associated Press. (2021b). *Wyoming lawmakers pursue 2 hate crimes bills for 2022.* Retrieved from https://apnews.com/article/wy-state-wire-wyoming-hate-crimes-bills-laws-9d7b2445adbc08d16536d368c7bd5627.

Berrill, K. T. (1990). Anti-gay violence and victimization in the United States: An overview. *Journal of Interpersonal Violence*, 5(3), 274–294.

Bornstein, D. R., Fawcett, J., Sullivan, M., Senturia, K. D., & Shiu-Thornton, S. (2006). Understanding the experiences of lesbian, bisexual and trans survivors of domestic violence: A qualitative study. *Journal of Homosexuality*, 51(1), 159–181.

Boswell, J. (1980). *Christianity, social tolerance, and homosexuality: Gay people in Western Europe from the beginning of the Christian era to the fourteenth century.* Chicago: University of Chicago Press.

Boyd, E. A., Berk, R. A., & Hamner, K. M. (1996). "Motivated by hatred or prejudice": Categorization of hate-motivated crimes in two police divisions. *Law and Society Review*, 819–850.

Briones-Robinson, R., Powers, R. A., & Socia, K. M. (2016). Sexual orientation bias crimes: Examination of reporting, perception of police bias, and differential police response. *Criminal Justice and Behavior*, 43(12), 1688–1709.

Bufkin, J. L. (1999). Bias crime as gendered behavior. *Social Justice*, 26(1), 155–176.

Bureau of Justice Statistics. (2019). *Bias-motivated/hate crime.* Retrieved from https://bjs.ojp.gov/topics/crime/hate-crime.

Cheng, W., Ickes, W., & Kenworthy, J. B. (2013). The phenomenon of hate crimes in the United States. *Journal of Applied Social Psychology*, 43(4), 761–794.

Comstock, G. D. (1991). *Violence against lesbians and gay men.* New York: Columbia University Press.

Dunbar, E. (2006). Race, gender, and sexual orientation in hate crime victimization: Identity politics or identity risk? *Violence and Victims*, 21(3), 323–337.

Federal Bureau of Investigation (FBI). (2021). *Hate crimes.* Retrieved from www.fbi.gov/investigate/civil-rights/hate-crimes.

Gerstenfeld, P. B. (2019). Hate crimes against the LGBTQ community. In *The encyclopedia of women and crime.* Hoboken, NJ: Wiley.

Giannasi, P. (2014). Policing and hate crime. In N. Hall, A. Corb, P. Giannasi, & J. Grieve (Eds.), *The Routledge international handbook on hate crime* (pp. 331–342). London: Routledge.

Giannasi, P., & Hall, N. (2016). Policing hate crime: Transferable strategies for improving service provision to victims and communities internationally. In J. Scweppe & M. A. Walters (Eds.), *The globalizaiton of hate: Internationalizing hate crime?* (pp. 190–212). Oxford: Oxford University Press.

Goodmark, L. (2013). Transgender people, intimate partner abuse, and the legal system. *Harvard Civil Rights Civil Liberties Law Review*, 48, 51–104.

Green, D. P., McFalls, L. H., & Smith, J. K. (2001). Hate crime: An emergent resarch agenda. *Annual Review of Sociology*, 27(1), 479–504.

Gruenewald, J., & Allison, K. (2018). Examining differences in bias homicide across victim groups. *Crime & Delinquency*, 64(3), 316–341.

Herek, G. M. (1990). The context of anti-gay violence: Notes on cultural and psychological heterosexism. *Journal of Interpersonal Violence*, 5(3), 316–333.

Herek, G. M., Gillis, J. R., & Cogan, J. C. (1999). Psychological sequelae of hate-crime victimization among lesbian, gay, and bisexual adults. *Journal of Consulting and Clinical Psychology*, 67(6), 945.

Iganski, P. (2001). Hate crimes hurt more. *American Behavioral Scientist*, 45(4), 626–638.

Iganski, P., & Lagou, S. (2015). Hate crimes hurt some more than others: Implications for the just sentencing of offenders. *Journal of Interpersonal Violence*, 30(10), 1696–1718.

Janssen, H. J., Oberwittler, D., & Koeber, G. (2021). Victimization and its consequences for well-being: A between- and within-person analysis. *Journal of Quantitative Criminology*, 37(1), 101–140. https://doi.org/10.1007/s10940-019-09445-6.

Kena, G., & Thompson, A. (2021). *Hate crime victimization, 2005–2019.* Bureau of Justice Statistics. Retrieved from https://bjs.ojp.gov/library/publications/hate-crime victimization-2005-2019.

King, R. D., & Sutton, G. M. (2013). High times for hate crimes: Explaining the temporal clustering of hate-motivated offending. *Criminology*, 51(4), 871–894.

Lantz, B. (2020). Victim, police, and prosecutorial responses to same-sex intimate partner violence: A comparative approach. *Journal of Contemporary Criminal Justice*, 36(2), 206–227.

Lantz, B., Gladfelter, A. S., & Ruback, R. B. (2019). Stereotypical hate crimes and criminal justice processing: A multi-dataset comparison of bias crime arrest patterns by offender and victim race. *Justice Quarterly*, 36(2), 193–224.

Lantz, B., & Kim, J. (2019). Hate crimes hurt more, but so do co-offenders: Separating the influence of co-offending and bias on hate-motivated physical injury. *Criminal Justice and Behavior*, 46(3), 437–456.

Lee, C. (2008). The gay panic defense. *U.C. Davis Law Review*, 42(2), 471–566.

Levin, J., & McDevitt, J. (1993). *The rising tide of bigotry and bloodshed: Hate crimes.* New York: Plenum Press.

Lyons, C. J. (2008). Individual perceptions and the social construction of hate crimes: A factorial survey. *The Social Science Journal*, 45(1), 107–131.

Lyons, C. J., & Roberts, A. (2014). The difference "hate" makes in clearing crime: An event history analysis of incident factors. *Journal of Contemporary Criminal Justice*, 30(3), 268–289.

Malcom, Z. T., & Lantz, B. (2021). Hate crime victimization and weapon use. *Criminal Justice and Behavior*, 48(8), 1148–1165.

Manza, J., & Uggen, C. (2006). *Locked out: Felon disenfranchisement and American democracy.* New York: Oxford University Press.

Masucci, M., & Langton, L. (2017). *Hate crime victimization, 2004–2015.* U.S. Department of Justice, Office of Justice Programs, Bureau of Justice Statistics.

Matthew Shepard Foundation. (2021). *Creating safer communities hate crimes prevention training.* Retrieved January 27, 2022, from www.matthewshepard.org/creating-safer-communities-hate-crimes-prevention-training.

McDevitt, J., Balboni, J., Garcia, L., & Gu, J. (2001). Consequences for victims: A comparison of bias- and non-bias-motivated assaults. *American Behavioral Scientist*, 45(4), 697–713.

McDevitt, J., Levin, J., & Bennett, S. (2002). Hate crime offenders: An expanded typology. *Journal of Social Issues*, 58(2), 303. https://doi.org/10.1111/1540-4560.00262.

McKay, T., Lindquist, C. H., & Misra, S. (2019). Understanding (and acting on) 20 years of research on violence and LGBTQ+ communities. *Trauma, Violence, & Abuse*, 20(5), 665–678.

Messner, S. F., McHugh, S., & Felson, R. B. (2004). Distinctive characteristics of assaults motivated by bias. *Criminology*, 42(3), 585–618.

Minter, S. (2020). *SPLC report is a wake-up call for LGBTQ people.* Southern Poverty Law Center. Retrieved from www.splcenter.org/news/2020/04/01/splc-report-wake-call-lgbtq-people.

Oudekerk, B. (2019). *Hate crime statistics.* Bureau of Justice Statistics, March 29. Retrieved from www.bjs.gov/content/pub/pdf/hcs1317pp.pdf.

Palmer, N. A., & Kutateladze, B. L. (2021). What prosecutors and the police should do about under-reporting of anti-LGBTQ hate crime. *Sexuality Research and Social Policy*, 1–15.

Perry, B. (2001). *In the name of hate.* London: Routledge.

Perry, B., & Alvi, S. (2012). 'We are all vulnerable' The in terrorem effects of hate crimes. *International Review of Victimology*, 18(1), 57–71.

Pezzella, F. S., & Fetzer, M. D. (2017). The likelihood of injury among bias crimes: An analysis of general and specific bias types. *Journal of Interpersonal Violence*, 32(5), 703–729.

Pezzella, F. S., Fetzer, M. D., & Keller, T. (2019). The dark figure of hate crime underreporting. *American Behavioral Scientist*. Advance online publication.

Rinaldi, C. (2020). Homophobic conduct as normative masculinity test: Victimization, male hierarchies, and heterosexualizing violence in hate crimes. In A. Balloni & R. Sette (Eds.), *Handbook of research on trends and issues in crime prevention, rehabilitation, and victim support* (pp. 100–124). Hershey, PA: IGI Global.

Schweppe, J., Haynes, A., & MacIntosh, E. M. (2020). What is measured matters: The value of third party hate crime monitoring. *European Journal on Criminal Policy and Research*, 26(1), 39–59.

Shields, D. M. (2021). Stonewalling in the brick city: Perceptions of and experiences with seeking police assistance among LGBTQ citizens. *Social Sciences*, 10(1), 16.

Stotzer, R. L. (2009). Violence against transgender people: A review of United States data. *Aggression and Violent Behavior*, 14(3), 170–179.

Stotzer, R. L. (2012). *Comparison of hate crime rates across protected and unprotected groups—An update.* The Williams Institute.

Stotzer, R. L., & Sabagala, A. P. (2020). "Message" crimes: Understanding the community impacts of bias crime. In R. J. Sternberg (Ed.), *Perspectives on hate: How it originates, develops, manifests, and spreads* (pp. 251–276). Washington, DC: American Psychological Association.

Straub, F. G., Cambria, J., Castor, J., Gorban, B., Meade, B., Waltemeyer, D., & Zeunik, J. (2017). *Rescue, response, and resilience: A critical incident review of the Orlando public safety response to the attack on the Pulse Nightclub.* Washington, DC: Department of Justice. Office of Community Oriented Policing Services.

United States Department of Justice. (2021a). *Federal hate crimes: Laws and policies.* Retrieved from www.justice.gov/hatecrimes/laws-and-policies.

United States Department of Justice. (2021b). *2020 FBI hate crimes statistics.* Retrieved from www.justice.gov/crs/highlights/2020-hate-crimes-statistics.

Walfield, S. M., Socia, K. M., & Powers, R. A. (2017). Religious motivated hate crimes: Reporting to law enforcement and case outcomes. *American Journal of Criminal Justice*, 42(1), 148–169.

Walters, M. A. (2011). A general theories of hate crime? Strain, doing difference and self-control. *Critical Criminology*, 19(4), 313–330.

Weinstein, J. (1992). First amendment challenges to hate crime legislation: Where's the speech? *Criminal Justice Ethics*, 11, 6–20.

Williams, M. L., & Tregidga, J. (2014). Hate crime victimization in Wales: Psychological and physical impacts across seven hate crime victim types. *British Journal Criminology*, 54(5), 946–967.

Wolff, K. B., & Cokely, C. L. (2007). "To protect and to serve?": An exploration of police conduct in relation to the gay, lesbian, bisexual, and transgender community. *Sexuality and Culture*, 11(2), 1–23.

Chapter 4

LGBTIQ Hate, Harassment, and Abuse Online

Luke Hubbard and Rachel Keighley

Introduction

LGBTIQ hate crime—the targeting of individuals with violence and abuse because of their sexual orientation or gender identity—has long been recognized as a significant social problem. It results in a range of emotional, physical, and behavioral impacts on those who are directly targeted (Herek et al., 2003; Williams & Tregidga, 2014), as well as the wider LGBTIQ community through knowledge of and/or exposure to such acts (Perry & Alvi, 2012).

However, LGBTIQ hate, harassment, and abuse (hereafter referred to as LGBTIQ online hate) has been transformed by the advent of the internet, now a key feature of contemporary society and everyday life (Law Commission, 2018). Approximately 96% of households in Great Britain have internet access (Office for National Statistics (ONS), 2020), and about 87% of adults use the internet on a daily or almost daily basis (ONS, 2019). As the internet has become increasingly prominent in our lives, so too has social media, with 82% of internet users having a social media profile (Ofcom, 2020). The development of social media platforms, such as YouTube, Twitter, Instagram, Facebook, and personal blogs and message-boards such as Reddit and Craigslist, have fundamentally changed the way people interact with one another and has transformed the ways content, data and information is generated and shared. While the internet has brought with it many benefits, making it easier to shop, bank, date, and communicate, it has also provided a platform and space in which LGBTIQ people can be subject to, and targeted with, hate, harassment, and abuse (see McGuire & Dowling, 2013).

Research by Galop, a UK based LGBT+ anti-abuse charity, found that 84% of LGBTIQ people had experienced at least one incident of online hate (Stray, 2017). Similarly, the Sussex Hate Crime Project found that 83% of LGBTIQ respondents had been personally targeted online, while 86% of LGBTIQ respondents reported being indirectly victimized at least once (Paterson et al., 2018). Powell et al. (2020) demonstrated how LGBTIQ individuals experience much higher rates of digital harassment and abuse compared with their heterosexual, cisgender counterparts. Consequently, LGBTIQ online hate is described as "endemic" (Bachmann & Gooch, 2017, p. 4), with the internet, and particularly social media, being labeled as "unsafe" for many LGBTIQ people (Government Equalities Office, 2018, p. 97). However, despite the prevalence of LGBTIQ online hate, very little is known about its nature and impact (Davidson et al., 2019; Rohlfing, 2014). Therefore, this chapter seeks to examine the nature and extent of online hate directed toward LGBTIQ individuals and the impact on LGBTIQ victims and the wider LGBTIQ community. The data presented draws on collated findings from two qualitative transnational studies, comprising a total of 1849 LGBTIQ people, who had all experienced some form of online hate. This chapter

DOI: 10.4324/9781003400981-5

will begin with a summary of this research's data collection before discussing LGBTIQ people's experiences of online hate and the need for a range of different responses to tackle this pervasive issue.

Method

This chapter draws on data collected from two qualitative transnational studies researching LGBTIQ online abuse. First, a large-scale survey of 1,674 LGBTIQ individuals and a transnational survey involving 175 LGBTIQ respondents, comprising a total of 1849 LGBTIQ people (Hubbard, 2020; Keighley, 2022). Data was collected using online surveys and follow-up, semi-structured interviews, publicised across a range of social media platforms through posts which provided a link to the survey. Participants were predominantly from the UK and Europe, representing a diverse range of ages, genders, sexualities, ethnicities, and religious backgrounds (see Keighley, 2021; Hubbard, 2020).

The research explored the nature, impacts, and responses to LGBTIQ online hate, as guided by LGBTIQ participants' understanding of victimization. To provide context, open-ended questions allowed participants to elaborate on their experiences of LGBTIQ abuse (Hennink et al., 2010). Consequently, participants defined their own parameters of hate, the nature and impacts of such abuse, and their experiences with support. This rich qualitative data was analyzed using Clarke and colleagues (2015) thematic analysis. Using an iterative process, the data was returned to over time to gain an in-depth understanding (Terry et al., 2017). The data presented delves into the nuances of LGBTIQ people's experiences for a more comprehensive understanding of the nature and impacts of LGBTIQ online hate.

Nature of LGBTIQ Online Hate

Given there is not a universal definition of online hate (Bakalis, 2016), a variety of concepts have been used by various scholars. Some definitions are narrow, focusing on specific forms of abusive online behaviors such as bullying (Tokunaga, 2010), harassment (Lindsay et al., 2016), and stalking (Dreßing et al., 2014). Others have focused on online hate which has taken place on particular mediums such as social media platforms (Burnap & Williams, 2015), while others have defined online hate in terms of its intent and a requirement to incite violence (Awan, 2016). This lack of agreement has repercussions for our understanding of and responses to LGBTIQ online hate. Therefore, to fully understand LGBTIQ online hate in all its forms, research participants were asked to define the parameters of their own experiences. This technique revealed a wide range of abusive online behaviors, ranging from extreme forms of physical and sexual violence to more common forms of everyday hate, such as name calling and insensitive humour. Our primary understanding of hate typically comprises the former. Indeed, participants reported death threats and threats of physical and sexual violence.

He sent videos of himself wielding a knife, saying he's going to stab me if he sees me in person.

(Gay, Male)

Detailed and graphic descriptions of how they were going to rape me and turn me straight.

(Lesbian, Female)

Privacy violations were also apparent, as demonstrated by numerous respondents who disclosed that they were blackmailed and threatened with having personal and private information published online without their consent, a process known as doxing (Hubbard, 2020). When related to their LGBTIQ identity, this would result in them being outed[1].

> *They threatened to tell people that I was gay and disclose my HIV status if I didn't do what they wanted me to.*
>
> (Genderqueer/Fluid, Queer)

> *After I was outed online my family disowned me and kicked me out.*
>
> (Nonbinary, Queer)

Insulting language, abusive personal comments, and name calling were also discussed by several participants as a form of online hate they had experienced.

> *People call me every name under the sun and insult me for being gay.*
>
> (Gay, Male)

> *On one of my Tik Tok posts, I said I wanted a girlfriend, and someone said, "no you want hell" with a clown emoji.*
>
> (Heterosexual, Trans Female)

Furthermore, participants reported more subtle forms of online hate including sharing false or inaccurate information, disingenuous debating, spreading rumors, insensitive humor, demanding proof of someone's LGBTIQ identity, deadnaming[2], and misgendering[3].

> *"I'm constantly having my gender invalidated by people intentionally and repeatedly misgendering and deadnaming me."*
>
> (Bisexual, Trans Man)

> *Hateful messages, mocking, joking, dragging someone down.*
>
> (Pansexual, Nonbinary)

While these comments suggest that some experiences are not criminal in nature, this does not undermine the impacts or harms experienced by the victim. Seemingly innocuous acts such as these are often experienced by LGBTIQ people multiple times and sometimes in conjunction with more serious acts.

> *I can't separate out the consequences of individual "incidents" this shit is literally every day, multiple times a day.*
>
> (Lesbian, Female)

> *There is no one "incident." Every day we hear insults of all kinds.*
>
> (Lesbian, Nonbinary, Trans)

Participants' descriptions of their victimization demonstrates that there is no fixed pattern of LGBTIQ online hate, both in terms of frequency and manifestations of hate. LGBTIQ people report experiencing acts ranging from persistent, highly threatening, and hateful incidents to comparatively infrequent, and less provocative, non-threatening messages. When discussing online hate, often it is the more extreme manifestations that attract our attention, with the "lower level," everyday forms being overlooked or dismissed (Hardy & Chakraborti, 2020). Moreover, it is these more extreme acts, such as threats of physical and sexual violence, that we consider to be impactful, while more mundane forms of hate are widely considered as something to be tolerated. However, to truly understand online hate, one needs to examine all its forms, not just those perceived as serious, harmful, or those that are deemed criminal. Therefore, rather than relying on a hierarchy of offenses, online abuse should be seen as a continuum, similar to that of sexual violence (Kelly, 1988). This more fluid approach allows for the full extent of LGBTIQ people's experiences to be captured and understood. It also allows for us to expand our understanding of the harms associated with LGBTIQ online hate, something this chapter addresses subsequently.

LGBTIQ participants' experiences of online hate were not limited to being directly targeted. Respondents also illustrated how they were vicariously victimized by having viewed fellow members of the LGBTIQ community being abused.

The sheer number of death threats and hurtful comments I've seen in the open on Facebook/Twitter has made me hate my sexuality.

(Gay, Male)

I regularly see comments or posts threatening physical violence towards and generally insulting other LGBTIQ people.

(Gay, Trans Man)

Similarly, LGBTIQ respondents discussed seeing a range of online comments that did not target specific individuals but were generally offensive and discriminatory toward the LGBTIQ communities.

It gets you down after a while; scrolling through comments sections and seeing all that venomous hatred.

(Bisexual, Female)

Even when it's not directed at me personally, it's there against ALL trans people on videos or posts.

(Heterosexual, Trans Man)

Online hate, whether directly experienced or observed in general circulation, much like offline hate, appears to send a message to the wider LGBTIQ communities that they are not welcome and are equally at risk of victimization (Iganski, 2001). Moreover, those who observe online hate experience strikingly similar emotional and behavioral impacts (Perry & Alvi, 2012), as will be detailed in due course. Furthermore, this message is transmitted much further and wider due to the nature of online communications (Williams, 2019). The permanency of the internet means that content is easy to find and available indefinitely, and is accessible for millions of other internet users, increasing the public visibility of the victimization. This reach can be further extended through the use of hashtags, retweeting, screenshotting, sharing and/or liking posts and tagging other users, bringing it to the attention of millions of other online users.

Given the nature of the online environment, the range of online hate documented by participants occurred across a wide variety of social media platforms and websites, including but not limited to Facebook, Twitter, Instagram, TikTok, Snapchat, chatrooms, email, blogs, WhatsApp, online gaming, dating apps, comment sections on websites, Tumblr, Reddit, and discussion forums. The range of online sites in which LGBTIQ individuals come across abusive material suggests that hateful content is widespread online. This point was reinforced by many survey respondents who described the online abuse they received or witnessed as *"constant," "all the time," "inescapable.' "never-ending," "relentless," and "everywhere"*; very rarely was online abuse described as one-off.

It was also not uncommon for LGBTIQ respondents to receive large volumes of abuse from groups or large numbers of perpetrators within a short space of time. These forms of online hate can be grouped into three types: cybermobbing, where a group of people rally against and attack an individual (or small group of people) in a coordinated, sustained, and organized way, or dogpiling, where abuse is directed at a person or group from multiple sources, and brigading, which involved online users inciting and encouraging their followers to target certain individuals and groups.

> *This group would constantly target all my social media with insults and threats.*
>
> (Pansexual, Trans Man)

> *After I posted about attending my local Pride parade, a lot of people started commenting in a very homophobic way such as insults, death threats, and physical violence.*
>
> (Gay, Unsure/Questioning)

> *He would post photos of trans women before and after transition, and publicly invite people to post abuse at them for being trans and how they look.*
>
> (Gay, Trans Female)

The above set of quotes demonstrate that witnessing abuse online can draw others into behaving in a similarly abusive manner. While abuse was often initiated by an individual or small group, often bystanders would replicate and mimic the behaviors and attacks that they had witnessed or been asked to carry out. The ability to tag people, use hashtags and to share content, features unique to online spaces, has aided the perpetration of LGBTIQ online hate, making it easier to find individuals to target as well as drawing others into similar behaviors.

As Perry and Olsson (2009) note, the internet has allowed hate movements to reinvent themselves as a viable collective on an international scale. Consequently, individuals who share similar prejudiced views, who previously would have been isolated from one another, are now able to come together virtually to share and discuss similar ideologies, and gain support and approval for such views, reinforcing these socially unacceptable behaviors, including spreading messages of hate. These attitudes and behaviors are further strengthened by additional features of the online world in that it allows individuals to conceal their identity and be physically distant from their target, removing any fear of being held accountable for their actions as well as any social cues which would otherwise prohibit them from engaging in harmful and offensive behavior (Rohlfing, 2014). Having discussed the nature of online hate, this chapter will now discuss the impacts upon the LGBTIQ community.

The Impact of LGBTIQ Online Abuse

Thus far, this chapter has detailed the spectrum of manifestations of LGBTIQ online hate. However, it is insufficient to merely recognize what constitutes online hate. There is a prerequisite for the harms to equally be acknowledged (Hardy & Chakraborti, 2020; Law Commission, 2018). Williams (2019) recognizes that online hate crimes have an intense, profound, and enduring effect on their victims. Similarly, the Law Commission (2018) found that while there is a spectrum of forms of online hate, the impacts are still devastating, life changing, and can be life ending. Moreover, the hate crime literature clearly demonstrates that hate online produces similar, if not more pronounced emotional responses in victims, as compared to offline hate due to some unique factors of the internet (Williams, 2019; Stray, 2017). The potential for anonymity online means perpetrators are more likely to offend, and these offenses can be more serious due to the disinhibition effect (Williams, 2019). However, very little research has sought to enumerate the impacts of online hate on LGBTIQ people in any detail. These impacts can largely be categorized as emotional and behavioral responses that typify LGBTIQ people's experiences of online hate. This chapter seeks to enhance our knowledge of these impacts, exploring each set of responses in turn.

Emotional Responses to LGBTIQ Online Hate

LGBTIQ people report a range of emotional responses to online hate. The most common emotional responses are anger, sadness, anxiety, depression, and loss of trust. Such feelings are rarely experienced in isolation, but as part of a wider set of emotional and behavior responses to repeat victimization. As discussed, the nature of LGBTIQ online hate is constant. This perpetuates the emotional impacts, which deepen in severity because of the relentless nature of LGBTIQ online hate, or the potential to be victimized again. Thus, those who expressed feeling upset, typically described subsequent feelings of anxiety.

> *The impact wasn't immediate. It's been years of it seeping into my mind, reinforcing feelings that I am broken.*
>
> (Asexual, Trans Male)

Evidence indicates that the rates at which LGBTIQ people experience depression and anxiety is greater than their heterosexual, cisgender peers (Williams et al., 2015). Experiences of online hate further amplifies this, as LGBTIQ online abuse acts as a catalyst to facilitate feelings of worthlessness. If sustained over time, or if exposed to large amounts of hate, LGBTIQ people report developing depression, anxiety, and panic disorders.

> *Online hate based on my sexual orientation has affected my mental state, to the point that my psychiatrist started me on antidepressants.*
>
> (Pansexual, Male)

> *It sets my anxiety off and can cause a panic attack.*
>
> (Pansexual, Gender Fluid)

There were no significant differences between the types of online hate experienced and subsequent emotional impacts reported. Therefore, experiences of microaggressions impact LGBTIQ people's mental well-being in the same way as more extreme forms of hate. To target a person's gender or sexuality on any level is sufficient to affect LGBTIQ people's self-worth, evoking feelings of shame, inferiority, and invalidity in their identity. Moreover, these experiences exacerbated a loss of trust in respondents. This extends further than potential perpetrators of hate, but to every new person encountered, as well as to friends and peers.

> *I lack any form of trust with others. I can easily detach now. I don't like spending much time with other people.*
>
> (Bisexual, Pansexual, Female, Gender Fluid)

This lack of trust is embedded in the majority of LGBTIQ people's associations with others, manifesting as a skepticism of the safety of society. Consequently, those who reported experiencing a loss of trust also reported experiencing fear. This fear referred to a general feeling of unsafety and uncertainty when meeting new people, and of repeat victimization.

> *The experience of continually having to "hide" my queerness online is a constant feeling of looking behind my shoulder and being overly careful online.*
>
> (Queer, Female)

With something so personal, fear and mistrust of repeat episodes are enough to amplify the negative mental health effects. This fear is not isolated to the online world but affects the wider physical spaces LGBTIQ people occupy. As discussed, we know online hate can extend into the offline world and vice versa as a continuity of victimization. Therefore, LGBTIQ people reported constantly feeling unsafe, even in spaces where they had not necessarily experienced hate. This has consequences for a person's behavioral choices to mitigate future victimization.

Notable differences were reported in relation to certain experiences of online hate. Those who would typify their experiences as microaggressions or everyday victimization, reported expressing anger, as opposed to sadness. For instance, LGBTIQ people who made references to anger also described experiencing more subtle and mundane forms of online hate.

> *Angers me we live in a society where people think it's ok to have an opinion on something they're not involved in, won't affect them and is just human.*
>
> (Gay, Female)

> *I think mainly upset but also angry. Because it annoys me that these people aren't educated and choose to be willfully ignorant.*
>
> (Gay, Lesbian, Female)

Expressions of anger were underpinned by an injustice at being targeted over your identity. LGBTIQ individuals described wishing they could be heterosexual or cisgender to avoid hate. They also reported feeling frustrated that they should have to assimilate into a heteronormative, cisgender society to avoid being the target of hate. However, anger is an unsustainable emotion, with LGBTIQ people subsequently reporting feeling exhausted due to maintaining high levels of resentment. Consequently, a loss of trust and exhaustion at trying to navigate online spaces meant LGBTIQ people reported an inability to form close, sustainable bonds.

Participants also minimized experiences of online hate through normalizing or seeing them as being an inevitable part of everyday life as a LGBTIQ person (Hardy & Chakraborti, 2020).

> *It's every day. For us, this is normal.*
>
> (Gay, Trans Man)

The burden of responsibility for LGBTIQ online hate often falls on the victim's shoulders. Thus, LGBTIQ people describe that normalizing their experiences acts as a safeguarding buffer against processing why they are being targeted. To normalize your experiences of hate is to downplay the fact that your gender and/or sexuality is viewed as objectionable and thus to mitigate feelings of worthlessness previously described. Furthermore, reports suggest experiences of internalized homophobia, either by downplaying the experiences or invalidating your own identity, can increase the rate at which online abuse is normalized. Stray (2017) suggests this is as a direct result of growing up in a hetero-/cis-normative society.

> *Like I was a terrible person and that I was disgusting, and I considered just "acting straight" to avoid it all.*
>
> (Pansexual, Female)

LGBTIQ people frequently report feelings of inferiority in their identity, as part of their self-blame for being visibly different. By appearing to accept that their identity is inferior, LGBTIQ people routinise experiences of abuse as deserved. This can perpetuate the underlying attitude that everyday experiences of hate are not serious, and therefore not worthy of any meaningful response. Consequently, LGBTIQ people also report engaging in behavioral responses as an alternative method for coping with online hate experiences.

Behavioral Responses to LGBTIQ Online Hate

Previous discussions on the emotional consequences of online hate illustrate the tangible impacts LGBTIQ people experience following exposure to hate. However, these consequences are not exclusively felt online. Nor do they manifest purely psychologically. Research demonstrates how experiences of online hate result in a range of physical behaviors and responses. Moreover, the boundaries between the online and offline world are blurred (Awan & Zempi, 2016). As identified previously, it can be difficult to isolate online threats from the possibility of them materializing in the real world. Thus, research suggests this has a continuity effect on subsequent behavioral actions in LGBTIQ people.

First, it is important to recognize the manifestation of physiological responses to online hate. LGBTIQ people report engaging in physiological responses or coping mechanisms. Reports suggest LGBTIQ people engage in self-harming behaviors, experience suicidal ideation, or suicide attempts at a rate greater than the general population. A recent study by Stonewall, a UK LGBT+ rights charity, estimated that LGBTIQ people are at more risk of suicidal behavior and self-harm than non-LGBTIQ people (Bachmann & Gooch, 2017). Physiological responses to hate are thought to be a way to control, internalize, or cope with victimization and abuse (Paterson et al., 2018).

I've had issues with self-harming due to the hate.

(Lesbian, Female, Gender Fluid)

I think of killing myself daily, and I don't always feel safe.

(Bisexual, Female)

The reason why LGBTIQ people experience these physiological responses is complex. However, research suggests rates of suicide and self-harm are exacerbated when targeted for abuse and hate because of your sexuality and/or gender identity (Powell et al., 2020). Notably, experiences of self-harm and suicide attempts were experienced differently by individuals within the LGBTIQ labels. Trans, nonbinary, and gender nonconforming individuals were more likely to suffer because of their victimization compared to cisgender respondents. Thus, when exploring the impacts of LGBTIQ online hate, it is important to recognize how certain identity characteristics may compound experiences of hate and associated impacts.

Fear of online abuse, or that threats online will be carried out in the real world leads to LGBTIQ people adopting certain behavioral modifications to reduce the likelihood of victimization. Manifesting as a form of self-censorship, primarily, LGBTIQ people reported a range of behavioral adaptations to prevent future victimization, including withdrawal from online and offline spaces, and measures such as changing one's appearance. Online, LGBTIQ people reduced their use of social media, removed LGBTIQ identifying information from personal profiles, and in extreme cases, came off the internet entirely.

I became fully anonymous online (not publishing any info about who I am, any photos of my face) so I can't be outed in real life or doxed.

(Queer, Agender, Nonbinary)

LGBTIQ people use the internet to explore their sexuality and gender, meet new people and form connections (De Ridder & Van Bauwel, 2015). Yet they often reported being scared to express their true self, feeling the need to lie about their sexuality or gender identity to remain safe online. LGBTIQ online hate appears to silence many individuals, who restrict their use of the internet to reduce risk of further victimization. Often, LGBTIQ people became reluctant to voice opinions, join conversations online, and share content. Many also tightened controls on their profiles, blocking large numbers of users, to limit the abuse they could receive.

As demonstrated above, however, behavioral changes do not relate solely to the online world. Just as hate spills into the offline world, so does a fear of victimization and adaptations to offline behavior in response. LGBTIQ people reported changing their appearance and movements to appear less Queer, and therefore be less likely to fall victim to a crime according to any visible difference identifiers.

I just changed how I presented online to keep myself safe.

(Queer, Trans Female)

I tried to suppress my identity. I stopped wearing make-up and toned down my clothes.

(Asexual, Male)

Consequently, LGBTIQ people often report withdrawing completely from the social world, preventing meaningful interactions with peers. This complete self-exclusion from online and offline spaces contributes to feelings of isolation, as LGBTIQ people report attempting to cope alone. Thus, when we look at the impacts of online abuse, we must consider the online/offline blurring of a person's life (Awan & Zempi, 2016). A person's life online does not sit in isolation from their offline life and vice versa. The online world is not some ephemeral place in which a person can separate their sense of self from reality. It is a part of LGBTIQ people's reality, and one that infiltrates the rest of a person's life and interactions. An incident of LGBTIQ online hate can affect your perceptions of how the entire world will view you (Williams, 2019). Consequently, LGBTIQ people adapt their behaviors online and offline to assimilate into normative identity categories, to hide their Queerness, or withdraw completely for protection.

Counternarratives to LGBTIQ Online Hate

When we are exploring the impacts of LGBTIQ abuse, our view must not be parochial. Not all LGBTIQ people report experiencing negative emotional and behavioral responses. Another category of responses to online hate, largely undocumented in the literature regards counternarratives against LGBTIQ online hate. Resilience to online hate comes in the form of activism behaviors, allyship, and support toward LGBTIQ peers and other marginalized communities. LGBTIQ people spoke about developing resilience in the face of repeated exposure to, or the potential to be exposed to, online hate.

It made me stronger. It makes me want to fight for further equality.

(Gay, Male)

It's made me a lot more determined to keep fighting for this stuff in the spaces that I am in. I'm trying to do more to normalize trans inclusion, like putting your pronouns in your email signature.

(Biromantic, Asexual, Trans Male)

Rather than accepting that this was the norm, the development of an inner strength was crucial for some LGBTIQ people to cope and set hopeful goals for a future without hate. LGBTIQ people reported a sense of responsibility to protect others from hate, while also pushing for justice and accountability for perpetrators of online hate. Moreover, positive affirmations of LGBTIQ identity acted as a buffer against negative adverse effects by reducing rates of anxiety, worthlessness, and shame. Despite the many negative changes to victims' behavior, it is encouraging that for some this did not deter them from engaging in LGBTIQ spaces, or wider society in general. An increased determination to engage with LGBTIQ content helps to affirm LGBTIQ identity and increases self-worth. Additionally, by fighting back against such abuse and helping others who may be subject to similar abuse the LGBTIQ community demonstrates a refusal to be silenced on important social harms issues but motivates change in society.

Conclusion

This chapter has explored the nature and impacts of LGBTIQ online hate, by drawing on LGBTIQ participants' own experiences of victimization. By considering the full spectrum of hate experiences, including microaggressions, to rape and death threats, this has significant implications for our understanding of online hate. Future research needs to ensure that they consider the wide range of acts that make up online hate to recognize the lived realities of LGBTIQ people experiencing adverse effects, including the variety of websites and platforms where online hate occurs and the impact on bystanders. By enumerating the emotional and behavioral impacts, this chapter challenges existing assumptions that online hate is not serious but demonstrates that it affects LGBTIQ people's lives both on and offline. Such is the illocutionary power of speech, and to dismiss words and verbal cues as low level is to undermine the tangible and long-term harmful consequences (Williams, 2019; Butler, 1997).

Moreover, when understanding the impacts of LGBTIQ online hate, it is important to recognize that you do not have to be a direct victim of hate to experience emotional and behavioral effects. Many respondents in this study were indirectly affected by observing the abuse of someone else, or by coming across hateful anti-LGBTIQ content and material that did not necessarily target an individual but was in general circulation online. Thus, any meaningful discussion of LGBTIQ online hate must consider both the community and individual impacts.

This broader understanding of LGBTIQ online hate has implications for how we respond. While legislation is welcome and is the primary way in which many countries (such as Germany and the UK) have sought to respond to online abuse, by only addressing the most serious incidents, it fails to address the full range of acts this research has identified as harmful to LGBTIQ people. We therefore need to consider alternative methods, such as the responsibilities of social media platforms and internet providers to regulate content online, as well as challenging the cultures and practices that allow LGBTIQ hate online to flourish.

Notes

1 Outing is the process by which a person's sexuality and/or gender identity is disclosed to others without their consent.
2 The process by which a transgender person is called by their birth name, which they have changed as part of their gender transition.
3 The use of a word, especially a pronoun or form of address, that does not correctly reflect the gender with which they identify.

References

Awan, I. (2016). Islamophobia on social media: A qualitative analysis of Facebook's walls of hate. *International Journal of Cyber Criminology*, 10(1), 1–20.

Awan, I., & Zempi, I. (2016). The affinity between online and offline Anti-Muslim hate crime: Dynamics and impacts. *Aggression and Violent Behaviour*, 27, 1–8.

Bachmann, C., & Gooch, B. (2017). *LGBT in Britain: Hate crime and discrimination*. London: Stonewall.

Bakalis, C. (2016). Regulating hate crime in the digital age. In J. Schweppe & M. A. Walters (Eds.), *The globalisation of hate: Internationalizing hate crime* (pp. 263–276). Oxford: Oxford University Press.

Burnap, P., & Williams, M. L. (2015). Cyber hate speech on twitter: An application of machine classification and statistical modelling for policy and decision making. *Policy and Internet*, 7(2), 223–242.

Butler, J. (1997). *Excitable speech: A politics of the performative*. London: Routledge.

Clarke, V., Braun, V., & Hayfield, N. (2015). Thematic analysis. *Qualitative psychology: A practical guide to research methods*, 3, 222–248.

Davidson, J., Livingstone, S., Jenkins, S., Gekoski, A., Choak, C., Ike, T., & Phillips, K. (2019). *Adult online hate, harassment and abuse: A rapid evidence assessment*. Retrieved from https://assets.publishing.service.gov.uk/government/uploads/system/uploads/attachment_data/file/811450/Adult_Online_Harms_Report_2019.pdf.

De Ridder, S., & Van Bauwel, S. (2015). The discursive construction of gay teenagers in times of mediatization: Youth's reflections on intimate storytelling, queer shame and realness in popular social media places. *Journal of Youth Studies*, 18(6), 777–793.

Dreβing, H., Bailer, J., Anders, A., Wagner, H., & Gallas, C. (2014). Cyber-stalking in a large sample of social network users: Prevalence, characteristics and impact upon victims. *Cyberpsychology, Behaviour and Social Networking*, 17(2), 61–67.

Government Equalities Office. (2018). *National LGBT survey research report*. Manchester: Government Equalities Office.

Hardy, S. J., & Chakraborti, N. (2020). *Blood, threats and fears: The hidden worlds of hate crime victims*. Springer Nature.

Hennink, M., Hutter, I., & Bailey, A. (2010). *Qualitative research methods*. London: Sage.

Herek, G. M., Cogan, J. C., & Roy Gillis, J. (2003). Victim experiences in hate crimes based on sexual orientation. In B. Perry (Ed.), *Hate and bias crimes: A reader* (pp. 243–259). London: Routledge.

Hubbard, L. (2020). *Online hate crime report 2020*. London: Galop.

Iganski, P. (2001). Hate crimes hurt more. *American Behavioural Scientist*, 45(4), 626–638.

Keighley, R. (2021). Hate hurts: Exploring the impact of online hate on LGBTQ+ young people. *Women & Criminal Justice*, 1–20. https://doi.org/10.1080/08974454.2021.1988034.

Keighley, R. (2022). *The dark side of social media: Exploring the nature, extent, and routinisation of LGB+ online hate* (Unpublished doctoral thesis). Leicester: University of Leicester.

Kelly, Liz. (1988). *Surviving Sexual Violence*, Cambridge: Polity.

Law Commission. (2018). *Abusive and offensive online communications scoping report*. Retrieved from https://s3-eu-west-2.amazonaws.com/lawcom-prod-storage-11jsxou24uy7q/uploads/2018/10/6_5039_LC_Online_Comms_Report_FINAL_291018_WEB.pdf.

Lindsay, M., Booth, J. M., Messing, J. T., and Thaller, J. (2016). Experiences of online harassment against emerging adults: Emotional reactions and the mediating role of fear. *Journal of Interpersonal Violence*, 31(19), 3174–3195.

McGuire, M., & Dowling, S. (2013). *Cyber crime: A review of the evidence, home office research report 75*. London: Home Office.

Ofcom. (2020). *Adults' media use and attitudes report 2020*. Retrieved from www.ofcom.org.uk/data/assets/pdf_file/0031/196375/adults-media-use-and-attitudes-2020-report.pdf.

Office for National Statistics. (2019). *Internet access—households and individuals, Great Britain statistical Bulletin*. Retrieved from www.ons.gov.uk/peoplepopulationandcommunity/householdcharacteristics/homeinternetandsocialmediausage/bulletins/internetaccesshouseholdsandindividuals/2019.

Office for National Statistics. (2020). *Internet access—households and individuals, Great Britain statistical Bulletin*. Retrieved from www.ons.gov.uk/peoplepopulationandcommunity/householdcharacteristics/homeinternetandsocialmediausage/bulletins/internetaccesshouseholdsandindividuals/2020.

Paterson, J., Walters, M., Brown, R., & Fearn, H. (2018). *The Sussex hate crime project*. Retrieved from http://sro.sussex.ac.uk/id/eprint/73458/1/__smbhome.uscs.susx.ac.uk_lsu53_Documents_My%20Documents_Leverhulme%20Project_Sussex%20Hate%20Crime%20Project%20 Report.pdf.

Perry, B., & Alvi, S. (2012). "We are all vulnerable": The in terrorem effects of hate crime. *International Review of Victimology*, 18(1), 57–71.

Perry, B., & Olsson, P. (2009). Cyberhate: The globalisation of hate. *Information and Communications Technology Law*, 18(2), 185–199.

Powell, A., Scott, A. J., & Henry, N. (2020). Digital harassment and abuse: Experiences of sexuality and gender minorities. *European Journal of Criminology*, 17(2), 199–223.

Rohlfing, S. (2014). Hate on the internet. In N. Hall, A. Corb, P. Giannasi, & J. Grieve (Eds.), *The Routledge international handbook on hate crime* (pp. 293–305). London: Routledge.

Stray, M. (2017). *Online hate crime report 2017*. London: Galop.

Terry, G., Hayfield, N., Clarke, V., & Braun, V. (2017). Thematic analysis. In *The Sage handbook of qualitative research in psychology* (pp. 17–37). Los Angeles, CA: Sage.

Tokunaga, R. S. (2010). Following you home from school: A critical review and synthesis of research on cyberbullying victimisation. *Computers in Human Behaviour*, 26(3), 277–287.

Williams, H., Varney, J., Taylor, J., Fish, J., Durr, P., & Elan-Cane, C. (2015). *The lesbian, gay, bisexual and trans public health outcomes framework*. Manchester: LGBT Foundation.

Williams, M. L. (2019). *Hatred behind the scenes: A report on the rise of online hatred*. Retrieved from http://orca.cf.ac.uk/127085/1/Hate%20Behind%20the%20Screens.pdf.

Williams, M. L., & Tregidga, J. (2014). Hate crime victimisation in Wales: Psychological and physical impacts across seven hate crime victim types. *British Journal of Criminology*, 54(5), 946–967.

Chapter 5

The Consequences of Polyvictimization Among Transgender and Gender Nonconforming People

Shanna Felix, Andia M. Azimi, and Dana L. Radatz

Introduction

Despite representing less than 1% of the total US population (Jones, 2021), transgender and gender nonconforming (TGNC) people experience incredibly high rates of victimization. Nationally representative studies, such as the 2015 United States Transgender Survey, find that nearly half of all TGNC people experience sexual assault, harassment, or intimate partner violence at some point in their lives (James et al., 2016). Victimization literature on the general population shows that those who are chronically victimized throughout their lives (i.e., polyvictimized) have the highest risk for negative outcomes, such as poor mental health (Finkelhor et al., 2007a, 2007b). However, despite the existing knowledge that TGNC people are at an especially high risk for victimization, polyvictimization research studies specific to TGNC people are sparse. Therefore, there is a need for more scholarly work in this area. This chapter provides a critical and scoping review of the existing literature on polyvictimization among TGNC people, along with implications for future research in this area.

Polyvictimization

All people carry various risk levels for potential victimization. However, there are some populations of people who carry higher rates of risk compared to other populations. These populations are considered to be vulnerable. For instance, research literature has historically demonstrated that children are one of the most vulnerable populations at risk for violence and victimization (Finkelhor & Dzuiba-Leatherman, 1994). In fact, scholars studying childhood victimization are responsible for conceptualizing the study of polyvictimization, which is the focus of this chapter (Finkelhor et al., 2007a, 2007b).

In 2007, David Finkelhor and his colleagues coined the term "poly-victim" to describe a child who had experienced multiple different types of victimization (e.g., physical victimization, sexual victimization, property victimization, witness/indirect victimization) to conceptualize and explain trauma symptoms (Finkelhor et al., 2007a). Up until then, studies on victimization among children had largely centered on singular, individual types of harm and the negative consequences that stemmed from the violence and victimization. Within their study, Finkelhor et al. (2007a) highlighted three notable concerns regarding the limitations of childhood victimization studies. The researchers first highlighted the potential to exaggerate the impact of one singular victimization type on mental health outcomes (for instance, over-emphasizing the impact of childhood trauma on lifetime mental health).

DOI: 10.4324/9781003400981-6

Second, existing research at the time did not account for interrelationships among victimization types and the effects of such interrelationships on mental health symptomatology. The third problem acknowledged that prior research had not examined subsamples of children within their study populations who were chronically victimized (p. 8), as those children with multiple victimizations could be particularly vulnerable. Taken together, these three problematic concerns led the researchers to expand the field of victimization research into the study of polyvictimization—the study of cumulative victimization and its negative consequences on polyvictims.

The study of polyvictimization has since been expanded to other populations of people that carry higher risks for victimization compared to the general population. For example, several studies have revealed that women who fall under the purview of the criminal justice system—for instance, women who are arrested, incarcerated, and so on—have extensive histories of victimization (e.g., Chesney-Lind & Pasko, 2012; McKee & Hilton, 2019; Pasko & Chesney-Lind, 2016; Smith, 2017). Some researchers have examined polyvictimization among incarcerated women with histories of victimization (e.g., Radatz & Wright, 2015). Similar to the noted limitations made by Finklehor and his colleagues in 2007, Radatz and Wright (2015) acknowledged that the study of victimization among adult women, both those within the general population and those who are incarcerated, had largely focused on individual types of harm. Their study findings revealed the extent of polyvictims within the incarcerated women sample was higher compared to the general population sample, as they also had a significantly higher average number of different victimization types. Notably, Azimi et al. (2019) further expanded the study of polyvictimization to include not only female people who are incarcerated, but also male people who are incarcerated, another widely acknowledged vulnerable population (DeHart, 2008; Wolff et al., 2009). Their findings indicated that women were more likely to be polyvictims, and have negative outcomes, such as poor mental health.

Like the above groups, national-level research findings reveal that lesbian, gay, bisexual, transgender, and Queer (LGBTQ+) people are also considered a vulnerable population due to their considerably high risk for victimization. For example, results from the National Crime Victimization Survey (NCVS) indicated LGBT people[1] are almost four times more likely to experience a violent victimization compared to non-LGBT people (Flores et al., 2020). The 2010 National Intimate Partner and Sexual Violence Survey (NISVS) results revealed similar patterns—lesbian, gay, and bisexual people are at an increased risk for most types of sexual violence compared to heterosexual people, with nearly 75% of bisexual women and almost half of bisexual men reporting sexual violence other than rape (compared to 43% of heterosexual women and 21% of heterosexual men; Walters et al., 2013, p. 1). As such, using NISVS data, Daigle and Hawk (2021) found that cisgender LGB people were at an increased risk for victimization, revictimization, and polyvictimization compared to heterosexual people, with 84% of LGB people being victimized in their lifetime, 79% being revictimized, and 66% being polyvictimized. These large-scale studies demonstrate high levels of polyvictimization among the entire LGBT population, and points to a need for more research on specific groups within the community.

Polyvictimization Among TGNC People

Even among LGBTQ+ individuals, not all carry the same risk of victimization. Transgender and gender nonconforming (TGNC) people are at an elevated risk for victimization compared to cisgender people, and they are particularly vulnerable to victimization with multiple layers of marginalization (Dilley et al., 2010; Downing & Przedworski, 2018; James et al., 2016; Kassing et al., 2021). For instance, the 2015 United States Transgender Survey (USTS) indicated that 47% of all respondents had been sexually assaulted in their lifetime, and 54% had experienced some form of intimate partner violence (James et al., 2016, p. 198). By contrast, NISVS reports that only 18% of cisgender women and 1% of cisgender men have been sexually assaulted in their lifetime, and 36% of cisgender women and 29% of cisgender men have experienced violence by an intimate partner in their lifetime (Black et al., 2011, pp. 1–2). Further, 58% of TGNC people were denied equal treatment or service, verbally harassed, and/or physically attacked in the past year for any reason; TGNC participants who were also participating in the underground economy (e.g., sex work), who had disabilities, or who were American Indian, Middle Eastern, or multiracial were also more likely to report those victimization experiences than TGNC people who were not multiply marginalized (James et al., 2016, p. 198). In fact, for all the types of violence surveyed by the USTS, having multiple layers of marginalization usually contributed—to varying extents—to victimization risk. For instance, sexual assault was higher among American Indian, Middle Eastern, and multiracial people, along with TGNC people who had female on their original birth certificates—with American Indian transgender men having the highest prevalence of lifetime sexual assault at 71% (James et al., 2016, pp. 205–206).

Given that TGNC people are at such an elevated risk for victimization, it logically follows that they might also be at an elevated risk for polyvictimization. However, the literature specifically examining polyvictimization among TGNC people is limited. Sterzing et al. (2019, p. 426) sought to establish the prevalence of polyvictimization among a sample of LGBTQ+ adolescents and found that genderQueer assigned-male-at-birth (AMAB) participants had the highest prevalence of lifetime polyvictimization, and TGNC adolescents in general were more likely to experience polyvictimization compared to cisgender LGB counterparts. The study findings also revealed African American participants had lower rates of polyvictimization compared to Caucasian participants. This is an unexpected finding given more recent literature. For instance, Sherman et al. (2020) found that Black and Latinx transwomen experienced extremely high rates of violence, with 91% of the participants experiencing one form of violence and 86% experiencing polyvictimization. Most recently, Messinger et al. (2021) used data on adult respondents to the USTS and noted that those with multiple layers of marginalization (e.g., being a racial/ethnic minority or impoverished in addition to being TGNC) were more likely to experience polyvictimization. These conflicting findings point to the need for further research.

The Consequences of Polyvictimization

Researchers have well-documented that experiences of victimization can leave lasting scars, often taking significant tolls on an individual, potentially affecting a variety of areas in one's life (Figley, 1988). Victimization not only can affect one's health and well-being, but it can also disrupt relationships and life trajectories. This is especially true for marginalized groups (e.g., Sigurvinsdottir & Ullman, 2016), including transgender and gender nonconforming (TGNC) people, as the magnitude of the consequences of victimization is higher for this group (Mustanski et al., 2016). Evidence suggests that TGNC people are especially susceptible to the negative consequences of victimization due to their compounded vulnerabilities, linked to characteristics associated with higher risk of harm (e.g., gender identity, social factors). The risk for polyvictimization emphasizes the marginalization of TGNC people on interpersonal and societal levels (Mitchell et al., 2018). For example, TGNC people are not afforded equal legal protections, which may exacerbate the consequences of polyvictimization, as less legal protection may contribute to a lack of resources and social capital. A lack of resources and social capital will negatively affect anyone who is dealing with the consequences of victimization, as they cannot access much-needed resources to help them cope. As mentioned before, these factors make the price of polyvictimization higher for TGNC people.

In general, the consequences of a single-instance victimization and its impact on an individual are dependent on an array of factors related to the victimization experience itself. For instance, factors such as the age of the victim, severity of the victimization, and relationship to the offender have all been shown to influence the magnitude of related consequences (Beitchman et al., 1991; Beitchman et al., 1992). In line with the development of the concept, polyvictimization has also been identified as an important factor that is known to impact the negative outcomes of victimization and trauma (Finkelhor et al., 2007a). Finkelhor's seminal work demonstrated the magnitude of the consequences for those who experience polyvictimization. When accounting for polyvictimization, the effect of any one type of victimization experience is diminished, suggesting that exposure to multiple types of victimization has lasting effects on individuals. In other words, compared to single-type victims, victims of polyvictimization report profoundly worse health and social consequences (Finkelhor et al., 2007a, 2007b). Higher rates of delinquency, trauma symptomology, low academic achievement, and alcohol use have been reported among those exposed to polyvictimization (Mitchell et al., 2018). Moreover, compared to non-polyvictims, those who experienced polyvictimization are more likely to come from single parent families and more likely to live in large cities. They are also more likely to be older, report higher rates of other adverse life events (such as serious illness, accidents, and family substance abuse problems), and experience serious forms of victimization (i.e., involving violence or sex offenses; Finkelhor et al., 2007b, 2009; Finkelhor et al., 2005). Polyvictimization, then, is a multifaceted problem that includes a diverse set of trauma experiences that have unique correlates among individuals.

Consequences of Polyvictimization Among TGNC People

Given that polyvictimization is a complex problem, adequate attention is needed on prevention and understanding mechanisms of the problem. Research on prevention and mechanisms of polyvictimization show that certain factors, such as gender or socioeconomic status (SES), interact with trauma exposure and can result in worse outcomes (Dilley et al., 2010; Kassing et al., 2021; Mitchell et al., 2018). The discussion surrounding the intersectionality of gender and social factors is especially pertinent to TGNC people who experience polyvictimization. For instance, it is well established in victimization literature that LGBTQ+ people generally are at an increased risk for single-instance victimization. The lived realties of many LGBTQ+ people include an increased risk for physical and sexual assault (Walters et al., 2013), harassment (Whitfield et al., 2019), and bullying (Kosciw et al., 2018; Martín-Castillo et al., 2020), with these risks being substantially higher than non-LGBTQ+ people (see also James et al., 2016). Furthermore, there is also a wealth of scholarly work to show that LGBTQ+ people are uniquely targeted for discriminatory violence based on sexual orientation and/or gender identity (Kehoe, 2020). Additionally, LGBTQ+ people are at an increased risk for victimization that is not directly the result of their gender identity or sexual orientation, such as sexual assault or intimate partner violence (James et al., 2016, p. 198; Walters et al., 2013). Further, the social structures in which LGBTQ+ people live often lead to limited access to resources for coping with victimization, meaning that LGBTQ+ will often struggle more with the consequences of victimization (for instance, see Acevedo-Polakovich et al., 2011; Calton et al., 2016; Ciarlante & Fountain, 2010).

This is especially the case due to the significant health disparities between LGBTQ+ people and heterosexual people. Not only are LGBTQ+ people at risk for negative health outcomes, they also have fewer protective health care practices compared to their heterosexual counterparts (Hasenbush et al., 2014). For TGNC people, specifically, data show that compared to cisgender people, they have worse mental health and disabilities, although there is little difference in access to healthcare (Downing & Przedworski, 2018). This issue is exacerbated given that access to trans-specific healthcare may be limited in certain areas, such as rural areas, and many health insurance companies do not cover trans-related healthcare (Johnson et al., 2020; Roberts & Fantz, 2014). Moreover, gender nonconforming people have higher odds of multiple chronic conditions, poor quality of life, and disabilities than both cisgender men and women (Downing & Przedworski, 2018). Health disparities create another layer of vulnerability that is compounded in the face of victimization.

The compounded effect of an increased risk for victimization and a lack of resources for coping means that victimization is a particularly salient problem among LGBTQ+ people that emphasizes the magnitude of subsequent negative health outcomes. Although all types of trauma can potentially lead to negative outcomes, those that involve repeated instances of interpersonal violence (i.e., polyvictimization) are especially damaging. Kassing et al. (2021) found that compared to those LGBTQ+ people who experienced fewer forms of interpersonal trauma, polyvictims (who experienced multiple forms of interpersonal trauma) were more likely to develop a range of negative mental health outcomes, including post-traumatic stress disorder (PTSD), depression, anxiety, and substance use issues.

Moreover, problems related to PTSD may stem from previous traumatic events and places one at risk for polyvictimization (Sterzing et al., 2017). Although literature on the consequences of polyvictimization among TGNC people is sparse, the existing evidence suggests that this is especially the case with this group. Among a sample of TGNC adolescents, Sterzing et al. (2017) found that higher levels of post-traumatic stress originating from family-level victimization increased the likelihood of experiencing past-year polyvictimization. Therefore, the interpersonal aspects in addition to the chronic nature of polyvictimization means that its effects are especially significant. In fact, polyvictimization is shown to be more salient in predicting traumatic stress symptoms compared to other life adversities, such as serious illness, family conflict, homelessness, death, and unemployment (Finkelhor et al., 2007b; Finkelhor et al., 2005). Additionally, Kassing et al. (2021) found that polyvictimization was associated with a far higher risk for a variety of negative mental health outcomes when compared to groups with less exposure to trauma, and although the authors found no difference in physical health outcomes between the two groups, those polyvictims were more likely to perceive their health as poor. Thus, the costs of polyvictimization for vulnerable groups like TGNC people may be too high to endure.

Similarly, polyvictimization is also a strong indicator of poor emotional and social functioning. Among youth who are not TGNC, those who experience high levels of polyvictimization are at an increased risk for both experiencing and perpetuating peer harassment (Mitchell et al., 2018). In a sample of LGBTQ+ college students, DeKeseredy et al. (2020)

found exceptionally high rates of polyvictimization among youth who received pro-abuse information or youth who had attachments to abusive peers. The implications for these findings are especially pertinent for TGNC people. Evidence suggests that they are a vulnerable group to bullying and harassment. Taken in context with DeKeseredy et al. (2020)'s findings, these experiences could also feed into the reasons why polyvictimization is related to higher trauma symptoms. In general, those who experience polyvictimization persistently over time are less likely to have supportive friends. TGNC people are very vulnerable to these types of experiences due to the level of bigotry and misinformation surrounding trans issues. Experiences of polyvictimization can further compound issues with interpersonal relationships. Research shows that polyvictimization can lead to induced hyperarousal and fear, both of which can interfere with peer interactions and social information processing (as cited in Mitchell et al., 2018). In turn, this can lead to TGNC people being excluded from peer group and increased risk to peer victimization.

Implications for Future Research

As previously noted, the literature on polyvictimization among TGNC people is limited. Given the dearth of knowledge surrounding polyvictimization and its consequences among TGNC people, some research implications can be inferred from what is currently known. First and foremost, it is recommended that researchers seek to design polyvictimization studies that intentionally center TGNC people as the sample population. Researchers should aim to not combine the experiences of cisgender LGB people with the experiences of TGNC people. While there is an undeniable overlap in the TGNC and LGB communities in that they both share a long history of pathologizing, and they both face similar issues of stigmatization related to gender expression or sexuality, which may overlap across both communities (Van der Ros & Motmans, 2016), the two groups ultimately deserve separate scholarly analysis (for instance, see the arguments presented in Worthen, 2013).

Additionally, the study of polyvictimization and its relation to vulnerable populations beyond children is relatively new. As noted earlier in this chapter, Finkelhor et al. (2007a, p. 8) identified three main problems within childhood victimization research that led to the development of the concept of polyvictimization. Indeed, the same three problems Finkelhor and his colleagues originally identified for research on victimization and its consequences among children have implications for the study of polyvictimization and its consequences among TGNC people, as polyvictimization research in this area is newly emerging. Finkelhor and his colleagues originally noted that the contribution of one instance of victimization may be exaggerated compared to polyvictimization, and research in this area among TGNC people is lacking. Mustanski et al. (2016) found that LGBT youths who had higher levels of cumulative victimization were more likely to suffer mental health consequences, but as of the writing of this chapter, it is the only study that directly compares the mental health outcomes of single-instance victimization with multiple instances of victimization that is inclusive of transpeople. There is also room for more research in this area that better accounts for diverse gender identities—such as nonbinary peoples' experiences.

Finkelhor and his colleagues also noted that the contribution of interrelationships among victimizations was understudied, and there is also a great need for exploratory literature in this area among TGNC people. For instance, DeKeseredy et al. (2020) found that the presence of negative peer support increased the prevalence of polyvictimization among

LGBTQ+ people, but the exact mechanism of how these peer associations might increase risk for polyvictimization is not clear from the data. Finally, Finkelhor and his colleagues identified a lack of literature altogether of those children who were chronically victimized because they might be especially vulnerable to negative outcomes. Messinger et al. (2021) is the only study, to date, that uses nationally representative data (the 2015 USTS) to measure the prevalence of polyvictimization among TGNC people. There is still a need for research that not only captures those TGNC people whom Finkelhor would define as "chronically" victimized (i.e., those who are "high polyvictims" who experience seven or more types of polyvictimization; Finkelhor et al., 2007a, p. 13), but which also captures the consequences of chronic victimization in comparison to other types of victimization. Finally, there is a need for more qualitative research to determine why TGNC people are particularly vulnerable to polyvictimization. Most notably, DeKeseredy et al. (2020, pp. 5–6) noted that those LGBTQ students studied were polyvictimized "both within categories and between categories," meaning that they were victimized not only by cisgender people, but also by other LGBTQ people. If this type of victimization is happening inside and outside of the TGNC community, there is a great need for culturally sensitive intervention techniques to address victimization in this community.

Conclusion

Polyvictimization is a serious form of victimization that carries heavy consequences for vulnerable groups. Although the literature on TGNC polyvictimization is sparse, the existing literature suggests that TGNC people may be particularly vulnerable to polyvictimization and subsequent adverse physical and mental health outcomes. This vulnerability may be exacerbated by multiple layers of marginalization, such as by being a racial/ethnic minority or impoverished in addition to being TGNC. Recently there has been an increased research focus on TGNC and victimization. Nevertheless, far more scholarly work is needed in this area in order to better understand the patterns and prevalence of polyvictimization among TGNC people, and to better develop inclusive policies and practice to address its harmful effects. This book chapter is one step toward that goal.

Note

1 Acronyms throughout this chapter are used intentionally. For instance, "LGBT" refers to lesbian, gay, bisexual, and transgender people, while "LGB" refers only to lesbian, gay, and bisexual people.

References

Acevedo-Polakovich, I. D., Bell, B., Gamache, P., & Christian, A. S. (2011). Service accessibility for lesbian, gay, bisexual, transgender, and questioning youth. *Youth & Society*, 45(1), 75–97. https://doi.org/10.1177/0044118X11409067.

Adams, Z. W., Moreland, A., Cohen, J. R., Lee, R. C., Hanson, R. F., Danielson, C. K., Self-Brown, S., & Briggs, E. C. (2016). Polyvictimization: Latent profiles and mental health outcomes in a clinical sample of adolescents. *Psychology of Violence*, 6(1), 145–155.

Azimi, A. M., Daquin, J. C., & Hoppe, S. J. (2019). Identifying poly-victimization among prisoners: An application of latent class analysis. *Journal of Interpersonal Violence*, 1–25.

Beitchman, J. H., Zucker, K. J., Hood, J. E., daCosta, G. A., & Akman, D. (1991). A review of the short-term effects of child sexual abuse. *Child Abuse & Neglect*, 15(4), 537–556.

Beitchman, J. H., Zucker, K. J., Hood, J. E., daCosta, G. A., Akman, D., & Cassavia, E. (1992). A review of the long-term effects of child sexual abuse. *Child Abuse & Neglect*, 16(1), 101–118.

Black, M. C., Basile, K. C., Breiding, M. J., Smith, S. G., Walters, M. L., Merrick, M. T., Chen, J., & Stevens, M. R. (2011). *The national intimate partner and sexual violence survey (NISVS): 2010 summary report*. Retrieved from www.cdc.gov/violenceprevention/pdf/NISVS_Report2010-a.pdf.

Calton, J. M., Cattaneo, L. B., & Gebhard, K. T. (2016). Barriers to help seeking for lesbian, gay, bisexual, transgender, and Queer survivors of intimate partner violence. *Trauma, Violence, & Abuse*, 17(5), 585–600.

Chesney-Lind, M., & Pasko, L. J. (2012). *The female offender: Girls, women, and crime* (3rd ed.). Los Angeles, CA: Sage.

Ciarlante, M., & Fountain, K. (2010). *Why it matters: Rethinking victim assistance for lesbian, gay, bisexual, transgender, and Queer victims of hate violence & intimate partner violence*. Washington, DC: National Center for Victims of Crime and the National Coalition of Anti-Violence Program.

Daigle, L. E., & Hawk, S. R. (2021). Sexual orientation, revictimization, and polyvictimization. *Sexuality Research and Social Policy*, 1–13. Advance online publication. https://doi.org/10.1007/s13178-021-00543-4.

DeHart, D. D. (2008). Pathways to prison: Impact of victimization in the lives of incarcerated women. *Violence Against Women*, 14(12), 1362–1381.

DeKeseredy, W. S., Schwartz, M. D., Kahle, L., & Nolan, J. (2020). Polyvictimization in a college lesbian, gay, bisexual, transgender, and queer community: The influence of negative peer support. *Violence and Gender*. Advance online publication. https://doi.org/https://doi.org/10.1089/vio.2020.0040.

Dilley, J. A., Simmons, K. W., Boysun, M. J., Pizacani, B. A., & Stark, M. J. (2010). Demonstrating the importance and feasibility of including sexual orietnation in public health surveys: Health disparities in the Pacific Northwest. *American Journal of Public Health*, 100(3), 460–467.

Downing, J. M., & Przedworski, J. M. (2018). Health of transgender adults in the U.S., 2014–2016. *American Journal of Preventive Medicine*, 55(3), 336–344.

Figley, C. R. (1988). Victimization, trauma, and traumatic stress. *The Counseling Psychologist*, 16(4), 635–641.

Finkelhor, D., & Dzuiba-Leatherman, J. (1994). Victimization of children. *American Psychologist*, 49(3), 173–183.

Finkelhor, D., Ormrod, R. K., & Turner, H. A. (2007a). Poly-victimization: A neglected component in child victimization. *Child Abuse & Neglect*, 31, 7–26.

Finkelhor, D., Ormrod, R. K., & Turner, H. A. (2007b). Polyvictimization and trauma in a national longitudinal cohort. *Development and Psychopathology*, 19, 149–166.

Finkelhor, D., Ormrod, R. K., & Turner, H. A. (2009). Lifetime assessment of poly-victimization in a national sample of children and youth. *Child Abuse & Neglect*, 33, 403–411.

Finkelhor, D., Ormrod, R. K., Turner, H. A., & Hamby, S. L. (2005). Measuring poly-victimization using the juvenile victimization questionnaire. *Child Abuse & Neglect*, 29, 1297–1312.

Flores, A. R., Langton, L., Meyer, I. H., & Romero, A. P. (2020). Victimization rates and traits of sexual and gender minorities in the United States: Results from the national crime victimization survey, 2017. *Science Advances*, 6(40).

Hasenbush, A., Flores, A. R., Kastanis, A., Sears, B., & Gates, G. J. (2014). *The LGBT divide: A data portrait of LGBT people in the midwestern, mountain, & southern states*. Retrieved from https://escholarship.org/uc/item/17m036q5.

James, S. E., Herman, J. L., Rankin, S. R., Keisling, M., Mottet, L. A., & Anafi, M. A. (2016). *The report of the 2015 U.S. Transgender survey*. Retrieved from https://transequality.org/sites/default/files/docs/usts/USTS-Full-Report-Dec17.pdf.

Johnson, A. H., Hill, I., Beach-Ferrara, J., Rogers, B. A., & Bradford, A. (2020). Common barriers to healthcare for transgender people in the U.S. Southeast. *International Journal of Transgender Health*, 21(1), 70–78.

Jones, J. M. (2021). LGBT identification rises to 5.6% in latest U.S. estimate. *Gallup*. Retrieved from https://news.gallup.com/poll/329708/lgbt-identification-rises-latest-estimate.aspx.

Kassing, F., Casanova, T., Griffin, J. A., Wood, E., & Stepleman, L. M. (2021). The effects of poly-victimization on mental and physical health outcomes in an LGBTQ sample. *Journal of Traumatic Stress*, 34, 161–171.

Kehoe, J. (2020). Anti-LGBTQ hate: An analysis of situational variables. *Journal of Hate Studies*, 16(1), 21–34.

Kerig, P. K. (2018). Polyvictimization and girls' involvement in the juvenile justice system: Investigating gender-differentiated patterns of risk, recidivism, and resilience. *Journal of Interpersonal Violence*, 33(5), 789–809.

Kosciw, J. G., Greytak, E. A., Zongrone, A. D., Clark, C. M., & Truong, N. L. (2018). *The 2017 national school climate survey: The experiences of lesbian, gay, bisexual, transgender, and Queer youth in our nation's schools*. Retrieved from www.glsen.org/sites/default/files/GLSEN%20 2017%20National%20School%20Climate%20Survey%20%28NSCS%29%20-%20Full%20 Report.pdf.

Martín-Castillo, D., Jiménez-Barbero, J. A., Pastor-Bravo, M. D. M., Sánchez-Muñoz, M., Fernández-Espín, M. E., & García-Arenas, J. J. (2020). School victimization in transgender people: A systematic review. *Children and Youth Services Review*, 119.

McKee, S. A., & Hilton, N. Z. (2019). Co-occurring substance use, PTSD, and IPV victimization: Implications for female offender services. *Trauma, Violence, & Abuse*, 20(3), 303–314.

Messinger, A. M., Guadalupe-Diaz, X. L., & Kurdyla, V. (2021). Transgender polyvictimization in the U.S. transgender survey. *Journal of Interpersonal Violence*. Advance online publication. https://doi. org/10.1177/08862605211039250.

Mitchell, K. J., Segura, A., Jones, L. M., & Turner, H. A. (2018). Poly-victimization and peer harassment involvement in a technological world. *Journal of Interpersonal Violence*, 33(5), 762–788.

Mustanski, B., Andrews, R., & Puckett, J. A. (2016). The effects of cumulative victimization on mental health among lesbian, gay, bisexual, and transgender adolescents and young adults. *American Journal of Public Health*, 106(3), 527–533.

Pasko, L., & Chesney-Lind, M. (2016). Running the gauntlet: Understanding commercial sexual exploitation and the pathways perspective to female offending. *Journal of Developmental and Life-Course Criminology*, 2, 275–295.

Radatz, D. L., & Wright, E. M. (2015). Does polyvictimization affect incarcerated and non-incarcerated adult women differently? An exploration into internalizing problems. *Journal of Interpersonal Violence*, 32(9), 1379–1400.

Roberts, T. K., & Fantz, C. R. (2014). Barriers to quality health care for the transgender population. *Clinical Biochemistry*, 47, 983–987.

Sherman, A. D. F., Poteat, T. C., Budhathoki, C., Kelly, U., Clark, K. D., & Campbell, J. C. (2020). Association of depression and post-traumatic stress with polyvictimization and emotional transgender and gender diverse community connection among Black and Latinx transgender women. *LGBT Health*, 7(7).

Sigurvinsdottir, R., & Ullman, S. E. (2016). Sexual orientation, race, and trauma as predictors of sexual assault recovery. *Journal of Family Violence*, 31(1), 913–921.

Smith, V. C. (2017). Substance-abusing female offenders as victims: Chronological sequencing of pathways into the criminal justice system. *Victims & Offenders*, 12(1), 113–137.

Sterzing, P. R., Gartner, R. E., Goldbach, J. T., McGeough, B. L., Ratliff, G. A., & Johnson, K. C. (2019). Polyvictimization prevalence rates for sexual and gender minority adolescents: Breaking down the silos of victimization research. *Psychology of Violence*, 9(4), 419–430.

Sterzing, P. R., Ratliff, G. A., Gartner, R. E., McGeough, B. L., & Johnson, K. C. (2017). Social ecological correlates of polyvictimization among a national sample of transgender, genderQueer, and cisgender sexual minority adolescents. *Child Abuse & Neglect*, 67, 1–12.

Van der Ros, J., & Motmans, J. (2016). Trans activism and LGB movements: Odd bedfellows? In D. Paternotte & M. Tremblay (Eds.), *The Ashgate research companion to lesbian and gay activism* (pp. 179–194). New York: Routledge.

Walters, M. L., Chen, J., & Breiding, M. J. (2013). *The national intimate partner and sexual violence survey (NISVS): 2010 findings on victimization by sexual orientation.* Retrieved from www.cdc.gov/violenceprevention/pdf/nisvs_sofindings.pdf.

Whitfield, D. L., Kattari, S. K., Langenderfer-Magruder, L., Walls, N. E., & Ramos, D. (2019). The crossroads of identities: Predictors of harassment among lesbian, gay, bisexual, and Queer adults. *Journal of the Society for Social Work and Research*, 10(2), 237–260.

Wolff, N., Shi, J., & Siegel, J. A. (2009). Patterns of victimization among male and female inmates: Evidence of an enduring legacy. *Violence and Victims*, 24(4), 469–484.

Worthen, M. G. F. (2013). An argument for separate analyses of attitudes toward lesbian, gay, bisexual men, bisexual women, MtF and FtM transgender individuals. *Sex Roles*, 68, 703–723.

Chapter 6

Sexual Consent, Sexual Coercion, and Victimization within the LGBTQA+ Community

Brooke A de Heer

Research on sexual consent and violence has traditionally focused on heterosexual, cisgender interactions between men and women. In other words, research in this area has had a heteronormative approach in that it has considered heterosexual cisgender experiences as standard, normal, and dominant to the exclusion of Queer or gender nonconforming experiences (Marchia & Sommer, 2019; Warner, 1993). This chapter seeks to situate sexually minoritized[1] people's experiences with sexual consent and victimization within Queer and feminist theoretical perspectives by briefly reviewing the relevant literature, identifying the gaps, and highlighting current research that investigates LGBTQA+[2] experiences with sexual victimization. This chapter strives to remove the gender binary that is typically studied in sexual violence; male perpetrator and female victim (for a review of the gender binary in sexual violence see Turchik et al., 2016); and focus on existing power structures and forces, regardless of gender or sexual identity. By shifting the focus to power, which is dynamic within dual identities (gender and sexual identities), the findings elucidate how sexual violence in LGBTQA+ populations present itself, and how and where power dynamics influence communication around sex.

Research on sexual violence and victimization typically involves two common themes: 1) violence perpetrated by heterosexual men against heterosexual women, and 2) explorations of risk factors that contribute to perpetration and victimization. Both themes are incredibly important for furthering our understanding of sexual violence from a heteronormative perspective. We know that women are the predominant victims of sexual violence perpetrated by men across both student and community samples (Koss et al., 1987; Krebs et al., 2016; Smith et al., 2018; Walters et al., 2013). Data also indicates that various factors increase an individual's risk of being a perpetrator or victim (Abrahams et al., 2014; Coulter et al., 2017; Mellins et al., 2017; Tharp et al., 2013). For example, one of the most widely researched variables in the campus sexual assault literature that is related to *both* perpetration and victimization is alcohol consumption (Abbey et al., 2014; Fedina et al., 2018; Krebs et al., 2009).

While research on sexual violence victimization across community and college samples has identified LGBTQ+ people as having elevated rates of sexual victimization (Ford & Soto-Marquez, 2016; Jones et al., 2016; Walters et al., 2013), few studies focus on Queer experiences exclusively. One such study found that LGBQ youth were almost twice as likely to experience sexual coercion compared to heterosexual youth, and transgender youth were more than three times as likely to experience sexual coercion compared to cisgender youth (Dank et al., 2014). Sexually minoritized adults also show elevated risk for sexual victimization (Rothman et al., 2011; Walters et al., 2013). Edwards et al. (2015) found that sexually minoritized college students reported twice as many incidents of sexual assault (24.3%)

DOI: 10.4324/9781003400981-7

compared to their heterosexual counterparts (11%). Unfortunately, outside of prevalence rates, we know very little about the experiences of sexual violence within the Queer community because of research's heteronormative foci.

One salient gap in our understanding of LGBTQA+ experiences of sexual violence is the social construction of sexual consent and its relationship with coercive behaviors and practices to gain sexual access. The topics of both sexual consent and coercion in sexual relationships have garnered research attention through a heteronormative lens, but Queer individuals and communities are often sidelined in these areas of scholarship. Given that the traditional power dynamic between heterosexual men and women presents differently in LGBTQA+ experiences of sexual violence, it is important to investigate the ways in which Queer experiences with sexual consent and coercion may be different.

Consent

Understanding the complexities of sexual consent is foundational to identifying how *non-consensual* sexual contact occurs. Rape and sexual assault laws, which vary by state, often refer to consent when it is missing or absent (lack of consent or non-consent). For example, Nevada law determines that lack of consent results from force, threat of force, or physical or mental incapacity of the victim (RAINN, 2021). Eleven states at the time of this writing use affirmative consent indications in their rape and sexual assault laws, meaning that consent is *not* present unless it is affirmative, voluntary, and freely given.[3] Even with the increasing popularity of affirmative consent, especially in college and university policy, what constitutes "voluntary" or "freely given" is debatable (Beres, 2007; Pugh & Becker, 2018).

Intersectional feminists offer an insightful critique of consent by considering the influence of people's race, class, gender, and sexual identity on their perceived agency to consent (Alcoff, 2018; Ehrlich, 2001; Loick, 2020; Mackinnon, 1989). The critique questions notions of true consent when the ability to consent is inherently entrenched in patriarchal constraints that confine and limit marginalized people from freely expressing wants and needs. In other words, meanings of consent are socially constructed by those in powerful, dominant positions. In an article that critically questions the role of choice in women's lives, Baker (2008) comments "consent is never freely or neutrally given in situations of inequality" (p. 58). This notion is supported empirically by research that investigates unwanted but consensual sex (Peterson & Muehlenhard, 2007; Thomas et al., 2017). Research has demonstrated that it is not uncommon for people to consent to sex but not actually want it and that there are many reasons for doing so. Studying only heterosexual encounters, scholars find that women often acquiesce to unwanted sex to maintain relationships, avoid tension or violence, and because it is easier and safer than refusing (Bay-Cheng & Eliseo-Arras, 2008; Hayfield & Clarke, 2012; O'Sullivan & Allgeier, 1998). In this context, women acquiesce or yield to sex to align with cultural and structural norms that are male dominated (Baker, 2008; Gavey, 2005; Mathieu, 1990). The critique argues that agreeing to sex under these contexts does not necessitate actual consent. This further problematizes the legal requirements around consent that are often hinged on the archaic "no means no, yes means yes" standard (Loick, 2020). Clearly there are examples of coerced consent in which yes is artificial and obligatory.

The limitation to this research is the exclusive focus on gender inequality in heterosexual encounters. While gender and heterosexual identity are salient and important characteristics when considering the nuance of consent, the heteronormative categories limit the full scope of the issue. Much of heteronormative focused research exclusively examines women's societal positioning and how secondary status (due to gender) prohibits an active choice to consent or not, given the structural barriers defined by gender. But gender is not the only category of difference that suffers the ramifications of a masculinized, gender normed society. LGBTQA+ individuals have historically existed on the margins of society, often forced to hide, or suppress their sexual identity. Queer people and communities have endured a long struggle with systemic oppression and inequitable treatment (Buist et al., 2018; Worthen, 2020), yet they have been largely left out of the conversation of structural barriers to sexual consent.

To fill that gap, recent research has investigated the nuance of sexual consent through LGBTQA+ peoples' own voices. Studies show that sexual consent within the Queer community is generally agreed upon as important and readily discussed in interpersonal interactions, which differs from heterosexual consent practices (de Heer et al., 2021; Hirsch & Khan, 2020). Using focus groups with LGBTQA+ individuals, de Heer et al. (2021) specifically notes the following barriers to navigating consent unique to the complexities of Queer relationships: 1) understanding what constitutes sex among the LGBTQA+ community, 2) the role of heteronormative sex education in perpetuating misconceptions about sexual consent, 3) the impact of trauma, coercion, and victimization on the Queer community, and 4) the importance of dual identities (gender and sexual identity) and discrimination as a result of those dual identities in framing attitudes, feelings, and experiences of sexual consent. One finding of particular importance is how power dynamics in Queer relationships are not based on gender, which was revealed when individuals reflected on their dual identities. For example, bisexual women expressed that, compared to heterosexual power dynamics that are rooted in gender (men are aggressors, women are passive receivers), their relationships with other women displayed similar power positions, with one woman taking more of the dominant role and the other woman being more submissive (de Heer et al., 2021).

While LGBTQA+ individuals appeared to be less restricted by stereotypical heterosexual and gender norms and/or power dyads in sexual expression and practice, in some ways those lowered restrictions may increase the complexity of sexual consent, given the social and structural oppression of the Queer community. LGBTQA+ individuals have historically existed on the margins of society, often forced to hide or suppress their sexual identity, therefore creating barriers in communication and acceptance of their sexual choices (Buist et al., 2018). Queer people and communities have endured a long struggle with systemic oppression and inequitable treatment (Worthen, 2020), yet they have been largely left out of the conversation of structural barriers to sexual consent. Most of the overarching themes identified by de Heer et al. (2021) highlight the marginalization and inequitable treatment of sexually minoritized people and the distribution of power in sexual interactions that have subsequent ramifications on experiences of sexual consent and trauma. Conversely, analyses also identified that participants viewed discriminatory experiences and trauma as a shared burden among the LGBTQA+ community, thus invoking an increased sense of responsibility to openly communicate about sexual wants and needs in an attempt to neutralize power inequities (see de Heer et al., 2021 for a detailed description of the study and findings).

Forced Consent

The concept of forced consent, or agreement to engage in a sexual act through coercive or manipulative tactics, is another way to compel a person to consent without actually wanting the sexual contact (Conroy et al., 2015; Koss et al., 1987; Ray et al., 2018; Testa et al., 2004). The vast majority of studies on sexual coercion and forced consent spotlight gender, with little consideration of intersectional analyses. Recent research shows that coercive interactions are not unique to heterosexual women. In fact, sexually minoritized women *and* men experience situations of coerced sexual victimization at a disproportionately high rate (Messinger & Koon-Magnin, 2019; Ray et al., 2021). Ray et al. (2021) is one of the first studies to both articulate substantial gaps in the literature on same-sex forced consent and empirically address them. Results from this study indicate that 58% of sexually minoritized females and 44% of sexually minoritized males report experiencing coerced sexual violence. This is substantially higher than heterosexual women (42%) and men (24%) in the study.

As demonstrated by the statistics above, forced consent elucidates the role of power and inequity in sexual negotiations, especially for LGBTQA+ victims. Thus, gender is likely not the most influential variable regarding forced consent, although it is an important factor (for research on heterosexual men using coercive tactics against women see Jozkowski & Peterson, 2013; Jozkowski et al., 2017; Pugh & Becker, 2018). Disparate power dynamics that foster coercive interactions can manifest in a number of ways outside of the gender binary. Renzetti's (1992) work on coercion with lesbian couples argued that power inequity transverses gender roles such that two women in a relationship can still engage in coercive practices determined by power differentials. For example, one woman in the relationship may take a more dominant role and coerce sexual consent through threats or manipulation. Scholars have argued to detach abusive behaviors from the gender dichotomy of men and women, and instead represent them as more masculine or more feminine behaviors (Donovan & Hester, 2015; for review of coercive control in LGBTQA+ relationships see Stark & Hester, 2019). This research identifies that perpetrators tend to fill what has been historically more masculine roles in relationships, such as setting the terms of the relationship and being the decision maker, while victims tend to take on more feminine roles, such as responsibility for caretaking and emotional happiness, *regardless of gender identity*. Similarly, Bedera and Nordmeyer (2020) found that perpetrators of sexual violence against Queer women are more likely to adopt expressions of masculinity independent of their gender identity. Research on Queer experiences of coercive practices and the relationship with power and gender/sexual identity is developing, but an understanding of the construction of sexual consent within that paradigm is still lacking.

LGBTQA+ Sexual Consent and Victimization: Current Research

The current study addresses the above identified gap in the literature on LGBTQA+ sexual consent and victimization through investigating the experience and impact of sexual victimization for LGBTQA+ people. Using one-on-one interviews with LGBTQA+ individuals with experiences of unwanted sexual contact or sexual assault, this research gives voice to Queer survivors to describe and define their experiences.

Methods

Fifteen semi-structured interviews were conducted with LGBTQA+ identifying individuals who had experienced sexual violence or unwanted sexual contact. Participants were recruited through flyers that were electronically and physically distributed to LGBTQA+

friendly organizations, businesses, and listservs. Identities included bisexual women, lesbian women, lesbian asexual women, Queer women, Queer gender nonconforming individuals, Queer transgender individuals, and Queer men. Incentives for participation were provided, which was important for both recruitment purposes and more importantly, to ensure that participants received compensation for sharing their time and personal stories. Interview questions broadly sought to understand if/how LGBTQA+ experiences of sexual violence differ from our understanding of cisgender heterosexual sexual violence experiences. Interviews were coded by two independent researchers using a deductive thematic analysis approach. Using relevant literature in the areas of consent and coercion, researchers identified specific themes representing coercive tactics or methods used by the perpetrators. These included coercion by means of lies, threats, or pressure; coercion by means of displeasure, critique, or anger; coercion by means of confusion usually representing a perpetrator taking advantage of an individual's age or relationship (child sexual abuse); coercion by means of making the victim feel they did not have the opportunity to say no (surprise); incapacitation; and threat of force (see Table 6.1; Canan et al., 2020; Koss et al., 2007).

A total of 31 experiences of unwanted sexual contact across the 15 participants were shared, with some having one experience (7 participants) and others having multiple experiences with sexual violence (8 participants). It should be noted that participants were asked to share as many or as few incidents as they were comfortable, thus the reported number of total *shared* incidents may not represent *all* the experiences of unwanted sexual contact experienced by the participants. Most participants (14 out of 15) experienced at least one of their unwanted sexual encounters at the hands of someone they know, either family and friends (21 incidents reported by 11 participants) or acquaintances (7 incidents reported by 6 participants).

Two participants shared three stories of stranger sexual assault/rape. Twenty-one perpetrators were assumed to identify as heterosexual cisgender men, six as lesbian or Queer women, two as heterosexual women, and two were unknown. Five of the reported incidents occurred when the participants were children (12 or under), nine occurred when they were teenagers (13–17), and 17 incidents occurred when they were adults (18 and up). In eleven of the shared experiences, participants classified the unwanted sexual contact as occurring with a partner and six of those were within a long-term relationship.

Table 6.1 Types of Coercion and Examples

Types of Coercion	Example
Lies, threats, or pressure	Telling someone they were asking for it by flirting or teasing and can't back out now; threatening to out a closeted person
Displeasure, critique, or anger	Telling someone they are unattractive or a bad partner if they don't engage in a sexual act; getting angry when someone does not comply with a sexual request
Confusion	Someone taking advantage of another person's age, mental capacity, or relationship (child sexual abuse)
Surprise	Making someone feel they did not have the opportunity to say no; Blitz style approach
Incapacitation	Using alcohol or drugs to intoxicate someone in order to gain sexual compliance
Threat of force	Someone threatening another with a weapon or physical force to gain compliance

Table 6.2 Descriptives of Unwanted Sexual Contact by Number of Incidents and Participants

Descriptives of Unwanted Sexual Contact	N (Incidents)	N (Participants)
Total	**31**	**15**
One experience of unwanted sexual contact		7
Multiple experiences of unwanted sexual contact		8
Age range at time unwanted sexual contact:		
12 years or under	5	3
13–17 years	9	8
18 years and above	17	10
Perpetrator:		
Family or friend	21	11
Acquaintance	7	6
Stranger	3	2
Heterosexual, cisgender men	21	12
Lesbian/Queer women	6	6
Heterosexual, cisgender women	2	2

Findings

Findings from the 15 interviews were grouped by prominent themes associated with the shared experiences of unwanted sexual contact. The presence of non-consent (or sexual contact that took place without the participants' agreement) was a dominant theme across the reported incidents, with forced sexual contact being common. Nonconsensual sexual contact was also discussed by participants in the context of relationships where it was difficult to retract consent once given. A second prominent and important theme was the role of the participant's Queer identity in the unwanted sexual contact such that some participants felt that their identity as LGBTQA+ was possibly associated with the incident(s). The use of coercion to gain consent was another major theme throughout the interviews, with tactics ranging from verbal manipulation to the threat of physical force. Lastly, the concept of power was an important theme as it was indirectly discussed in most incidents of unwanted sexual contact, whether the incident involved a different-sex, presumably heterosexual person, or same-sex person.

The Manifestation of Non-Consent

Consent was *not* sought by the perpetrator or given by the victim in 25 of the 31 incidents (15 participants) of unwanted sexual contact. In five of the 31 shared experiences (four participants), participants were in relationships at the time that sometimes involved consent practices and other times consent was not sought or given. These reported incidents typically involved interactions that started off consensual, but when the participant tried to stop it at a later point, those requests were not heard or acknowledged. Relative to consent clearly *not* being sought, two participants shared:

> And unfortunately, I also suffered sexual assault from the guy I was dating. I would express, I'm just, I can't, I'm just not . . . and he'd be like "can't isn't part of my vocabulary—I literally won't hear that." That's kind of haunted me, you know, for a while.
>
> I think he realized what he did was wrong. I think during the moment, he thought I was awake or something. I think after a couple months passed, he realized, "Oh! She wasn't awake. She was actually knocked out because of Benadryl."

Two participants expressed the issue with wanting to retract consent by explaining:

> It was a situation where we were already having sex, but I was like, experiencing a lot of pain and asked him to stop, but he continued.
>
> but at the beginning of that relationship things were consensual. I really did like that person and loved that person a lot and wanted to be intimate with them. But then some things started happening in that relationship that made me feel really unsafe, so I started to not want to be physically intimate with them.

The Role of Queer Identity

In ten of the shared incidents (nine participants), participants felt they may have been targeted because of their Queer identity. Most reported being openly out at the time and that this status possibly contributed to their victimization. In an additional three incidents (three participants), participants felt confident they experienced unwanted sexual contact as a direct result of their Queer identity. This feeling was typically linked to the perpetrator knowing and acknowledging the participants' LGBTQA+ identity. One participant who felt that the knowledge of their Queer status directly contributed to the assault and who was placed in a vulnerable position because of intoxication commented:

> She was someone who joked around a lot about, y'know, how easy she could get women, and her sister and her would have kind of a competition of who could bed the most people . . . She somehow coerced me to walk home with her, and she pulled me into her room, and pulled me onto her bed, and just kind of took advantage of my state, knowing that it would be just another number for her.

In another instance where a participant felt they had been targeted, they were out and a performer, which they felt contributed to the unwanted sexual contact.

> I was out one night, and we were drinking, and there were some lesbians, like a group of lesbians that came up as I was going out to my car, and they surrounded me by my car, and they were like, "We know what kind of girl you are, you should come party with us," and I was like, "I'm not into that." . . . And uh, one of the bigger of the girls pinned me up against the vehicle by my neck, and reached her hand under my skirt, as I was trying to fight her off, *[pause]*, and then she put her finger inside of me a few times, and she was like, "We know you like stuff like this."

Coercion and Consent

Coercive tactics used by the perpetrator were present in the vast majority (28 out of 31) of shared experiences. For the three experiences that were not classified as involving coercion, the participants were not comfortable sharing explicit details about the incident, so the use of coercion is unknown. Coercive means were highly variable and spread across the full range of coercive tactics ranging from verbal manipulation and deceit to threat of force. Many incidents (23) involved more than one type of coercive tactic. Fifteen of the shared experiences also involved the use of physical force. Below are the types of coercion participants expressed being used to gain sexual access and corresponding quotes that exemplify that method of coercion.

Twelve shared incidents of sexual victimization involved coercion by means of lies, threats, or pressure:

And my anxiety was pretty clear to him, cuz like, I wouldn't look him in the eyes. I wouldn't do anything, like I didn't want to kiss him. I didn't wanna do any of that. But I felt coerced into doing just like one step further. . . . But overall, I had said no, previously. Like when I look back at it, it's like I had said no from the get-go, kind of, and he just kept, kept pushing to do more.

Six incidents involved coercion by means of displeasure, critique, or anger:

And he would not take no for an answer. And it ended up just being me and him in the living room area. Everyone else was in the other room. And he would just not stop. He was very persistent on what he wanted, didn't care about what I wanted or what I said. And then, after, I left to just go back to my room, and he followed me and brought me . . . came in my room and pinned me against the wall and things. And was like, "you need to think about what you're doing. I told you I wanted this, and I want you to do this," and it turned into a very big fiasco and he wouldn't leave me alone.

Two experiences involved coercion by means of confusion where the person perpetrating the offense took advantage of an individual's age or relationship (child sexual abuse):

And I remember at first when I woke up and saw him sitting, I was sleeping, and I woke up, and he was sitting on the bed and his hand was on me. I remember at first, I was wondering; did this really happen? Because all of these other things had been going on, but it was hard for me to initially just actually take that in that he did that.

Nine incidents involved a method of incapacitation:

Since I was drunk and on molly a little bit, it had felt kind of good, but it had felt really kind of painful at the same time. In the moment I remember feeling really confused.

Nine shared experiences exhibited the threat of force:

He goes over and he locks his door. I was like, that's really weird, but maybe he's just trying to keep people out? But he starts to like, he sits back down, we're both sitting on the couch, and he starts pushing me closer and closer to the edge, and kind of like, pinning me and trapping me. Then he puts his hand on my leg, and he starts just trying to get handsy, and I'm like, "woah hey, we're just hanging out. It's cool, like, I'm really sorry but I'm not feeling this at all."

Eight incidents involved the victims being surprised by the behavior and feeling they did not have the chance to say no:

that came up as I was going out to my car, and they surrounded me by my car, and they were like, "We know what kind of girl you are. You should come party with us," and I was like, "I'm not into that." . . . one of the bigger of the girls pinned me up against the vehicle by my neck, and reached her hand under my skirt, as I was trying to fight her off.

Consent, Coercion, and Power

Findings from this study suggest that not explicitly seeking consent combined with coercive strategies are often used to gain sexual access within LGBTQA+ experiences of sexual violence. While physical force falls outside the parameters of coercive tactics, it was used in 15 incidents, and all those incidents involved other coercive methods such as verbal manipulation or incapacitation. Additionally, when consent was given, coercive tactics were also in play, indicating the potential for situations of forced consent in which agreement was not freely given and/or voluntary.

While coercion is used in many instances of sexual violence, cisgender heteronormative or other, the intersection of coercion and Queer identity is particularly complex and may provide unique insight into power dynamics related to sexual violence. Of particular importance is that most of the participants identified as bisexual, Queer, or lesbian women and most incidents are presumed to be perpetrated by heterosexual cisgender men, with a smaller number of incidents perpetrated by lesbian or Queer women. Concepts of power dynamics between perpetrator and victim, and more commonly, lack of power on the part of participants, was conveyed in all incidents regardless of gender or sexual orientation of the parties. For example, in one experience shared by a participant, they reflect on their first abusive Queer relationship, their perceived agency (related to power dynamics), and the coercive means used to engage them in nonconsensual sex:

> There's so many instances, just with this one relationship alone where I had basically not experienced having agency over my body. And so, it's not like a one-time thing, you know? It's kind of just like the [sic] nature of the relationship itself, the lack of sex education that included anything about consent.

This quote elucidates how aspects of agency, power, and heteronormative value systems impact sexual situations and negotiations within Queer relationships. This would suggest that power representations within Queer relationships mirror heterosexual power dynamics *without* the exclusive reliance on gender to determine who is dominant and who is passive. This participant describes being sexually violated by a Queer partner as a product of lack of agency due to inadequate education, and the nature of the Queer relationship. While issues with agency related to inadequate education and accompanying social scripts is also common in cisgender heterosexual instances of sexual violence, this participant indicates that there may be an additional element imbedded in some LGBTQA+ relationships that adds complexity to consent practices. This participant indicates that they may not have the tools to navigate sexual consent in a relationship that lies outside the heteronormative sphere.

Conclusion and Implications

There is a long history of heterosexual cisgender normativity, whereby everything ranging from policy development to parenting to education has been centered around heterosexual cisgender people's experiences and realities. As Worthen (2020) explains this heterosexual cisgender system "organizes social power around sexual identity and gender identity" (p. 25). This likely has adverse ramifications for the sexually minoritized, particularly in situations of sexual contact, because they are positionally placed with less power and subsequently less perceived and experienced agency. This then opens the door for coercive interactions to be particularly impactful and effective. Additionally, following work by Stark and Hester (2019), power inequity, coercive methods, and consent practices are often represented within LGBTQA+ relationships outside of the traditional gender binary. In other words, regardless of identification as a man or woman, dominance and control of one individual by another often influences consent and coercive practices.

The current study reviewed above sought to fill an existing gap in our understanding of LGBTQA+ experiences of sexual violence, including the impact and meaning of the social construction of sexual consent and coercive interactions. Findings suggest that LGBTQA+ people can offer profound insight into the complex relationship between power, marginalization, and sexual violence. It should be noted that as critical researchers and LGBTQA+ activists advocate for inclusion of gender nonconforming and sexual minoritized individuals in research paradigms and social inquiry, the LGBTQA+ community is vastly diverse, and attention needs to be paid to intersecting identities. As van Anders (2015) states

> The collapsing of diverse sexual minority groups into one sexual minority category can be problematic given differences in lived experiences. For example, the conflation of gender minorities (e.g., trans-identified people) and sexual minorities (e.g., LGB individuals) can obfuscate the disparate challenges these groups face and the types of social change they might seek. Other times, shared experiences of stigmatization might be a push to collective action among sexual minorities (p. 1185).

It is particularly important to recognize that diversity in the investigation of the experiences of sexual violence within sexually and gender minoritized communities because different identities and varying kinds of relationships have different influences on power dynamics and subsequent consent and coercion experiences.

Past research on stigma associated with sexual victimization identified stigmatization and help-seeking barriers as more prominent for survivors from disadvantaged social locations (i.e., marginalized groups; Kennedy et al., 2012). Thus, sexual victimization experiences for LGBTQA+ people likely incorporate additional layers of self-doubt, blame, powerlessness, and questions of acceptance that are accentuated in cases where coercion and consent are tangled. Given the historical marginalization of LGBTQA+ people and with an understanding of trauma related to sexual violence victimization, researchers and clinicians should be well informed of the negative effects of heteronormative assumptions and value systems when working with the Queer community. Research designs and best practice protocols should center inclusivity, affirmation, and safe spaces for Queer individuals.

Notes

1 The term *minoritized* is used over *minority* to emphasize that social and structural forces marginalize certain groups and create systemic discrimination and stigma (Smith, 2016)

2 The term LGBTQA+ is used to describe individuals who identify as homosexual, bisexual, asexual, transgender or any nonconforming sexual orientation and/or identify. Highlighting differences in social identity (similar to work by Schulze & Koon-Magnin, 2017) is critically important to understanding how different identities within the LGBTQA+ community experience consent and sexual violence. The term Queer is also utilized as an inclusive representation of this diverse group.

3 Laws that use affirmative consent phrasing: CA, CO, FL, HI, IL, MN, NH, NJ, OK, WA, WI

References

Abbey, A., Wegner, R., Woerner, J., Pegram, S. E., & Pierce, J. (2014). Review of survey and experimental research that examines the relationship between alcohol consumption and men's sexual aggression perpetration. *Trauma, Violence, & Abuse*, 15(4), 265–282.

Abrahams, N., Devries, K., Watts, C., Pallitto, C., Petzold, M., Shamu, S., & García-Moreno, C. (2014). Worldwide prevalence of non-partner sexual violence: A systematic review. *The Lancet*, 383(9929), 1648–1654.

Alcoff, L. M. (2018). *Rape and resistance*. Hoboken, NJ: John Wiley & Sons.

Baker, J. (2008). The ideology of choice. Overstating progress and hiding injustice in the lives of young women: Findings from a study in North Queensland, Australia. *Women's Studies International Forum*, 31(1), 53–64.

Bay-Cheng, L. Y., & Eliseo-Arras, R. K. (2008). The making of unwanted sex: Gendered and neoliberal norms in college women's unwanted sexual experiences. *Journal of Sex Research*, 45(4), 386–397.

Bedera, N., & Nordmeyer, K. (2020). An inherently masculine practice: Understanding the sexual victimization of Queer women. *Journal of Interpersonal Violence*, 0886260519898439.

Beres, M. A. (2007). 'Spontaneous' sexual consent: An analysis of sexual consent literature. *Feminism & Psychology*, 17(1), 93–108.

Buist, C. L., Lenning, E., & Ball, M. (2018). Queer criminology. In *Routledge handbook of critical criminology* (pp. 96–106). New York: Routledge.

Canan, S. N., Jozkowski, K. N., Wiersma-Mosley, J., Blunt-Vinti, H., & Bradley, M. (2020). Validation of the sexual experience survey-short form revised using lesbian, bisexual, and heterosexual women's narratives of sexual violence. *Archives of Sexual Behavior*, 49(3), 1067–1083. https://doi.org/10.1007/s10508-019-01543-7.

Conroy, N. E., Krishnakumar, A., & Leone, J. M. (2015). Reexamining issues of conceptualization and willing consent: The hidden role of coercion in experiences of sexual acquiescence. *Journal of Interpersonal Violence*, 30(11), 1828–1846.

Coulter, R. W., Mair, C., Miller, E., Blosnich, J. R., Matthews, D. D., & McCauley, H. L. (2017). Prevalence of past-year sexual assault victimization among undergraduate students: Exploring differences by and intersections of gender identity, sexual identity, and race/ethnicity. *Prevention Science*, 18(6), 726–736.

Dank, M., Lachman, P., Zweig, J. M., & Yahner, J. (2014). Dating violence experiences of lesbian, gay, bisexual, and transgender youth. *Journal of Youth and Adolescence*, 43(5), 846–857.

de Heer, B., Brown, M., & Cheney, J. (2021). Sexual consent and communication among the sexual minoritized: The role of heteronormative sex education, trauma, and dual identities. *Feminist Criminology*, 15570851211034560.

Donovan, C., & Hester, M. (2015). *Domestic violence and sexuality: What's love got to do with it?* Bristol, UK: Policy Press.

Edwards, K. M., Sylaska, K. M., Barry, J. E., Moynihan, M. M., Banyard, V. L., Cohn, E. S., . . . Ward, S. K. (2015). Physical dating violence, sexual violence, and unwanted pursuit victimization: A comparison of incidence rates among sexual-minority and heterosexual college students. *Journal of Interpersonal Violence*, 30(4), 580–600.

Ehrlich, S. L. (2001). *Representing rape: Language and sexual consent*. New York: Psychology Press.

Fedina, L., Holmes, J. L., & Backes, B. L. (2018). Campus sexual assault: A systematic review of prevalence research from 2000 to 2015. *Trauma, Violence, & Abuse*, 19(1), 76–93.

Ford, J., & Soto-Marquez, J. G. (2016). Sexual assault victimization among straight, gay/lesbian, and bisexual college students. *Violence and Gender*, 3(2), 107–115.

Gavey, N. (2005). *Just sex? The cultural scaffolding of rape*. New York: Routledge.

Hayfield, N., & Clarke, V. (2012). 'I'd be happy with a cup of tea': Women's accounts of sex and affection in long-term heterosexual relationships. *Women's Studies International Forum*, 35(2), 67–74.

Hirsch, J. S., & Khan, S. (2020). *Sexual citizens: A landmark study of sex, power, and assault on campus*, 1st edition. New York: W. W. Norton & Company.

Jones, L., de Heer, B., & Prior, S. (2016). Campus sexual assault: Conceptualizing vulnerable groups in an unfolding legal context. In *Campus action against sexual assault: Needs, policies, procedures, and training programs* (pp. 25–47). Westport, Connecticut, CA: Praeger.

Jozkowski, K. N., Marcantonio, T. L., & Hunt, M. E. (2017). College students' sexual consent communication and perceptions of sexual double standards: A qualitative investigation. *Perspectives on Sexual and Reproductive Health*, 49(4), 237–244.

Jozkowski, K. N., & Peterson, Z. D. (2013). College students and sexual consent: Unique insights. *Journal of Sex Research*, 50(6), 517–523.

Kennedy, A. C., Adams, A., Bybee, D., Campbell, R., Kubiak, S. P., & Sullivan, C. (2012). A model of sexually and physically victimized women's process of attaining effective formal help over time: The role of social location, context, and intervention. *American journal of Community Psychology*, 50(1–2), 217–228.

Koss, M. P., Abbey, A., Campbell, R., Cook, S., Norris, J., Testa, M., . . . White, J. (2007). Revising the SES: A collaborative process to improve assessment of sexual aggression and victimization. *Psychology of Women Quarterly*, 31, 357–370.

Koss, M. P., Gidycz, C. A., & Wisniewski, N. (1987). The scope of rape: Incidence and prevalence of sexual aggression and victimization in a national sample of higher education students. *Journal of Consulting and Clinical Psychology*, 55(2), 162.

Krebs, C. P., Lindquist, C. H., Berzofsky, M., Shook-Sa, B., Peterson, K., Planty, M., & Stroop, J. (2016). *Campus climate survey validation study: Final technical report* (p. 218). Washington, DC: BJS, Office of Justice Programs.

Krebs, C. P., Lindquist, C. H., Warner, T. D., Fisher, B. S., & Martin, S. L. (2009). College women's experiences with physically forced, alcohol-or other drug-enabled, and drug-facilitated sexual assault before and since entering college. *Journal of American College Health*, 57(6), 639–649.

Loick, D. (2020). ". . . as if it were a thing." A feminist critique of consent. *Constellations*, 27(3), 412–422.

MacKinnon, C. A. (1989). *Toward a feminist theory of the state*. Cambridge, MA: Harvard University Press.

Marchia, J., & Sommer, J. M. (2019). (Re) defining heteronormativity. *Sexualities*, 22(3), 267–295.

Mathieu, N. C. (1990). When yielding is not consenting: Material and psychic determinants of women's dominated consciousness and some of their interpretations in ethnology. *Feminist Issues*, 10(1), 51–90.

Mellins, C. A., Walsh, K., Sarvet, A. L., Wall, M., Gilbert, L., Santelli, J. S., . . . Hirsch, J. S. (2017). Sexual assault incidents among college undergraduates: Prevalence and factors associated with risk. *PLoS One*, 12(11), e0186471.

Messinger, A. M., & Koon-Magnin, S. (2019). Sexual violence in LGBTQ communities. In *Handbook of sexual assault and sexual assault prevention* (pp. 661–674). Cham: Springer.

O'Sullivan, L., & Allgeier, E. R. (1998). Feigning sexual desire: Consenting to unwanted sexual activity in heterosexual dating relationships. *The Journal of Sex Research*, 35(3), 234–243.

Peterson, Z. D., & Muehlenhard, C. L. (2007). Conceptualizing the "wantedness" of women's consensual and nonconsensual sexual experiences: Implications for how women label their experiences with rape. *Journal of Sex Research*, 44(1), 72–88.

Pugh, B., & Becker, P. (2018). Exploring definitions and prevalence of verbal sexual coercion and its relationship to consent to unwanted sex: Implications for affirmative consent standards on college campuses. *Behavioral Sciences*, 8(8), 69.

RAINN. (2021). *Consent laws*, May 3. Retrieved from https://apps.rainn.org/policy/policy-crime-definitions.cfm?state=Nevada&group=9&_ga=2.192678568.304148368.1620066281-843366111.1620066281.

Ray, C. M., Tyler, K. A., & Gordon Simons, L. (2021). Risk factors for forced, incapacitated, and coercive sexual victimization among sexual minority and heterosexual male and female college students. *Journal of Interpersonal Violence*, 0886260518758332.

Renzetti, C. M. (1992). *Violent betrayal: Partner abuse in lesbian relationships*. Los Angeles, CA: Sage Publications.

Rothman, E. F., Exner, D., & Baughman, A. L. (2011). The prevalence of sexual assault against people who identify as gay, lesbian, or bisexual in the United States: A systematic review. *Trauma, Violence, & Abuse*, 12(2), 55–66.

Schulze, C., & Koon-Magnin, S. (2017). Gender, sexual orientation, and rape myth acceptance: Preliminary findings from a sample of primarily LGBQ-identified survey respondents. *Violence and Victims*, 32(1), 159–180.

Smith, I. E. (2016). *Minority vs. minoritized: Why the noun just doesn't cut it*. Odyssey, September 2. Retrieved from www.theodysseyonline.com/minority-vs-minoritize.

Smith, S. G., Zhang, X., Basile, K. C., Merrick, M. T., Wang, J., Kresnow, M. J., & Chen, J. (2018). *The national intimate partner and sexual violence survey: 2015 data brief—updated release*. Atlanta: National Center for Injury Prevention and Control, Centers for Disease Control and Prevention. Retrieved from www.cdc.gov/violenceprevention/pdf/2015data-brief508.pdf.

Stark, E., & Hester, M. (2019). Coercive control: Update and review. *Violence Against Women*, 25(1), 81–104.

Testa, M., VanZile-Tamsen, C., Livingston, J. A., & Koss, M. P. (2004). Assessing women's experiences of sexual aggression using the sexual experiences survey: Evidence for validity and implications for research. *Psychology of Women Quarterly*, 28(3), 256–265.

Tharp, A. T., DeGue, S., Valle, L. A., Brookmeyer, K. A., Massetti, G. M., & Matjasko, J. L. (2013). A systematic qualitative review of risk and protective factors for sexual violence perpetration. *Trauma, Violence, & Abuse*, 14(2), 133–167.

Thomas, E. J., Stelzl, M., & Lafrance, M. N. (2017). Faking to finish: Women's accounts of feigning sexual pleasure to end unwanted sex. *Sexualities*, 20(3), 281–301.

Turchik, J. A., Hebenstreit, C. L., & Judson, S. S. (2016). An examination of the gender inclusiveness of current theories of sexual violence in adulthood: Recognizing male victims, female perpetrators, and same-sex violence. *Trauma, Violence, & Abuse*, 17(2), 133–148.

van Anders, S. M. (2015). Beyond sexual orientation: Integrating gender/sex and diverse sexualities via sexual configurations theory. *Archives of Sexual Behavior*, 44(5), 1177–1213.

Walters, M. L., Chen, J., & Breiding, M. J. (2013). *The national intimate partner and sexual violence survey (NISVS): 2010 findings on victimization by sexual orientation*. Atlanta, GA: National Center for Injury Prevention and Control.

Warner, M. (1993). *Fear of a queer planet: Queer politics and social theory*. Minneapolis: University of Minnesota Press.

Worthen, M. G. (2020). *Queers, bis, and straight lies: An intersectional examination of LGBTQ stigma*. New York: Routledge.

Chapter 7

Intimate Partner Violence within the LGBTQ+ Community

Prevalence, Unique Experiences, and Critical Needs

Danielle C. Slakoff and Stacie Merken

Regardless of gender identity or sexual orientation, intimate partner violence (IPV) victimization may include experiences with physical, sexual, verbal, and/or emotional/mental abuse, and can lead to a variety of health risks (National Center for Injury Prevention and Control, Division of Violence Prevention [NCIC], 2020). Negative health conditions such as digestive, reproductive, heart, and nervous system dysfunction can result from IPV, many of which become chronic conditions. IPV survivors may also experience depression and post-traumatic stress disorder (PTSD), which can lead to a host of risk engaging behaviors, such as increased binge drinking, smoking, and drug use (NCIC, 2020). Intimate partner violence can cause a myriad of consequences.

Most nationally published statistical data on IPV refers only to IPV in cisgender, heterosexual partnerships. The National Coalition Against Domestic Violence (NCADV) (2020) provides many resources and statistics; however, the special populations list does not include data on LGBTQ+ people's IPV victimizations. Although men's victimization is addressed within this resource, there is no data about the gender of the perpetrator (e.g., man, woman, nonbinary, etc.). Similarly, the Center for Disease Control (CDC)'s National Intimate Partner and Sexual Violence Survey (NISVS) (NCIC, 2020) addresses victimization for women and men, but does not include data on LGBTQ+ people and IPV on their website. This data fails to consider the approximately 5.6% of American adults (around 18 million people) who identify as LGBTQ+, with 54.6% of this group identifying as bisexual, 24.5% as gay, 11.7% as lesbian, and 11.3% as transgender (Jones, 2021). The lack of data on this specific population is indicative of a social construction of IPV that suggests IPV cannot occur between members of the LGBTQ+ community, which may result in low levels of reporting from LGBTQ+ victims.

In this chapter, the authors will explain the prevalence of IPV within the LGBTQ+ community, discuss unique needs and challenges that LGBTQ+ victims face, as well as describe critical needs to support this at-risk group. Although some programs and national organizations are working toward improving inclusivity, this chapter will address LGBTQ+ victims' experiences with minority stress and issues when reporting IPV to police, medical professionals, and/or formal IPV service providers.

Prevalence

While extant research has largely focused on intimate partner violence (IPV) within cisgender, heterosexual relationships, there is now a growing body of literature about IPV within LGBTQ+ relationships. Comparing lifetime IPV victimization for LGB and heterosexual

DOI: 10.4324/9781003400981-8

survivors, researchers have estimated that LGB IPV victimization is significantly higher than heterosexual victimization (Bartholomew et al., 2008; Goldberg & Meyer, 2013; Houston & McKirnan, 2007; Messinger, 2011; Tjaden & Thoennes, 2000; Turell, 2000; Walters et al., 2013). Indeed, in their examination of IPV in same-sex (gay or lesbian) relationships, Burke and colleagues (2002) found 68% of their sample had experienced at least one form of IPV during their lifetime. In their meta-analysis of IPV in lesbian relationships, Badenes-Ribera and colleagues (2015) found 48% of lesbians had experienced IPV over their lifetime. Moreover, college students who identify as lesbian, gay, bisexual, or other (LGBO) experienced higher rates of physical, sexual, and psychological victimization than their heterosexual peers (Porter & Williams, 2011). In their study examining the experiences of IPV in LGB people in Canada, Barrett and St. Pierre (2013) found bisexual people were at higher risk for IPV than lesbian and gay folks. Moreover, bisexual people reported more violent attacks and a higher rate of physical injury than their gay and lesbian counterparts (Barrett & St. Pierre, 2013).

Transgender people are also at high risk of IPV victimization. In a national survey of over 27,700 transgender people, 54% stated that they had experienced some form of IPV in their lifetime (James et al., 2016). In fact, trans people are "at 2 to 3 times higher risk of physical and sexual IPV compared with cisgender individuals" (Peitzmeier et al., 2020, p. e9). According to the National Coalition of Anti-Violence Programs (NCAVP) (2013), transgender women had a higher likelihood of experiencing physical injury, harassment, and intimidation in comparison to LGBQ survivors and transgender men. In sum, LGBTQ+ people experience high rates of IPV, and their experiences should be centered and explored more within criminology and victimology studies.

Minority Stress

Minority stress refers to the numerous stressors that compound upon those with minority status within a society or culture (Stephenson & Finneran, 2017). Minority stress theorists argue that people within stigmatized groups face various forms of adversity due to their minority status (Meyer, 2003). Specifically, sexual minority folks experience distal/external minority stress as well as proximal/internal minority stress (Mason et al., 2016; Rollè et al., 2018). Forms of external minority stress include discrimination, harassment, and/or victimization due to homophobia, transphobia, biphobia, racism, poverty, and more. An example of external minority stress is verbal harassment that an LGB person may receive when holding hands with their same-sex partner. Given experiences with external minority stress, LGBTQ+ people may then face internal forms of minority stress, such as internalized negativity toward one's identity (i.e., internalized homophobia) or anticipated rejection (Edwards & Sylaska, 2013). Put simply, minority stress—and the "stigma, prejudice, and discrimination" that comes with it—can "create a hostile and stressful social environment" for LGBTQ+ people (Meyer, 2003, p. 674)

The minority stress that LGBTQ+ people face impacts IPV in a variety of ways. First, research suggests that the perpetration of IPV may be impacted by minority stress. For example, in their study on lesbian IPV, Mason and colleagues (2016) found that lesbians who perpetrated intimate partner violence experienced minority and life stressors. In their study on gay and bisexual men, Stephenson and Finneran (2017) found that internalized homophobia, a common form of internal minority stress, was linked to IPV perpetration. Second, research similarly supports the notion that minority stress is linked to victimization experiences. Finneran and Stephenson (2014) found, in their study of men who have sex with men, that non-White race and positive HIV status, which both are connected to experiences of discrimination, were significantly associated to violence. Third, research suggests that folks experiencing minority stress are more likely to experience mental health problems (Fingerhut et al., 2010). Mental health problems may be worsened or exacerbated by IPV.

Research suggests that LGBTQ+ people who have suffered from discrimination (i.e., a form of external minority stress) may hesitate to speak out about their abuse (Rollè et al., 2018), as they do not want to further stigmatize their community (Hassouneh & Glass, 2008). And, given the lack of information about IPV in LGBTQ+ relationships, LGBTQ+ people being victimized may struggle to identify the behavior as abusive (Bornstein et al., 2006). Further, due to internalized homophobia or negative feelings LGBTQ people may have about themselves and their identity (Edwards & Sylaska, 2013), IPV victims may feel that they are deserving of punishment and/or abuse (Balsam & Szymanski, 2005). Moreover, LGBTQ+ people may hesitate to call authorities due to fear of discrimination or assault from police (Lewis et al., 2012).

Stigma and Reporting IPV to Police

Due to a variety of discrimination and abuse experiences, LGBTQ+ people are not as likely to report their IPV victimization (Bornstein et al., 2006). Carvalho and colleagues (2011) examined three internalized sexual minority stressors in gay and lesbian same-sex relationships, where participants identified as a victim and/or perpetrator of IPV (n = 581). The researchers utilized various scales, including Pinel's (1999) Stigma Consciousness Questionnaire (SCQ) scale, which assesses gay and lesbian people's expectation of stereotyping by others. Carvalho et al. (2011) found survivors of IPV that are involved in same-sex partnerships have a stronger likelihood to experience stigma consciousness. The same results were found for perpetrators of IPV in same-sex partnerships, although it must be noted that most perpetrators of IPV in same-sex partnerships also were victims previously. While IPV victimization is underreported in general, the percentage of LGBTQ+ reporting to police is drastically lower than heterosexual IPV victimization (Langenderfer-Magruder et al., 2016).

The decrease in reporting could be due to police distrust/lack of legitimacy by the LGBTQ+ community. Owen et al. (2018) compared LGBT and heterosexual respondents to better understand public perceptions of police interaction with LGBT communities, police fairness and equality, and overall policing qualities. The results showed higher levels of negative perceptions by LGBT people, and when other variables were controlled for (e.g., race, income, type of geographical area, and history of interactions with police), the negative perceptions by LGBT people significantly increased. Moreover, LGBTQ people may be concerned that reporting a crime to police will out them to their neighbors, friends, and other individuals.

Although IPV survivors overall reported dissatisfaction with police response to their victimization, heterosexual IPV survivors have reported higher levels of police trust/legitimacy than LGBTQ+ IPV survivors (Fedina et al., 2019). In interactions with police, many IPV victims report being blamed for the incident, not having their IPV report taken seriously as a crime, and higher levels of officer disrespect (Du Mont et al., 2003; Potter, 2010). Moreover, due to a lack of training regarding LGBTQ+ IPV, officers may misidentify the perpetrator and victim in LGBTQ+ IPV incidents (Morin, 2014) and/or may conduct a dual arrest. Dual arrests/mutual restraining order laws perpetuate a misconstrued notion regarding same-sex couples—they are viewed as simply fighting. These arrests reinforce the belief that police officers do not take LGBTQ+ IPV as seriously as heterosexual IPV (Andreano, 2020; Du Mont et al., 2003; Potter, 2010) or are not as well-trained in determining who the primary aggressor is when called to the scene of IPV between members of the LGBTQ+ community.

Resource Differences

LGBTQ+ victims who experience IPV need support and care but may face various obstacles when seeking help. First, many IPV-focused service providers assume that survivors are heterosexual and cisgender (Calton et al., 2016). Many agencies do not screen for sexual orientation or gender identity, so LGBTQ+ folks seeking services may be unable to access help tailored to their unique needs and experiences (Ford et al., 2013). Alternatively, LGBTQ+ people may choose not to disclose their sexual orientation or gender identity to service providers (Ford et al., 2013) due to past experiences with negative treatment or fear of discrimination.

Second, many LGBT survivors have had negative experiences at non-LGBT-specific agencies or programs (Bornstein et al., 2006), and LGBTQ+ IPV survivors are generally unsatisfied with support services (Turell & Cornell-Swanson, 2005). Service providers may feel ill-equipped to support LGBTQ+ survivors (Slakoff & Siegel, 2022), as levels of training on LGBT-specific issues are low across agencies (Ford et al., 2013). Research suggests that service providers or other people seeking services may feel uncomfortable with trans women (Apsani, 2018) or lesbian women (Simpson & Helfrich, 2005) being housed within shelter spaces. Service providers must work to ensure that all people are comfortable within the space (Mottet & Ohle, 2006)—this requires that service providers *not* center heterosexual ciswomen (Apsani, 2018) and instead focus on all survivors' needs.

Service providers recognize that their services are not always inclusive. For example, Simpson and Helfrich (2005) found, in their examination of IPV service providers working with lesbian clients, that service providers wanted to serve lesbian survivors but felt they faced significant limitations in doing so. Similarly, Ford and colleagues (2013) found that service providers wanted to improve services but felt they lacked the knowledge to provide better services. In their examination of service providers in Canada, Furman and colleagues (2017) found that "all participants felt their organizations could become more inclusive of LGBTQ2S survivors through modifying their organizational policies, practices, and structures" (p. 370). Put simply, IPV service providers recognize the need to make their spaces more inclusive.

While there is still much work that needs to be done on the national level, some IPV service providers are doing an admirable job of meeting the needs of their LGBTQ+ client base. Bolton Refuge House, located in Wisconsin, provides LGBTQ+ IPV and sexual assault survivors with emergency shelter space and a variety of other resources, including legal advocacy, outreach services, and support groups (Bolton Refuge House, 2021). As an organization, Bolton Refuge House serves Eau Claire (emergency shelter), Buffalo, and Jackson counties. Services are confidential with an option for anonymity if needed, and youth over fourteen are not required to communicate with any type of guardian (e.g., parents, caregivers). Survivors have access to staff support twenty-four hours a day, 365 days a year, and all services including shelter are at no cost to the survivors. There are five major community resources including, but not limited to, The Chippewa Valley LGBTQ+ Community Center, Planned Parenthood Gender Affirming Care, and the Queer Menomonie

Community Center (Bolton Refuge House, 2021). More organizations like the Bolton Refuge House are needed in the US.

Critical Needs

LGBTQ+ IPV survivors desperately need trauma-informed and culturally competent care from a variety of providers, including police, medical professionals, and IPV service providers (including shelter spaces). Across all of these groups, training and education are essential components to providing LGBTQ+ IPV survivors with better care.

LGBTQ+ IPV survivors report negative experiences with police when reporting IPV. Negative experiences with police include being deadnamed (i.e., being called by their name at birth or former name), misgendered (Slakoff & Siegel, 2022), and/or dual arrested alongside the perpetrator (Andreano, 2020; Hirschel & McCormack, 2021). Further, 58% of transgender folks report facing discrimination, harassment, and/or abuse from police officers (National Center for Transgender Equality, 2018). Police officers—as essential first responders—need extensive training in how to best support LGBTQ+ survivors. This training should give special attention to differences and similarities between hetero-cis-normative couples and those in relationships within the LGBTQ+ community. These trainings should affirm that IPV can occur in all types of relationships, regardless of the gender identity and sexual orientation of the people involved. In addition, policies and laws (e.g., dual arrests/mutual restraining orders) should be reexamined and reevaluated for more inclusivity toward LGBTQ+ IPV survivors.

Many IPV victims experience negative physical and mental health outcomes due to victimization experiences (Coker et al., 2002), and LGBTQ+ youth who have experienced physical violence commonly seek medical treatment and support (Scheer & Baams, 2019). Medical providers should recognize physical signs of IPV, including bruising, cuts, broken blood vessels in the eyes, hoarse voice, broken bones, etc, (Snyder, 2019; World Health Organization, 2012). In terms of mental health outcomes, victims of IPV may experience depression, anxiety, and post-traumatic stress disorder (PTSD), amongst other mental health issues (Reuter et al., 2017). Given these physical and mental health outcomes, medical providers are in a unique position to help victims of IPV, including LGBTQ+ people (Bermea et al., 2021).

For various reasons (e.g., minority stress, fear of outing, etc.), LGBTQ+ IPV victims may not feel comfortable sharing their abuse experiences with medical providers. As such, it is important that medical providers screen all people for IPV, regardless of gender identity or sexual orientation (Bermea et al., 2021). These screenings should include questions about various forms of abuse, including psychological abuse, medication withholding, and forced isolation (Stephenson & Finneran, 2013). Further, medical providers should take care not to make hetero-cis-normative assumptions about patients during their intake or screening procedures (Bermea et al., 2021).

Medical providers can affirm LGBTQ+ people by creating an inclusive and safe physical environment. For example, medical providers can have affirming visuals and images on websites, in waiting rooms, and in screening areas (Bermea et al., 2021). These images should include diverse family configurations beyond the hetero-cis-normative norm (Bermea et al., 2021). Further, gender-inclusive restrooms and inclusive gender and sexuality options on paperwork can alert LGBTQ+ folks that they are in an affirming space (Bermea et al., 2021).

In some instances, medical care providers may refer LGBTQ+ victims to other facilities, such as shelter spaces or mental health counselors. It is important for medical providers to refer patients to gender- and sexuality-affirming locations (Ard & Makadon, 2011). Given the negative experiences LGBTQ+ people report in shelter and IPV-focused spaces, it is important that medical providers do not send patients to spaces that can cause more harm. Medical providers should take care to find safe spaces to refer LGBTQ+ clients to, even if it takes time and energy to find these spaces.

LGBTQ+ IPV survivors need access to safe support services. In some locations, LGBTQ+-specific shelter spaces (or service providers) are non-existent or are extremely limited in number (Parry & O'Neal, 2015). For this reason, service providers in all locations need training on LGBTQ+ IPV. This training should be specific, thorough, and focused on unique issues that LGBTQ+ people face (Ford et al., 2013). For example, it is important staff understand that perpetrators may threaten to out victims (e.g., threatening to out a survivor to an ex to make sure custody of children is dissolved), control access to their medications, pretend to be a victim in order to access the shelter in which the survivor resides, and/ or manipulate the individual by stating the abuse is not real (e.g., women cannot abuse women, men cannot abuse men) (Ford et al., 2013; FORGE, 2016).

The *thoroughness* of trainings is another important point to consider, as service providers have shared those introductory trainings on the topic of LGBTQ+ IPV "only skimmed the surface on effectively working with LGBTQ2S clients" (Furman et al., 2017, p. 370). Put differently, many of those who received LGBT-specific IPV training felt the training was inadequate (Furman et al., 2017). It is not enough to mandate training for all service providers—the training needs to be high quality and thorough in its scope and breadth.

Both FORGE and Futures without Violence are national organizations that provide high quality and thorough training support for IPV service providers. FORGE was formed in 1994 and became federally funded in 2009, while Futures without Violence began as a non-profit in 1989, receiving government and private grants and donations (FORGE, 2016; Futures Without Violence, 2021). FORGE works with Futures without Violence as one partner organization providing resources. Both organizations include a variety of training methods for IPV service providers, such as training videos, safety cards, conference workshops, training webinars, quick tips regarding a more inclusive setting (e.g., pronoun use, no assumptions, including other types of options besides male and female on intake forms), interactive learning modules, and other aids. Both organizations provide national resources and have main locations: FORGE is based in Wisconsin and Futures without Violence has three primary offices in California, Massachusetts, and Washington, DC. Although national training programs exist, the need for all IPV service providers to incorporate and reiterate these methods is still relevant. All IPV shelters should be provided with federal funding to implement LGBTQ+ survivor client training.

We argue that *all* IPV service providers should be adequately and thoroughly trained on LGBTQ+ IPV; as such, more government funding should be made available to open LGBTQ+ specific spaces or to support the ones already in existence. For the various reasons outlined in this chapter, LGBTQ+ survivors may feel safer going to LGBTQ+ specific locations rather than to general service providers. Importantly, the LGBTQ+ service providers that do exist may be overwhelmed with patients/clientele, a major concern considering the high rate of burnout and compassion fatigue across IPV service providers (Voth Schrag et al., 2021). Moreover, even in locations with LGBTQ+ specific agencies, survivors may not realize that these services exist (Simpson & Helfrich, 2014). More funding for LGBTQ+

specific service providers can 1) alleviate stress on existing programs, 2) give survivors more options for care, and 3) provide service providers with funding to publicize their inclusive services. Moreover, service providers would be able to hire more LGBTQ+ folks to support survivors (a suggestion for improvement made by Furman and colleagues [2017]).

Finally, shelter spaces must be made LGBTQ+ friendly *in practice*. The *Equal Access Rule (EAR)* prohibits discrimination in government-funded shelters based on sexual orientation and/or gender identity (U.S. Dept. of Housing and Urban Development, 2021). While this mandate is an important step toward more inclusive shelter spaces, the reality is that many domestic violence shelters still function as cis woman only spaces (Shelton, 2015). Specifically, trans people (Shelton, 2015) and men (Côté et al., 2018) are often excluded from IPV shelter spaces, and are sometimes transferred to other spaces (hotels, homeless shelters) instead (Apsani, 2018). In order to safely house LGBTQ+ survivors, shelter spaces must grow in number and in size to accommodate all people. This growth will require more funding for domestic violence shelter programs.

In this chapter, the authors discussed the prevalence of IPV in the LGBTQ+ community, LGBTQ+ people's unique experiences with IPV, and the critical needs facing this group. Whether LGBTQ+ IPV survivors call the police, seek medical attention, or seek IPV-specific services, they are deserving of inclusive and safe help and assistance. As it stands, LGBTQ+ survivors report negative experiences when seeking help for IPV (Calton et al., 2016). In order to remedy this, changes must be made at multiple levels to assist LGBTQ+ survivors in their healing. To this end, the authors call for more extensive funding for IPV service providers and for better training for service providers, police personnel, medical staff, and more. It is past time that all survivors receive the help and support that they need.

References

Andreano, J. (2020). The disproportionate effect of mutual restraining orders on same-sex domestic violence victims. *California Law Review*, 108(3). Retrieved from www.californialawreview.org/print/mutual-restraining-orders-same-sex-domestic-violence-victims/#clr-toc-heading-4.

Apsani, R. (2018). Are women's spaces transgender spaces: Single sex domestic violence shelters, transgender inclusion, and the equal protection clause. *California Law Review*, 106(5). Retrieved from www.californialawreview.org/print/6-are-womens-spaces-transgender-spaces-single-sex-domestic-violence-shelters-transgender-inclusion-and-the-equal-protection-clause/.

Ard, K. L., & Makadon, H. J. (2011). Addressing intimate partner violence in lesbian, gay, bisexual, and transgender patients. *Journal of General Internal Medicine*, 26(8), 930–933. https://doi.org/10.1007/s11606-011-1697-6.

Badenes-Ribera, L., Frias-Navarro, D., Bonilla-Campos, A., Pons-Salvador, G., & Monterde-i-Bort, H. (2015). Intimate partner violence in self-identified lesbians: A meta-analysis of its prevalence. *Sexuality Research & Social Policy*, 12(1), 47–59.

Balsam, K. F., & Szymanski, D. M. (2005). Relationship quality and domestic violence in women's same-sex relationships: The role of minority stress. *Psychology of Women Quarterly*, 29, 258–269.

Barrett, B. J., & St. Pierre, M. (2013). Intimate partner violence reported by lesbian-, gay-, and bisexual-identified individuals living in Canada: An exploration of within-group variations. *Journal of Gay & Lesbian Social Services*, 25(1), 1–23. https://doi.org/10.1080/10538720.2013.751887.

Bartholomew, K., Regan, K. V., White, M. A., & Oram, D. (2008). Patterns of abuse in male same-sex relationships. *Violence & Victims*, 23(5), 617–636.

Bermea, A. M., Slakoff, D. C., & Goldberg, A. E. (2021). Intimate partner violence in the LGBTQ+ community. *Primary Care: Clinics in Office Practice*, 48(2), 329–337. https://doi.org/10.1016/j.pop.2021.02.006.

Bolton Refuge House. (2021). *LGBTQ+ advocacy*. Retrieved from www.boltonrefuge.org/lgbtq.

Bornstein, D. R., Fawcett, J., Sullivan, M., Senturia, K. D., & Shiu-Thornton, S. (2006). Understanding the experiences of lesbian, bisexual and trans survivors of domestic violence: A qualitative study. *Journal of Homosexuality*, 51(1), 159–181. https://doi.org/10.1300/J082v51n01_08.

Burke, T. W., Jordan, M. L., & Owen, S. S. (2002). A cross-national comparison of gay and lesbian domestic violence. *Journal of Contemporary Criminal Justice*, 18(3), 231–257. https://doi.org/10.1177/1043986202018003003.

Calton, J. M., Cattaneo, L. B., & Gebhard, K. T. (2016). Barriers to help seeking for lesbian, gay, bisexual, transgender, and queer survivors of intimate partner violence. *Trauma, Violence, & Abuse*, 17(5), 585–600. https://doi.org/10.1177/1524838015585318.

Carvalho, A. F., Lewis, R. J., Derlega, V. J., Winstead, B. A., & Viggiano, C. (2011). Internalized sexual minority stressors and same-sex intimate partner violence. *Journal of Family Violence*, 26(7), 501–509.

Coker, A. L., Davis, K. E., Arias, I., Desai, S., Sanderson, M., Brandt, H. M., & Smith, P. H. (2002). Physical and mental health effects of intimate partner violence for men and women. *American Journal of Preventive Medicine*, 23(4), 260–268. https://doi.org/10.1016/s0749-3797(02)00514-7.

Côté, I., Damant, D., & Lapierre, S. (2018). The inclusion of men in domestic violence shelters: An everlasting debate. *Journal of Gender-Based Violence*, 2(2), 373–391. https://doi.org/10.1332/239868018X15265562721544.

Du Mont, J., Miller, K. L., & Myhr, T. L. (2003). The role of "real rape" and "real victim" stereotypes in the police reporting practices of sexually assaulted women. *Violence Against Women*, 9(4), 466–486.

Edwards, K. M., & Sylaska, K. M. (2013). The perpetration of intimate partner violence among LGBTQ college youth: The role of minority stress. *Journal of Youth and Adolescence*, 42(11), 1721–1731. https://doi.org/10.1007/s10964-012-9880-6.

Fedina, L., Backes, B. L., Jun, H., DeVylder, J., & Barth, R. P. (2019). Police legitimacy, trustworthiness, and associations with intimate partner violence. *Policing*, 42(5), 901–916.

Fingerhut, A. W., Peplau, L. A., & Gable, S. L. (2010). Identity, minority stress and psychological well-being among gay men and lesbians. *Psychology and Sexuality*, 1, 101–114. DOI: 10.1080/19419899.2010.484592.

Finneran, C., & Stephenson, R. (2014). Intimate partner violence, minority stress, and sexual risk-taking Among U.S. men who have sex with men. *Journal of Homosexuality*, 61(2), 288–306. https://doi.org/10.1080/00918369.2013.839911.

Ford, C. L., Slavin, T., Hilton, K. L., & Holt, S. L. (2013). Intimate partner violence prevention services and resources in Los Angeles: Issues, needs, and challenges for assisting lesbian, gay, bisexual, and transgender clients. *Health Promotion Practice*, 14(6), 841–849. https://doi.org/10.1177/1524839912467645.

FORGE. (2016). *Training and events*. Retrieved from https://web.archive.org/web/20161026180523/http://forge-forward.org/trainings-events/.

Furman, E., Barata, P., Wilson, C., & Fante-Coleman, T. (2017). "It's a gap in awareness": Exploring service provision for LGBTQ2S survivors of intimate partner violence in Ontario, Canada. *Journal of Gay & Lesbian Social Services*, 29(4), 362–377. https://doi.org/10.1080/10538720.2017.1365672.

Futures Without Violence. (2021). *Lesbian, gay, bisexual, trans/GNC, and Queer IPV*. Retrieved from www.futureswithoutviolence.org/health/lgbtq-ipv/.

Goldberg, N. G., & Meyer, I. H. (2013). Sexual orientation disparities in history of intimate partner violence. Results from the California health interview survey. *Journal of Interpersonal Violence*, 28(5), 1109–1118.

Hassouneh, D., & Glass, N. (2008). The influence of gender role stereotyping on women's experiences of female same-sex intimate partner violence. *Violence Against Women*, 14(3), 310–325. https://doi.org/10.1177/1077801207313734.

Hirschel, D., & McCormack, P. D. (2021). Same-sex couples and the police: A 10-year study of arrest and dual arrest rates in responding to incidents of intimate partner violence. *Violence Against Women*, 27(9), 1119–1149. https://doi.org/10.1177/1077801220920378.

Houston, E., & McKirnan, D. J. (2007). Intimate partner abuse among gay and bisexual men: Risk correlates and health outcomes. *Journal of Urban Health*, 84(5), 681–690.

James, S. E., Herman, J. L., Rankin, S., Keisling, M., Mottet, L., & Anafi, M. (2016). *The report of the 2015 U.S. transgender survey*. Washington, DC: National Center for Transgender Equality.

Jones, J. M. (2021). LGBT identification rises to 5.6% in latest U.S. estimate. *Gallup*. Retrieved from https://news.gallup.com/poll/329708/lgbt-identification-rises-latest-estimate.aspx.

Langenderfer-Magruder, L., Whitfield, D. L., Walls, N. E., Kattari, S. K., & Ramos, D. (2016). Experiences of intimate partner violence and subsequent police reporting among lesbian, gay, bisexual, transgender, and Queer adults in Colorado: Comparing rates of cisgender and transgender victimization. *Journal of Interpersonal Violence*, 31(5), 855–871.

Lewis, R. J., Milletich, R. J., Kelley, M. L., & Woody, A. (2012). Minority stress, substance use, and intimate partner violence among sexual minority women. *Aggression and Violent Behavior*, 17(3), 247–256. https://doi.org/10.1016/j.avb.2012.02.004.

Mason, T. B., Lewis, R. J., Gargurevich, M., & Kelley, M. L. (2016). Minority stress and intimate partner violence perpetration among lesbians: Negative affect, hazardous drinking, and intrusiveness as mediators. *Psychology of Sexual Orientation and Gender Diversity*, 3(2), 236–246. https://doi.org/10.1037/sgd0000165.

Messinger, A. M. (2011). Invisible victims: Same-sex IPV in the national violence against women survey. *Journal of Interpersonal Violence*, 26(11), 2228–2243.

Meyer, I. H. (2003). Prejudice, social stress, and mental health in lesbian, gay, and bisexual populations: Conceptual issues and research evidence. *Psychological Bulletin*, 129(5), 674–697. https://doi.org/10.1037/0033-2909.129.5.674.

Morin, C. (2014). Re-traumatized: How gendered laws exacerbate the harm for same-sex victims of intimate partner violence. *New England Journal on Criminal and Civil Confinement*, 40(2), 477–498.

Mottet, L., & Ohle, J. (2006). Transitioning our shelters: Making homeless shelters safe for transgender people. *Journal of Poverty*, 10(2), 77–101. https://doi.org/10.1300/J134v10n02_05.

National Center for Injury Prevention and Control, Division of Violence Prevention. (2020). *Preventing intimate partner violence*. Retrieved from www.cdc.gov/violenceprevention/intimatepartnerviolence/fastfact.html.

National Center for Transgender Equality. (2018). *Ending abuse of transgender prisoners: A guide for advocates on winning policy change in jails and prisons*. Retrieved from https://transequality.org/endingabuseoftransprisoners.

National Coalition Against Domestic Violence. (2020). *Statistics*. Retrieved from https://ncadv.org/STATISTICS.

National Coalition of Anti-Violence Programs. (2013). *Lesbian, gay, bisexual, transgender, Queer, and HIV-affected intimate partner violence*. Retrieved from www.avp.org/storage/documents/ncavp_2012_ipvreport.final.pdf.

Owen, S. S., Burke, T. W., Few-Demo, A. L., & Natwick, J. (2018). Perceptions of the police by LGBT communities. *American Journal of Criminal Justice*, 43(3), 668–693.

Parry, M. M., & O'Neal, E. N. (2015). Help-seeking behavior among same-sex intimate partner violence victims: An intersectional argument. *Criminology, Criminal Justice, Law and Society*, 16(1), 17.

Peitzmeier, S. M., Malik, M., Kattari, S. K., Marrow, E., Stephenson, R., Agénor, M., & Reisner, S. L. (2020). Intimate partner violence in transgender populations: Systematic review and meta-analysis of prevalence and correlates. *American Journal of Public Health*, 110(9), e1–e14. https://doi.org/10.2105/AJPH.2020.305774.

Pinel, E. C. (1999). Stigma consciousness: The psychological legacy of social stereotypes. *Journal of Personality and Social Psychology*, 76(1), 114–128.

Porter, J., & Williams, L. M. (2011). Intimate violence among underrepresented groups on a college campus. *Journal of Interpersonal Violence*, 26(16), 3210–3224. https://doi.org/10.1177/08862 60510393011.

Potter, H. (2010). I don't think a cop has ever asked me if I was ok: Battered women's experiences with police intervention. In V. Garcia & J. E. Clifford (Eds.), *Female victims of crime: Reality reconsidered* (pp. 191–212). Upper Saddle River, NJ: Prentice Hall.

Reuter, T. R., Newcomb, M. E., Whitton, S. W., & Mustanski, B. (2017). Intimate partner violence victimization in LGBT young adults: Demographic differences and associations with health behaviors. *Psychology of Violence*, 7(1), 101–109. https://doi.org/10.1037/vio0000031.

Rollè, L., Giardina, G., Caldarera, A. M., Gerino, E., & Brustia, P. (2018). When intimate partner violence meets same sex couples: A review of same sex intimate partner violence. *Frontiers in Psychology*, 9, 1506. https://doi.org/10.3389/fpsyg.2018.01506.

Scheer, J. R., & Baams, L. (2019). Help-seeking patterns among LGBTQ young adults exposed to intimate partner violence victimization. *Journal of Interpersonal Violence*, 0886260519848785. https://doi.org/10.1177/0886260519848785.

Shelton, J. (2015). Transgender youth homelessness: Understanding programmatic barriers through the lens of cisgenderism. *Children and Youth Services Review*, 59(1), 10–18. https://doi.org/10.1016/j.childyouth.2015.10.006.

Simpson, E. K., & Helfrich, C. A. (2005). Lesbian survivors of intimate partner violence: Provider perspectives on barriers to accessing services. *Journal of Gay & Lesbian Social Services*, 18(2), 39–59. https://doi.org/10.1300/J041v18n02_03.

Simpson, E. K., & Helfrich, C. A. (2014). Oppression and barriers to service for Black, lesbian survivors of intimate partner violence. *Journal of Gay & Lesbian Social Services*, 26(4), 441–465. https://doi.org/10.1080/10538720.2014.951816.

Slakoff, D. C., & Siegel, J. A. (2022). Barriers to reporting, barriers to services: Challenges for transgender survivors of intimate partner violence and sexual victimization. In C. Buist & L. Kahle (Eds.), *Queering criminology in theory and praxis*. Bristol, UK: Bristol University Press.

Snyder, R. L. (2019). *No visible bruises*. New York: Bloomsbury.

Stephenson, R., & Finneran, C. (2013). The IPV-GBM Scale: A new scale to measure intimate partner violence among gay and bisexual men. *PLoS One*, 8(6), 1–10. https://doi.org/10.1371/journal.pone.0062592.

Stephenson, R., & Finneran, C. (2017). Minority stress and intimate partner violence among gay and bisexual men in Atlanta. *American Journal of Men's Health*, 11(4), 952–961.

Tjaden, P., & Thoennes, N. (2000). Prevalence and consequences of male-to-female and female-to-male intimate partner violence as measured by the national violence against women survey. *Violence Against Women*, 6(2), 142–161.

Turell, S. C. (2000). A descriptive analysis of same-sex relationship violence for a diverse sample. *Journal of Family Violence*, 15(3), 281–293.

Turell, S. C., & Cornell-Swanson, L. (2005). Not all alike: Within-group differences in seeking help for same-sex relationship abuse. *Journal of Gay & Lesbian Social Services*, 18(1), 71–88. https://doi.org/10.1300/J041v18n01_06.

United States Department of Housing and Urban Development. (2021). *HUD withdraws proposed rule, reaffirms its commitment to equal access to housing, shelters, and other services regardless of gender identity*. Retrieved from www.hud.gov/press/press_releases_media_advisories/HUD_No_21_069.

Voth Schrag, R. J., Wood, L. G., Wachter, K., & Kulkarni, S. (2022). Compassion fatigue among the intimate partner violence and sexual assault workforce: Enhancing organizational practice. *Violence Against Women*, 28(1), 277–297.

Walters, M. L., Chen, J., & Breiding, M. J. (2013). *The national intimate partner and sexual violence survey (NISVS): 2010 findings on victimization by sexual orientation*. Atlanta, GA: National Center for Injury Prevention and Control, Centers for Disease Control and Prevention.

World Health Organization. (2012). *Intimate partner violence*. Retrieved from https://apps.who.int/iris/bitstream/handle/10665/77432/WHO_RHR_12.36_eng.pdf.

Chapter 8

The Limitations of a Statute

Jane E. Palmer

The first time I was in the back of a police car, I sat next to a man who had just tried to rape me. I was 13 and he was 20. I reached for the door to try to escape, but there were no door handles in the back of police cars.

It was 1992, one month after my 8th grade graduation, and I was 1000 miles from my suburban Chicago home. My parents sent me to a college preparation summer camp in a feeble attempt to address my academic mediocrity. To get the college feel, as if that would inspire academic excellence, I attended classes and stayed in a dorm on a college campus in a suburb of Boston. The other kids in the program were entering their junior or senior year of high school and had little interest in me: a 13-year-old hippie tomboy from the Midwest.

The college prep program had financial problems, so when the teachers didn't show up, I spent time at a picnic table in front of my dorm, smoking cigarettes, and writing or drawing in my journal. The dorm next door housed a computer science day camp for elementary-aged kids. The camp counselors lived there full-time, and they would hang out with me when they were bored. One of the counselors, Adam,* came to the picnic table often. I just wanted to be left alone to write bad poetry, but he persisted in talking to me.

I wasn't supposed to go off campus, but one night, shortly before the end of the program, a group of older girls invited me to go to a bar in Boston that didn't card. They enjoyed dressing me in a girly outfit, with rolled up socks as fake boobs, hairspray in my hair, and lots of make-up on my face. I let them do it because I knew it was the only way they'd hang out with me. We got on the T and went to a bar, where at my new friends' urging, I ordered a drink called "Sex on the Beach." The bartender looked at me, laughed, and promptly kicked me out. As I was escorted out of the bar, I glanced back to see my "friends" laughing harder than the bartender.

I found my way back to campus and ran into Adam at the picnic table in front of my dorm. I told him the story, still feeling the sting of being set up, but also realizing how funny it was as I extracted the rolled up socks from my bra. Upon hearing that I had given myself permission to go off campus, he asked me to go to dinner with him the next night, my second-to-last night at the program. He said he had a car and promised there would be alcohol, so I accepted.

I began drinking alcohol and smoking cigarettes a couple months earlier. This was my first opportunity to drink in four weeks; well, second, if you count the fiasco at the bar in Boston. He seemed safe enough; he was a nerdy computer science camp counselor. We went to dinner at an Indian restaurant. He drank but wouldn't let me. It was getting late, and I wanted to go back to my dorm. I had to pack and get ready to fly home. He said we'd

DOI: 10.4324/9781003400981-9

head back soon but wanted to show me his university first, which was on our way back to the college where I was staying.

We walked around the campus, which was beautiful. We sat down on a bench and listened to the resident crickets welcome dusk with their song. He told me that he was attracted to me but knew it was wrong, and he was trying to not act on his feelings. I was curious what it would be like to kiss him, so I moved closer and tilted my head toward his. He said, "wait," and stood up, beckoning me to follow him. He was a resident assistant, so he had keys. I followed him into a nearby dorm, feeling the thrill of going into a place I knew we were not supposed to enter. When we entered a dorm room, I wasn't expecting it to be vacant. He turned on the lights and pushed me onto an empty mattress, unzipped his pants, and began to force mine off. Making out was one thing, but this was something else. I didn't know what to do and could feel my body go limp. He stopped suddenly when we could see a light from a flashlight and a knock on the window.

"University police. Who's in there?"

Adam quickly zipped up his pants while I pulled mine back on. As we walked out of the dorm, Adam ordered me to be quiet and threatened to hurt me if I said anything to the cop.

"Good evening, officer."

"Well, hello Adam. It's you. What are you doing here this time of night?"

"Oh, my little cousin is in town. She'll be looking at colleges soon, so I thought I'd show her around on our way back from dinner with family." The officer looked at me. I smiled wanly.

"Well, my shift is almost over. Can I give you a lift back to your car?"

"That would be wonderful. Thanks, officer."

I sat in the backseat staring at the back of the officer's head with Adam next to me. Wanting to scream but unable to speak. Wanting to run but unable to escape.

After the officer dropped us off at his car on the other side of campus, Adam drove us to a nearby parking lot and forced my seat back in his Volkswagen Rabbit. I hadn't said a word, and I remained silent as he began to take my clothes off again. I just wanted it to be over. It was dark, and I had no idea where we were or how I'd get back to my dorm room. In a time before cell phones, I couldn't fathom how to find my way back to campus. As his hand entered me, I cried out in pain. He covered my mouth, then flattened on top of me as another car entered the parking lot. He got back in the driver's seat and told me to stay where I was. He started the car and, as I lay there in the reclined passenger seat with tears streaming down my face, I tried not to make any sounds. I tried to make myself invisible. I wanted to disappear. He drove somewhere else, and when we got there, he took me out of the car, and raped me in a field on damp grass.

I do not remember the rest of the evening or coming back to the dorm, but I woke up in my bed the next morning in pain. I stayed in bed all day until a note was pushed under my door. It was from Adam:

Meet me by the athletic field so we can talk in private. 8:00 pm.

I went so that I could ask him why he did it. I rehearsed what I was going to say as I walked across the small campus. But when I arrived, words would not come out of my mouth. He pinned me down again and told me I must have wanted more since I agreed to meet with him again.

The next day, as I brought my hurriedly packed suitcases to the dorm parking lot to wait for the airport shuttle, he was there with a look I'll never forget. It was a look that combined pity and menace. My mom always said, "Keep your wits about you." I clearly did not heed her advice when I put myself in this situation with him not once, but twice in two days.

As I got on the plane at Logan airport, I breathed a sigh of relief. Although I couldn't escape from the back of the police car, or from him, I was alive. In a couple of hours, I would be 1000 miles away from Boston and that horrible experience would be behind me. Two nights earlier, when I was in a field with him on top of me, I thought I would die. But I didn't. I was heading home.

I had no plans to tell anyone other than my friend Natalie about what happened in Boston. I knew I'd brought it upon myself. I got in his car, went to dinner, invited a kiss, and didn't run away when it was clear where the night was going. I thought that if I told anyone that it was rape, I would not be believed. I didn't even think of it as rape at first. I could not admit to myself or others that the sex was unwanted. When I told Natalie, I bragged about getting with an older guy because she was always dating older men, and she liked to tease me for being a prude. As I entered high school, I tried to put the experience behind me with alcohol, weed, whippits (nitrous oxide), Robitussin (when I couldn't get alcohol), and my favorite: LSD.

On the first day of high school, I wore a tank top dress, combat boots, no bra, and strategically placed a fake tattoo of a rose on my upper arm because I wanted to make a very specific first impression: *I do not give a fuck what you think.* As I walked through the halls on that first day of school, I wanted everyone to know I was a tough girl. I could see the disappointment on my high school teachers' faces when they realized I wasn't the "Little Palmer" they were expecting. Many of the kids I knew from middle school avoided me. The druggies, skaters, and punks welcomed me to their favorite spot in a nearby park to smoke and get high.

The problem with a first impression of "I do not give a fuck" is that it prevents people from giving a fuck about you. I maintained my tough exterior and didn't let anyone get close. The "burnouts" I hung out with only cared about whether you had a cigarette to bum or a bag of weed, and my parents had money, so I always had both. I continued my tough girl act, self-medicating my post-traumatic stress symptoms. We didn't talk about our shitty lives. If anyone got too close, or if I thought I might be falling in love, I walked by them in the school hallways as if I didn't see them and stopped returning their calls.

This didn't stop me from becoming sexually involved with other men while I was high, men who I didn't care about, and who typically had easy access to drugs. I had escaped Boston after the rape, but I could not escape the rape. I suffered from intense flashbacks during sex, and sometimes flashbacks would also come, unexpectedly, as I was walking down the hall or lying in bed. I could still feel him on top of me. Inside me. I had trouble sleeping, and when I did sleep, I had nightmares. I started hearing voices. I was 14, and I had to drink or get high every day, just to get through the day.

One morning, about six weeks into freshman year of high school, I opened my eyes to sirens and red lights and realized I was in an ambulance. My best friend Daisy, who I'd known since third grade, had spent the night and woke up to me having a seizure. She called 911. Eventually, the neurologist diagnosed me with nocturnal epilepsy brought on by sleep deprivation. I was put on heavy prescription drugs that made me sleepy. I was addicted to drugs, depressed, cutting, and suicidal, but the neurologist didn't screen for any of that.

The following summer, I went back to the recreational summer camp in Wisconsin as a counselor-in-training. While at camp, I could be me. I could let my imperfections show. I could let my guard down. My friends, who were also misfits in their hometown, were there each summer. Through them I learned what it felt like to be loved.

That summer I fell in love. Ally had long brown hair and green eyes. Like me, or at least like my façade, Ally did not give a fuck what other people thought. We would sneak out at night to smoke cigarettes in the woods and talk. We read Anaïs Nin and listened to The Cure together. We danced in the rain. I didn't know how to name my love for her. Did I want to be like her? When she told me she was bisexual, I realized what I was feeling. It was intoxicating. But it was also confusing. Was I attracted to her because she wasn't a man? Did rape cause people to be gay? Would I love her if I hadn't been raped? Ally didn't love me the way I loved her but meeting her opened a door I didn't know was there. Like Alice exiting the rabbit hole into the "loveliest garden you ever saw," I never wanted to return to where I came from. By the end of the summer, I embraced the idea that women could love women. When I got home, I sat on the floor among the dusty shelves of my local library to read all the books that mentioned gay people. (There weren't many.) It was the early-1990s, so I started listening to feminist punk riot grrrl bands and Ani DiFranco. Once my parents got dial up internet, I connected with gay communities online.

My sophomore year of high school I was still using fake tattoos to make an impression. I was in Geometry class, staring out the window, when my teacher tapped me on the shoulder and asked to speak with me outside of the classroom. She asked to see my hand, where I had written **HATE** in all caps with a magic marker. I showed it to her, along with my other hand, where I'd written **LOVE**. I was emulating Meatloaf from *Rocky Horror Picture Show*, but she was not interested in my explanation.

"I'm worried about you."

"There's nothing for you to worry about. It's just a movie."

"If you ever want to talk . . ."

"I'm fine." I walked away. I needed a smoke.

I wasn't fine. I was still having flashbacks and panic attacks. The drugs and alcohol weren't helping as much as they once did. I was exhausted. I couldn't believe somebody gave a fuck about a girl who pretended she didn't need anyone. This teacher seemed genuinely concerned, and I wanted to tell her everything. She was also my seventh period study hall teacher, the last class of the day. I decided I would tell her then. I felt sick. I wanted to leave school and get high. But I made it to seventh period, sat down at my seat in the cafeteria, and wrote about the camp counselor. I folded the note and placed it on her desk as I walked out of the room. I went directly to the bathroom, threw up, then cried for the first time in two years. When I came back to study hall, she handed me an eleven-word note: *"Something similar happened to me. You are going to be OK."*

I believed her.

I told my friend's mom next, that day after school. She told me that she regretted not reporting her own sexual assault, and I should consider reporting. Until that conversation, I did not realize that what happened was a crime. I just thought it was a shitty thing that I clearly brought upon myself. Learning that the first two grown-ups I told were raped when they were teenagers enraged me. I looked at them and saw that rape could happen to anyone. I also saw that you could become a reasonably put together grown-up after rape. I saw that they found a way for smiling to come easy, something I couldn't yet figure out how to do.

I decided I wanted to report, which meant I had to tell my parents. I dreaded telling them. I had clearly disregarded my mother's advice to keep "my wits about me" by getting in a car with that man. What daughter of a feminist does that?

I sat at the kitchen table and told them everything. I told them I wanted to report. They convinced me not to. They said it was too complicated because we were in Illinois, and it happened in Massachusetts. They told me if I reported, I would have to see him again, and I didn't want that, did I?

They were right. I did not want to see him again. He had sent two letters to me a couple weeks after it happened. He wrote that I had "a lot of growing up to do" and that sexual relationships should be more "give and take." He also sent a letter to my parents telling them to be kinder to me. In my mind (and his?), I was a delinquent while he was a computer science major at a prestigious university. I used drugs and fooled around with men—even before I met him. I intuitively knew then that I wasn't a perfect victim, and that reporting was a bad idea.

I decided to focus on physically getting out of my hometown, instead of the mental escape I had attempted with my regular use of drugs and alcohol. My parents said they'd pay for the best college I could get into. I had an escape route if I wanted it. I quit drinking and drugs and joined clubs to keep busy and stay clean. A teacher had been asking me to come to a club she had started, so I went. It was a peer education theater troupe about racism and prejudice. I also became friends with a trio of older girls, seniors, who called themselves the Bitter Battle Maidens. They were feminist, and badass, and believed in the castration of men who harmed women. This seemed reasonable to me after what I had been through! My new friends were also editors of the literary magazine, so I joined them and began to cultivate my passion for writing. I got a part-time job taking care of an elderly woman after school on the days my clubs didn't meet. I found purpose, a community, and began to envision a different future. (During this time, I also began a habit—that I still have—of staying busy to avoid dealing with my shit.)

It was 1994, and despite being raised by a self-proclaimed feminist, this was the year of my actual feminist awakening. A teacher lent me *Outrageous Acts and Everyday Rebellions* by Gloria Steinem. My hometown was conservative and home to a fundamental Christian college, so when she lent it to me, she asked me not to tell anyone. It was also the year that Lorena Bobbitt, a rape survivor, went on trial for cutting off her husband's penis. In one of my first "outrageous acts," I showed up to school wearing sandwich boards that said, "**FREE LORENA**." It was a couple of years after Anita Hill's testimony, which, to be honest, I first learned about from a *Sonic Youth* song. But when I looked into her story to learn more, I was inspired by her truth telling.

When my friends and I tried to speak out against a racist incident at our school, there was no response from administrators. The next day we showed up with duct tape on our mouths with the word CENSORED written on it. My theater troupe started to travel to local schools where we put on short skits based on our personal experiences. My peers wrote and performed stories about racism, xenophobia, violence, and homophobia. I remained distant, serving as director and producer of their stories, because I wasn't ready to tell my truth yet. But it was incredible to see the power of personal experiences on stage. But I began to understand that the personal is indeed political.

I got my grades up, and at my request, my parents sent me to a different summer academic enrichment program at a college in Boston during the summer before my senior year of high school. While there, I tried to redeem myself by co-organizing a *Take Back the Night* rally and becoming a peer mentor for younger teens who were coming out as gay. Two field trips that summer were pivotal to my discovery of the possibility of Queer joy. The first was to the 1995 Newport Folk Festival where I saw Ani DiFranco, Indigo Girls, Joan Baez, and others play in front of a sea of lesbians experiencing pure Queer joy as we danced and sang in the rain. The second was to visit five colleges that I had never heard of in western Massachusetts. As we explored Smith College and Northampton, I knew where I needed to go to escape my hometown.

My dad and my guidance counselor wanted me to set my sights on the University of Illinois, where they both attended. They didn't want me to get my hopes up about going to Smith College—especially because my grade point average was not stellar. In my applications, I used the excuse of side effects of my prescription drugs for the seizures to explain my poor grades during the first half of high school. For my personal statement, I wrote about my budding activism and the protests I organized.

Unlike many of my friends, I had a ticket out of town due to my parents' wealth. Many of them, especially those I used drugs with in the first part of high school, did not go to college. In the days before email, you watched your mailbox to see if letters from colleges were in a big envelope (you got in!) or a small envelope (we regret to inform you . . .). When a big envelope arrived from Smith, there was no question I was on my way out of Illinois.

When my parents dropped me off at Smith, I knew I was where I belonged—socially, at least—but academically, I had a severe case of imposter syndrome. The more the other girls talked about being valedictorian of their private schools, the more I shut myself in my room to study and prove to myself I belonged there. I was sober, and my best friend at college was straight edge; while our friends went to parties, we went to the library.

I knew I wanted to get involved with campus activism, so my best friend and I joined the feminist club at the end of our first year. There were two clubs at Smith that focused on violence and abuse, but I was terrified to come out as a survivor. I stayed on the periphery of these groups until my senior year, periodically attending their events with my heart racing, but unable to say out loud, "I'm like you." Instead, I joined a club focused on child advocacy and focused my studies on making the world better for children and families.

One day, a professor handed me a newspaper article about a Northampton man who was starting an advocacy organization called Camp Safety Project. He was looking for college volunteers to help him get the organization off the ground. She thought I might be interested in helping him out.

I couldn't believe it: this man's son had been sexually abused in a summer camp and now he was looking to do something about it. With funding from my college, I spent the summer after my junior year as his paid intern. We conducted a survey that we sent—via fax, no less—to all child-serving organizations in the state to determine the extent of sexual abuse in summer camps. We collected over 100 stories of camp sexual abuse. I created a website—no small feat in 1999—to catalog and share these stories. I posted news articles about camp abuse, developed policies and procedures for camps looking to prevent abuse, and shared resources for parents who were looking to send their kids to camp.

I also started to tell my story publicly as part of our legislative advocacy efforts. I wrote letters to the editor and op-eds. I was interviewed on television about what happened to me. By telling our stories and sharing the data we collected, we convinced the Massachusetts legislature to change the camp oversight laws from the Office of Sanitation to the Office of Child Care Services. We educated camp administrators and parents that sex offender registry background checks were not enough, due to underreporting and lack of convictions. I became a survivor-activist and realized I had the power to make real change.

When I graduated from Smith, I moved to Chicago to work with kids by day and, apparently, to be a total mess in my personal life. Two formative intimate relationships in my early 20s were with people no one would want to fuck with: Elena, a Chicago cop, and Alejandro, a former Marine. I still walked through the world like I did on that first day of high school, projecting an image of fierce badassery, but it was all a performance. I did not feel safe in my own skin. With Elena and Alejandro, I thought I would be protected if anyone tried to harm me. The problem was that the risk of harm wasn't external to my relationships with them. It was with them.

One night, I was drinking and playing pool with friends at my favorite gay bar. I was surrounded by gay boys, and I noticed there was only one other woman in the bar. She approached me and made a joke that made me laugh. We started to play pool and talk. Elena was several years older than me. She had a broken arm and was on administrative leave from her position with the Chicago Police Department, the details of which I never really learned or asked about. We started dating and as we grew closer, we talked about the traumas we had experienced in our childhood. The extent of her trauma was heartbreaking—and made my childhood feel easy in comparison. She told me she became a cop for the same reasons I wanted to be a social worker: to help people and protect them from harm.

We dated twice. After not seeing her for several months after our first break up, I ran into her on the street, and she invited me to her 30th birthday party. I was 23. We started dating again. One night, I was in my apartment, and I received an instant message from Elena. She worked nights, so I wasn't expecting to hear from her. Elena was indeed at work and not sitting at her computer in her apartment. The person on the other end of the message was a woman using her account, someone she was also dating at the time, who knew about me even though I didn't know about her. She reached out to me to tell me to get as far away from Elena as I could. I didn't know if I should believe her, this stranger. I thought she was jealous of my connection with Elena. I was the new woman, but also an ex-, and I was convinced that Elena would be different with me.

But the next time I was at Elena's apartment, I saw evidence of where she punched the wall, barely missing the woman who had been so kind to reach out to me. I thought I could change her. But the truth was I couldn't leave her because I needed her to help *me*. To protect *me* from harm. One morning, she pulled her gun on a worker from the utilities company who she thought was trespassing on her property. I had to scream at her to make her put it down. When her buddies from work would come over, I heard how they would talk about the gang members and homeless people they encountered in her job. They weren't helping or protecting people. They actively harmed and threatened them. She did not hurt me, but she controlled me through my fear of her. I was afraid of making her mad because I saw what she did to others when she was angry. I was afraid of the prospect of violence at her hand. Each time we broke up, it was her idea, and I was relieved. I couldn't say out loud that I didn't want to be with her—to her or my friends.

The last time I saw her it was a couple years after our final break up. My friend and I were walking to a coffee shop, and she drove by, on patrol, and offered us a ride. It was a hot summer day in Chicago, so we accepted. When she shut the door with us inside, I remembered there are no door handles in the back seat. I started to panic, unable to breathe. It was the second time I felt trapped in the back of a police car, unable to open the doors. When we got to the coffee shop, I sobbed.

Around the same time that I was dating Elena on and off, I had a supervisor named Alejandro, who was a former Marine, a trained sniper who liked to brag about the number of kills he got in Iraq. Although I was a lesbian and was staunchly anti-war, I was attracted to him. We went on a couple of dates; he took me salsa dancing and to dinner. He was older than me and had a five-year-old kid. Over time I learned that his ex-girlfriend had an order of protection against him for punching (and shattering) the back window of a car when his ex-wouldn't let him have visitation. His child was in the backseat at the time. As I began to distance myself from him, in part due to the prospect of violence at his hand, he became more aggressive toward me. One day, after we finished a drug prevention presentation for fourth graders at an elementary school, we got into his car to go back to our office. I was refusing to see him outside of work, and he was pissed. As he drove away from the school, he locked the car doors, turned up a Nine Inch Nail's song with the lyrics "I want to fuck you like an animal," and drove 60 miles an hour—on a 30-mph section of road—ignoring other cars, stop signs, and red lights along the way. I grabbed onto the arm rest and froze, once again trapped in a car with someone who could harm me.

I didn't think I could tell anyone about the ongoing harassment and intimidation I experienced over the several months we worked together. On the day he sexually assaulted me in our shared office, the executive director interrupted it by knocking on the door. He jumped off me, and we pulled ourselves together before the director came in. I was relieved that for the second time in my life, an assault was interrupted by a timely knock. Once again, though, I was silent in the wake of what had just happened to me.

I still couldn't tell my truth. I didn't think anyone would believe me. I had gone on dates with him, but I was a lesbian. He was abused as a child, and I thought maybe I could change or help him. I was a feminist survivor-activist, but I couldn't stop being abused.

He eventually got a new job as an immigration enforcement agent, which, although he was the child of immigrants, was his dream job. The last time I saw him he was working at O'Hare. I was walking to baggage claim in a jetlagged haze after getting off an international flight. He appeared beside me, in his uniform, and under his breath said, "I could really fuck you over right now." I kept walking, looking straight ahead. I saw my bag, picked it up, and walked out of baggage claim. When I got outside the airport, I sat on the sidewalk and wept.

I was promoted to the supervisor position after his departure, and I started attending graduate school for my Master of Social Work part-time. For one of the requirements for my MSW program, I interned as a counselor for kids who had been sexually abused. One kid I worked with, around eleven years old, was brought to counseling because the order of protection against his uncle was running out and couldn't be renewed without a new incident. He was terrified. I helped him the best I could, but I felt helpless to truly make a difference in his life. On his last day of counseling with me, he thanked me and after giving me a quick, shy hug, he gave me a necklace with a St. Rita charm on it, the saint of impossible causes. I gave him a toy turtle that he had used during play therapy to symbolize himself. I still have the St. Rita necklace, and I still wonder if my causes are truly impossible.

With each client I worked with in that internship, it became clear that kids were not protected by our laws. I saw kids tell their truths to teachers or police or judges and not be believed. I made a mandatory report to child protective services (CPS) on behalf of a teenage client and CPS deemed it "low risk to an adult child." In other situations, children were removed from their families and placed into foster care when sexual abuse was alleged. Or mothers left with their children in the middle of the night to go to a shelter or stay at a relative's house. Why was it that the victims' lives were disrupted, while the lives of the offenders continued as if nothing happened? I thought about my struggles with alcohol, back pain, intimacy, and claustrophobia. Did the man who raped me have any lasting impact on his life? Should I have reported him, so he'd have to pay for what he did?

Toward the end of my internship, in 2003, I started looking for activism I could get involved with to change the criminal justice and child welfare systems, so they could actually help people instead of harming them. I learned about an organization in the Bay area called Generation Five (Gen5). I applied to join their Community Response Project, which was a training program for activists and organizers dedicated to a community-based, transformative justice-oriented, non-carceral model of ending child sexual abuse. I was accepted but had to fund my travel to New York City to participate every six weeks for a year or so. It was well worth the increase in credit card debt.

Part of Gen5's philosophy was that if we really wanted to end violence, we had to work with those who harmed, not just with those who had been harmed. But to me, offenders were monsters. How could I look at a monster with empathy? One of the sessions of the training featured a panel with a man convicted of child sexual abuse, his wife, and a therapist. After the husband and wife told their stories, the questions from the audience flooded in—all directed toward the wife, including accusations, blame, and judgement about her not intervening soon enough. How could she not know? How could she allow this to happen to her grandchildren? The facilitator stepped in and asked us to consider our questions, to think how we might rephrase them toward the husband. And herein was the problem: we couldn't look at his humanity in the eye.

Another guest speaker told us a story about an information and referral hotline that had been set up to help survivors of child sexual abuse and their loved ones. They set up the number, advertised it on billboards and elsewhere, trained their volunteers, and when the first call came in, it was from someone who wanted to stop sexually abusing children but didn't know how. He wanted help. They hadn't prepared for this type of caller.

Soon, they collected resources and helped many callers find the support they needed to get help to stop perpetrating abuse. Then, in the mid-1990s, Megan's Law was passed, which created a public sex offender registry and required community notification of registered sex offenders. The guest speaker told us that once Megan's Law passed, the number of people seeking help to stop perpetrating abuse who called the hotline went down to zero.

For my second MSW practicum, I was hired by a non-profit to serve as a victim advocate in Chicago's domestic violence court and a children's counselor at the non-profit's location in the community. Any last shred of faith that I had in the criminal justice system being just or helpful to victims was eliminated within a month of working at the court. I was once again a mandated reporter, which I had to mention upon introducing myself as an advocate or counselor. With the victims at the domestic violence court, this was code for "please don't tell me your children are being harmed. I can't help you." The women knew from this introduction that if they mentioned child abuse, their kids would be removed by CPS. So they couldn't tell me their whole truths if they wanted to keep their children. As women came in for orders of protection, and I advocated for them, I knew that it was likely putting them in more danger, instead of less. Women of color twice my age sat across from me, wondering what a 26-year-old White girl could do to help them. I often wondered the same thing.

As I sat in the courtroom observing case after case of victims telling their stories to convince judges they needed orders of protection, I saw how they were treated. Courts are, by design, focused on the rights of offenders to receive due process, to confront witnesses, to have an attorney, etc. In a criminal domestic violence case, it becomes the state's case, and the victim is a witness to the crime that occurred against them. In the process, victims lose agency. They are only allowed to speak about the specific incident that was associated with a police report, not the pattern of abusive behavior they'd experienced over a longer period of time. When my colleagues and I would go out for drinks after work, we were in absolute agreement that we would never recommend a friend go through this process. I became more and more grateful that I had made the decision not to report my rape so many years prior.

Meanwhile, as I continued the training with Gen5, I was coming to realize that a transformative justice response, based on the fundamental belief that people can and do change, was the key to ending violence. My head told me this was true, but my heart resisted. It made my blood boil to think about people who committed child sexual abuse. It brought me back to my Bitter Battle Maiden crew in high school, where we'd discussed castration as the only option over lunch in the cafeteria, with Lorena Bobbitt as our patron saint. Transformative justice also recognizes, in a way I refused to at the time, that harm-doers and victims of harm exist in a Venn diagram. As Mariame Kaba says, "hurt people hurt people." But then I thought about the abuse and trauma that Elena and Alejandro experienced as children, and how their career choices reflected an attempt at gaining and maintaining power over others, after childhoods of feeling so powerless. I remembered that one time when we were talking at the picnic table in Boston, before the night we went out for dinner, Adam told me he was a rape survivor. If I truly wanted to end violence, I needed to recognize that the current legal responses to abuse, and all my energies working with victims, were merely Band-Aids placed on a bullet wound.

I left Chicago a couple years later when I fell in love with a woman who lived in St. Louis. For the first time, I was in a long-term relationship based on mutual respect and care. It was incredible. My first job in St. Louis was as a supervisor for advocates for children in foster care, but again, I found myself working in a system that harmed, instead of helped, families. I was trying to figure out how to transition my career into working with men who had harmed women or children. I learned about an organization called RAVEN, which was founded by male feminists in the 1970s to end men's violence against women. When they were hiring a new executive director, I applied and, to my surprise, was hired for the position.

I was 28 and in charge of a batterer intervention program and youth violence prevention program that was founded in 1978, the year I was born. The organization's funding through the Violence Against Women Act meant that we had to work closely with probation and parole officers and report whether the men were coming to the 48-week program. We also had to assess whether we thought they were changing their behavior. I was profoundly hopeful that we could make an impact but had no way of knowing if we were. If they were still harming people in their life, the men had no incentive to tell the truth since compliance was associated with fulfilling the terms of their probation or parole. I had no idea if women were safer or—like in the domestic violence court—in more danger due to a false belief that we would fix their abusers' behaviors. So I applied for a Ph.D. program in Washington DC so that I could try to fix the law instead. All of the work to change individuals didn't mean anything when the structures set people up to fail.

In 2009, when my partner and I moved to DC, it struck me that I was living 15 miles from Adam's hometown in Virginia. I began to have nightmares about running into him. I was still afraid of him 17 years later. I needed to know he could not harm me.

One August night, I typed his name into the sex offender registry search box for the thousandth time, but he wasn't there. I had been searching for him for years with no luck. I wanted to find him, and the registry was the only place I thought to look. I assumed he had reoffended. I prayed that someone else had reported him. From my work with the Camp Safety Project and elsewhere, I knew the limits of the registry. But I still had faith that he would be there. Or maybe I was afraid to find him somewhere else.

I decided to try Google. I knew his full name, where he went to college, and his hometown. Each time I clicked a link in my search results my heart skipped a beat. I scrutinized the details on each website, and when I realized it wasn't him, I didn't know whether to feel disappointed or relieved.

I clicked a LinkedIn profile. There he was. The guy who had raped me when I was 13 was completing a doctoral degree at an ivy league university instead of serving a prison sentence.

I looked up the statute of limitations for Massachusetts. For victims under age 16, the statute of limitations was 15 years after the victim turns 16 or reports to police, whichever is earlier. Since I never reported, the statute of limitations would have run out 15 years after I turned 16, or on my 31st birthday, which I'd celebrated the day before.

For the second time that evening, I didn't know whether to feel disappointed or relieved. There I was, reconsidering reporting the crime, and I was one day too late. I could not reconcile that I had let the man who raped me go free. He faced no accountability for what he had done. But since nothing could be done, I closed my laptop and stopped searching the registry. Instead, I immersed myself in my studies, with a focus on the legal and policy response to gender-based violence, hoping to advocate for changes to the legal system I had avoided.

In spring of 2016, while working on a research project in Massachusetts, I learned that the statute of limitations in the state had changed. For rape or abuse of a child under 16, there was no statute of limitations, but if it has been more than 27 years since the offense, there needed to be *"independent evidence that corroborates the victim's allegation. Such independent evidence . . . shall not consist exclusively of the opinions of mental health professionals."* I had two years from that moment to decide to report because if I waited any longer, I would need *"independent evidence."*

I didn't have any evidence. My life wasn't like a CSI episode. I had delayed disclosing. I never went to the hospital. I didn't report it to the police. I have people in my life that could validate that I was quite troubled after I returned home from Boston that summer, but I was also troubled before I left for Boston. People could attest to my flashbacks, but they probably thought they were bad LSD trips. I contacted his university to see if there were any records of the officer finding us that night. A lieutenant replied:

Apparently, the University Police switched to electronic records the month after your assault occurred, so she is digging to see if there are paper files remaining. She expressed that she feels terrible about the timing and remains hopeful that she will be able to find some remaining paper trail to share with you. She agreed that she would be in touch with you to let you know what/if she finds anything.

I never heard from them.

Curious, I decided to see if I could find him again online, although seven years had passed since I first found his LinkedIn page. It did not take long to find his C.V. He was a researcher who regularly presented at academic conferences. I looked up where and when I could attend a conference that he regularly spoke at. I was familiar with the conference because some of my colleagues attended. He was presenting in two weeks in Washington, DC, a couple of miles from my apartment.

My heart raced. I began to imagine various scenarios where I would confront him, in front of a room of academics, for what he did to me. For the pain he caused. For the way he has been able to live his life for 24 years without consequences.

Through Google, I found his home address. I found the name of the woman he had married. I found records of his contributions to the Democratic party and other progressive causes. I imagined writing a letter to him—or maybe his wife—to call him out as a rapist and a despicable human being. I sent an email to Daisy, my best friend who called an ambulance when I had a seizure, to tell her all I had learned about this man and that I was considering writing or reporting him. Her response, as always, was what I need to hear:

Okay. First of all, I need to tell you that I love you so much . . . having said that, I have a few hard things to say about this guy in Boston.

Please!!!!! STOP giving this man any more control over your life! He is consuming your thoughts! Girl . . . please, be kind to yourself. This man is not deserving of this much control. . . .

Jane, I love you so much, and this letter was not easy to type because I would rather be here to listen and would love to agree with you . . . but this is how I truly feel about the man in Boston. . . . Just send him the bill for all your years in therapy!

She was right. I ripped up the post-it where I had written his address and let the conference dates pass.

I was 13, and he was a 20-year-old college student who took advantage of my vulnerability. Legally, I could not have consented to what occurred. It was statutory rape, so I could probably get a conviction.

But would a conviction be possible in 2016, I wondered? And to what end? I had spent my career working to end violence. The most powerful positive impacts in this work—where I had a glimmer of hope that another world is possible—were in the community-led and community-based initiatives. The most negative impacts were made worse by the harm inherent in the criminal legal system.

I was angry that the statute of limitations had been extended. That a door that was closed for me had reopened, trying to invite me back in. I wondered if my silence meant he was able to go on with his life as if it never happened, while I struggled with chronic back pain, nightmares, flashbacks, intimacy, and an inability to feel safe. At the time that I ripped up the post-it note, I couldn't sit in a room without facing the door. I was always on edge. I took the stairs instead of the elevator so I couldn't get trapped. I even had trouble taking cabs because I wasn't in the driver's seat. Yet I realized it was not me that let the man who raped me go free. And it was not because of me that he faced no accountability for what he had done.

Pursuing charges wouldn't unrape me, it wouldn't take away the pain I've experienced. It wouldn't pay for the years of therapy, and it likely wouldn't put him in prison. He could hire an expensive lawyer and call me a liar. I had no "independent evidence," after all. Even if he did go to prison, it wouldn't be for very long, and it wouldn't have prevented any other offenses he may have committed in the intervening years. And it wouldn't hold him accountable in any meaningful way to me and my life.

The reopening of the possibility to press charges was an opportunity for me to reflect on what I, as a survivor, needed to heal. I needed to ask my heart what felt right to me. I was an activist, professor, researcher, and a former social worker. My head was filled with data and survivors' stories that said loud and clear: the police will not protect you, and the courts will not keep you safe. I realized my head and my heart were saying the same thing: pressing charges would help no one. The legal system would not change our culture that raised men to want to control women. It would not heal me. It would break me. It cannot heal the men that harm women. It cannot magically make a survivor feel whole again. As Mariame Kaba (2021) writes, "It does nothing to change a culture that makes this harm imaginable, to hold the individual perpetrator accountable, to support their transformation, or to meet the needs of survivors" (p. 3).

I do not know what would have happened if I had reported my rape at any point, whether it was 1992, 1994, 2003, 2009, 2016, or yesterday. What I do know is that I needed what I would argue most survivors need: to be able to tell my truth, for my truth to be believed, to feel safe, and for my power to be restored. What I also know from my work over the past two decades is that the criminal legal system is not a place where victims are believed, where victims can feel safe, or where victim power is restored.

Collectively, we must create a world where we can "build support and more safety for the person harmed, figure out how the broader context was set up for this harm to happen, and how that context can be changed so that this harm is less likely to happen again" (Kaba, 2021, p. 59). This is the only way forward to create a world without violence. The criminal legal system cannot do this—it cannot provide justice, safety, healing, or voluntary (and meaningful) accountability.

As I reflect on my story, I think about the support and safety I could have used; the context of my harm(s); and how the harm I experienced could have been prevented. I can blame my parents or my context as a Gen X latch-key kid, but that is too easy. Instead, I pivot to consider the multiple moments that made me whole again. I think of the first person I told, a high school math teacher, who believed me. I think of the kids who sat across from me in a counseling room, who told me their stories with puppets or other toys, who I validated and said, like the math teacher said to me, "You're going to be OK." I think of the emails I received from other survivors via the Camp Safety Project website. I think of my lovers who held me and helped me feel safe. I think of the community of people—a community of survivors and Queer people—who I have surrounded myself with over the years. I think of my chosen family, who have helped me know what it is like to be loved, to be cared for, and to reciprocate such care. I think of my therapists and acupuncturists who helped me discover that my nervous system was stuck in a trauma (fight/flight/freeze) response and who are working with me to learn to be present in my body again. I can now sit with my back to a door and, as I age, I welcome an opportunity to take an elevator over the stairs. I remember the highway in front of me as I drove the moving truck to St. Louis, and then to DC, so I could make my own life, chart my own path, and be in the driver's seat instead of trapped in a passenger seat with no escape.

Statutes of limitations are artificial boundaries on when a survivor can tell their truth. The sex offender registry doesn't make us safer. The legal system is designed to protect defendants' rights, not to support victims. What we need, as survivors, are community-led and community-based solutions that don't require "independent evidence" and instead center hope, healing, and community transformation. From my earliest memories, I lived in the shadow of the "prospect of violence"[1] and let it control me. In the summer of 2022,

I realized it had been 30 years since that night in 1992. I am at peace with the decisions I've made and the life I've built. I am proud of how far I've come in my healing. My decision not to report centered my needs, my healing, and my belief that systems can't fulfill the needs of survivors—or the needs of people who cause harm, either.

I will never forget a moment during the Gen5 training when I heard a spoken word poet, Aya de Leon,[2] declare the words **"risk hope."** These two words are what get me out of bed each morning and help me imagine—and work to create—a different world, one without violence or the prospect of it. Without hope, we remain trapped. With hope—and a vision—that a different world is possible, and that it is on us to create it, we can be free.

Acknowledgements

I am eternally grateful to Hannah Grieco, who is an incredible editor, kind soul, and friend. I am also very grateful for dear friends who took the time to read drafts and provide feedback: L.S., V.R, S.W., A.D.R., and F.O.

Note.

An excerpt of this essay, called "Independent Evidence," was published in the online magazine, *You Might Need to Hear This*, on December 9, 2021. www.youmightneedto hearthis.com/stories/independent-evidence

Notes

1 Das (2007) writes about how, for survivors of abuse, "violence can present in everyday life as a possibility, eventuality, and actuality" (as cited in Henze-Pedersen, 2021, p. 9).
2 Aya de Leon (https://ayadeleon.wordpress.com/about-aya/)

References

Das, V. (2007). *Life and words. Violence and the descent into the ordinary.* Oakland, CA: University of California Press.

Henze-Pedersen, S. (2021). The ghost of violence: The lived experience of violence after the act. *Violence Against Women.* Online First. https://doi.org/10.1177/1077801221994910.

Kaba, M. (2021). *We do this 'til we free us.* Ed. Tamara Nopper. Chicago, IL: Haymarket Books.

Queer Victimology and Queer Identities

Chapter 9

Victimization Among Transgender and Gender Diverse Youth

Research Poems on Family, Religion, Identity, and Resilience

Megan S. Paceley, Rey Flores, Isaac Sanders, Emera Greenwood, Patricia Sattler, and Jacob Goffnett

Introduction

Transgender and gender diverse (TGD) youth are at an elevated risk of experiencing victimization compared to cisgender youth. Victimization occurs across social contexts, including communities, schools, and families, and may take numerous forms, such as family violence and rejection; stigma and anti-TGD rhetoric; bullying and harassment; hate crimes; and intimate partner violence (Garthe et al., 2021; Johns et al., 2019; Paceley et al., 2020; Reisner et al., 2015). For example, one US-based study found TGD students experienced bullying in schools at more than twice the rate of their cisgender peers (Johns et al., 2019). Additionally, empirical research finds family rejection to be associated with psychological distress and self-harm (Bariola et al., 2015; Grossman & D'Augelli, 2007), and hostile community climates are associated with high rates of victimization, depression, and anxiety (Paceley et al., 2020). Societal stigmatization of TGD identities—and the privileging of cisgender and binary ones—underpins this elevated risk of victimization (Delozier et al., 2020; Hendricks & Testa, 2012). Furthermore, experiences of victimization are related to behavioral health difficulties, including substance misuse, depression, anxiety, and suicidality (Garthe et al., 2020; Johns et al., 2019; Reisner et al., 2015).

Despite the overwhelming risk of experiencing victimization, TGD youth demonstrate resilience and perseverance in developing their identities and well-being. For example, Goffnett and Paceley (2020) asked TGD youth advice they had for other TGD youth. While all participants acknowledged strife associated with identity development, they also encouraged youth to persevere in developing their identities because the journey was worth the rewarding connections, authenticity, and feelings of pride. Other researchers have documented mechanisms that facilitate resilience among TGD youth. One study found five methods TGD youth used to build resilience: self-conceptualization of gender identity; self-advocacy; supportive educational systems; reframing mental health challenges; and family support (Singh et al., 2014). Collectively, this body of work documents the cognitive, emotional, and behavioral labor TGD youth must shoulder to resist victimization and precursory stigma systemic in the US sociopolitical environment.

This chapter aims to illustrate the victimization and resilience experiences of TGD youth in the Midwest—an area of the US marked by increased risks of violence and stigma (Kosciw et al., 2016). Given the high rates of victimization experienced by TGD youth, it is essential that researchers engage in strategies that challenge and reduce stigma while emphasizing the strengths and expertise of TGD individuals and communities. One such strategy is

DOI: 10.4324/9781003400981-11

the use of research poems (Jen & Paceley, 2021), a form of arts-based methodology that weaves qualitative data into a poem (Cousik, 2014; Leavy, 2015). Research poems, as a method, allow us to share stories and "convey strong emotion" that arises in qualitative data (Furman, 2004, p. 163). Given our goal of illustrating the victimization and resilience experiences of TGD youth in the Midwestern US, research poems are a creative, innovative strategy to challenge stigma, highlight TGD youth experiences, and have an affective impact beyond that of traditional research endeavors.

TGD Youth in the Midwest Study

This study utilized the expertise of a transgender youth advisory board (TYAB) to conceptualize the study, and assist with study design, recruitment strategies, and data analysis. The nine members of the board met biweekly to provide ongoing feedback during data collection and early data analysis. In-depth interviews were conducted with 19 transgender and gender diverse young people (13–24 years old; M = 18) living in two Midwestern states between September 2017 and December 2018. Most of the interview participants were White (74%) and identified as trans-masculine (42%) or gender nonbinary (42%). Interviews were conducted in-person or via video conferencing; all youth received a $20 gift card for their time. Interviews explored how TGD youth navigate identity across diverse social contexts to include family, school, and community. Thematic analysis (Braun & Clarke, 2006) was used to sort and categorize the data through numerous rounds of data analysis for various publications.

Research Poem Development

To develop the research poems, interview transcripts were read for familiarity by three members of the research team who identify as Queer and/or TGD. During this process, they coded segments of text as "victimization" so that all aspects of interviews that related to victimization were included. Consistent with prior research on victimization among TGD and Queer youth (Kosciw et al., 2010, 2013), we include discussion of physical, sexual, and emotional abuse, as well as bullying, stigmatizing experiences and language, and discrimination and oppression in our conceptualization of victimization. Next, three members of the research team who identify as TGD read the victimization excerpts to identify key themes or stories they felt needed to be told through one or more poems. They consulted the first author as needed but took leadership over this process as TGD individuals and scholars. They then began the process of creating found poems—poems in which all aspects of the poem are found in the participant's words, rather than from the researcher or other sources (Patrick, 2013). Through several virtual meetings, they co-constructed four research poems that highlight the harm of victimization by families, religious institutions, and intersecting forms of oppression, but also the survival and resilience of TGD youth in the Midwest. The poems that follow illustrate lived experiences of victimization, trauma, resilience, and survival.

Research Poems

My Parents Broke Me

Growing up with messages that gay people are gross and not normal.
Hearing messages from friends, family, the community, the media,

This wasn't a real thing.
I'm really shy. I'm anxious.
I felt really ashamed to say that I am trans

After I came out, I felt broken

My dad told me I was retarded every day.
I was scared to come back to my mom or my dad.
I wanna kill myself because my family doesn't accept me.

It felt like my parents broke me

They weren't happy with it.
They didn't want me to tell anyone.
They tried to make sure I didn't talk to anyone about it.

I felt broken

So I kind of only come out to people where I know it's going to be safe,
that does not include my family.
My dad kicked me out of the house
He said that my way of life was interfering with his
My parents broke me

[I'm] trying to just prove myself.
It's kind of all for show.
My parents said that I was worthless and that I wasn't deserving

I
Felt
Broken

Just because they're family
Doesn't mean they know what's right for you
I chose my family
Believe in yourself

Don't think it's your fault.
You deserve to be respected.
You're valid.
"Hey princess, get your chin up or don't let something fall off my head."

I found a new family.

~~"Trans people are going to hell"~~
I used to be Christian. I'm not anymore
I ended up being publicly humiliated in front of the whole church

So I quit going

> "Why are we letting men into women's spaces?"

I had some friends that were super religious that won't even talk to me anymore
You never really know, I guess. Terrifying knowing what you do
I am just nervous about talking to religious people

> "Well, you're messed up"

They put me in conversion therapy

> "You were **born a girl**"
> "You should be happy with **the body** God gave you"

Everyone they follow seems to kind of attack the community
> "I'm sorry I can't do that because of what it says in the Bible"
> "That's not right because my religion says so"
> "You need to go back to church and get this out of your system"
> "I'm going to hell or that I am sinning"

They use my birth name and the wrong pronouns out of spite
My dad kicked me out once he figured out that I was going on testosterone
He said that my way of life was interfering with his family's religion
~~"Trans people are going to hell"~~

Religious people have not been very accepting
Her reasoning is all religion
I just wanna know it's okay
I'm not really sure where I'm at religiously right now

In Their Mind

> There's a specific look associated with them
> Androgynous and White and thin

But my blackness is centred
We navigate so many intersections of oppression and resistance
As a Black woman, as a trans Black woman my work will always be questioned

> They're uncomfortable
> They don't understand
> They can't classify you
> To them you can't be non-White and Queer

> Maybe they'll use the right pronouns if I cut my hair

When I cut it, I felt empty

It's part of my identity as a Native American
I'm really far away from my tribe
My hair is a reminder they're still there
But it makes people think I'm not enough

If I spend more on masc-fitting clothes

> They'll respect me for who I am

If I drop $50 on a binder

> They'll respect me for who I am
> "So dumb, attention seeking"

Hispanics, we don't really believe in LGBT

> We have strong gender roles

Expectations of masculinity
Women cook, and clean, and care for the children

> [We] don't look like what society paints in their mind
> You don't see many people of color
> We only see Black trans women who have died

Sorry, Not Sorry

You never stop coming out.
Whether you're gay *or trans*
You have to explain to 40 people, yet again,

But I'm that trans girl that everyone knows.

You see Queer people rocking it,
It makes you happy
You can be that way for someone else.
Trans is not one thing.

It waxes and wanes.

For the first two years of my transition,
I took a picture every single day.
Some I'm just sobbing on my bathroom floor
Some I'm having the best time of my life and I feel the most beautiful

It's about repainting *our* narrative.

I am a woman.
I am a goddess.
I am nonbinary.
I am Black, and my blackness is centred
into all of those other aspects of who I am.

It means not apologising

My friends call it my "sassy gay walk"

Yes, I have a boyfriend.
Yes, I am transgender.
Yes, this is who we are.
Hey, yeah, it is not gonna change, buddy.
Sorry, not sorry.

Conclusion

Although tempting to end this chapter with the words of one TGD youth, "sorry, not sorry," we feel it is our responsibility as Queer and TGD scholars to end with a brief reflection and call to action. The TGD youth in this study expressed a range of victimization and traumatic experiences, from overt and violent behaviors to stigmatizing rhetoric and language. From family rejection to stigmatizing religious rhetoric and the intersections of racism and cissexism, these poems illustrate the damaging impact of these experiences on TGD youth. Importantly, they also highlight TGD youth's immense capacity for resilience and, indeed, their resistance to the expectations from others about who or what they should be. The poems created from their words represent 19 individual stories woven together to tell a collective story of trauma and survival. We ask you to read them again (and again) and consider how each of us can act in response to their words, within ourselves, our families, and communities, and in broader society, so that TGD youth do not have to be so resilient and can tell a different set of stories next time. Because they're worth it.

"Sorry, not sorry."

References

Bariola, E., Lyons, A., Leonard, W., Pitts, M., Badcock, P., & Couch, M. (2015). Demographic and psychosocial factors associated with psychological distress and resilience among transgender individuals. *American Journal of Public Health*, 105, 2108–2116. https://doi.org/10.2105/AJPH.2015.302763.

Braun, V., & Clarke, V. (2006). Using thematic analysis in psychology. *Qualitative Research in Psychology*, 3(2), 77–101. https://doi.org/10.1191/1478088706qp063oa.

Cousik, R. (2014). Research in special education: Using a research poem as a guide for relationship building. *The Qualitative Report*, 19(26), 1–16. https://doi.org/10.46743/2160-3715/2014.1210.

Delozier, A. M., Kamody, R. C., Rodgers, S., & Chen, D. (2020). Health disparities in transgender and gender expansive adolescents: A topical review from a minority stress framework. *Journal of Pediatric Psychology*, 45(8), 842–847. https://doi.org/10.1093/jpepsy/jsaa040.

Furman, R. (2004). Using poetry and narrative as qualitative data: Exploring a father's cancer through poetry. *Families, Systems, & Health*, 22(2), 162–170. https://doi.org/10.1037/1091-7527.22.2.162.

Garthe, R. C., Hidalgo, M. A., Goffnett, J., Hereth, J., Garofalo, R., Reisner, S. L., Mimiaga, M. J., & Kuhns, L. M. (2020). Young transgender women survivors of intimate partner violence: A latent class analysis of protective processes. *Psychology of Sexual Orientation and Gender Diversity*, 7(4), 386–395. http://dx.doi.org/10.1037/sgd0000379.

Garthe, R. C., Kaur, A., Rieger, A., Blackburn, A. M., Kim, S., & Goffnett, J. (2021). Dating violence and peer victimization among male, female, transgender, and gender-expansive youth. *Pediatrics*, 147(4). https://doi.org/10.1542/peds.2020-004317.

Goffnett, J., & Paceley, M. S. (2020). Challenges, pride, and connection: A qualitative exploration of advice transgender youth have for other transgender youth. *Journal of Gay & Lesbian Social Services*, 32(3), 328–353. https://doi.org/10.1080/10538720.2020.1752874.

Grossman, A. H., & D'Augelli, A. R. (2007). Transgender youth and life-threatening behaviors. *Suicide and Life-Threatening Behavior, 37*(5), 527–537. https://doi.org/10.1521/suli.2007.37.5.527.

Hendricks, M. L., & Testa, R. J. (2012). A conceptual framework for clinical work with transgender and gender nonconforming clients: An adaptation of the Minority Stress Model. *Professional Psychology: Research and Practice, 43*(5), 460–467. https://doi.org/10.1037/a0029597.

Jen, S., & Paceley, M. S. (2021). Capturing queer and trans lives and identities: The promise of research poems to inform stigma research. *Stigma and Health, 6*(1), 62–69. https://doi.org/10.1037/sah0000282.

Johns, M. M., Lowry, R., Andrzejewski, J., Barrios, L. C., Demissie, Z., McManus, T., . . . & Underwood, J. M. (2019). Transgender identity and experiences of violence victimization, substance use, suicide risk, and sexual risk behaviors among high school students—19 states and large urban school districts, 2017. *Morbidity and Mortality Weekly Report, 68*(3), 67–71. https://doi.org/10.15585/mmwr.mm6803a3.

Kosciw, J., Greytak, E., Diaz, E., & Barkiewicz, M. J. (2010). The 2009 National School Climate Survey. *The experiences of lesbian, gay, bisexual, and transgender youth in our nation's schools.* Gay, Lesbian and Straight Education Network. Retrieved from https://files.eric.ed.gov/fulltext/ED535177.pdf.

Kosciw, J. G., Greytak, E. A., Giga, N. M., Villenas, C., & Danischewski, D. J. (2016). *The 2015 National School Climate Survey: The experiences of lesbian, gay, bisexual, transgender, and queer youth in our nation's schools.* Gay, Lesbian and Straight Education Network. Retrieved from https://files.eric.ed.gov/fulltext/ED574780.pdf.

Kosciw, J. G., Palmer, N. A., Kull, R. M., & Greytak, E. A. (2013). The effect of negative school climate on academic outcomes for LGBT youth and the role of in-school supports. *Journal of School Violence, 12*(1), 45–63. https://doi.org/10.1080/15388220.2012.732546.

Leavy, P. (2015). *Method meets art: Arts-based research practice.* New York City, NY: Guilford Press.

Paceley, M. S., Fish, J. N., Thomas, M. M., & Goffnett, J. (2020). The impact of community size, community climate, and victimization on the physical and mental health of SGM youth. *Youth & Society, 52*(3), 427–448. https://doi.org/10.1177/0044118X19856141.

Patrick, L. (2013). *Found poetry: A tool for supporting novice poets and fostering transactional relationships between prospective teachers and young adult literature* (Doctoral Dissertation, The Ohio State University). OhioLINK. https://etd.ohiolink.edu/apexprod/rws_etd/send_file/send?accession=osu1376439323&disposition=inline.

Reisner, S. L., Vetters, R., Leclerc, M., Zaslow, S., Wolfrum, S., Shumer, D., & Mimiaga, M. J. (2015). Mental health of transgender youth in care at an adolescent urban community health center: A matched retrospective cohort study. *Journal of Adolescent Health, 56*(3), 274–279. https://doi.org/10.1016/j.jadohealth.2014.10.264.

Singh, A. A., Meng, S. E., & Hansen, A. W. (2014). "I am my own gender": Resilience strategies of trans youth. *Journal of Counseling & Development, 92*(2), 208–218. https://doi.org/10.1002/j.1556-6676.2014.00150.x.

Chapter 10

Indigenous Victimization and the Colonized Rainbow

Sheena L. Gilbert and Karen Z. Armenta Rojas

Introduction

The unique make-up of Indigenous communities (e.g., poverty, substance abuse) (Bohn, 2003; Bubar, 2009; Sapra et al., 2014; Yuan et al., 2006), embracing Indigenous culture outwardly (Bryant-Davis et al., 2009; Yuan et al., 2006) and identifying as LGBTQ2S (Wilson, 2011) place Indigenous people at an increased risk of victimization. As a result, Indigenous people experience trauma-related health effects (Bryant-Davis et al., 2009) and high rates of discrimination and oppression (Grant et al., 2011). Given the historical oppression, violence, and racism Indigenous people continue to experience, those working with and responding to Indigenous victims (e.g., police, medical personnel, advocacy groups) should consider their history, culture, traditions, and beliefs and use culturally sensitive methods (e.g., storytelling, sweat lodges, beadwork gatherings, ribbon skirt-making classes, and healing circles) when working with Indigenous populations as this is important to utterly understand the context of Indigenous victimization and gaining their trust (Jones, 2008).

Research gaps remain regarding identifying risk factors for Indigenous LGBTQ2S victimization, the impact of violence on Indigenous victims and ways to respond. This warrants more action as Indigenous people suffer from higher victimization rates than other races/ethnicities (Rosay, 2016), including those who identify as LGBTQ2S (Grant et al., 2011). Knowing and understanding Indigenous and Indigenous LGBTQ2S victimization helps those in criminology and criminal justice gain a better understanding of the dynamics of victimization for *all* populations. Therefore, research should be more inclusive of Indigenous voices to provide better insight and policy recommendations regarding protecting Indigenous and Indigenous LGBTQ2S people.

History of the Colonized Rainbow

According to the Indian Health Services (2021), the term "two-spirit" may now be included in the umbrella of LGBTQ. However, the term "two-spirit" does not simply mean someone Indigenous and someone who identifies as a member of the LGBTQ community. Though the label has only been used since the '90s (Lougheed, 2016), the Indian Health Services (2021) discuss how traditionally, Indigenous two-spirit people were male, female, and sometimes intersex individuals who combined activities of both men and women with traits unique to their status. However, it is crucial to understand that most Indigenous two-spirited are considered neither men nor women (Garnets & Kimmel, 2003); thus, fulfilling the third gender. More importantly, Indigenous two-spirited is recognized as having more gender-fluid roles

DOI: 10.4324/9781003400981-12

and sexuality beyond what is recognized in the traditional American ideology of male/female and homosexual/heterosexual (Wilson, 2011).

Indigenous people and the First Nations intentionally introduced the term to find common ground to help and educate traditional teachings in a contemporary context. Thus, this term is rooted in the spiritual teachings that *all* life is sacred. In 1990, in Winnipeg, Manitoba, Canada, at the 3rd North American LGBT Indigenous gathering, the term *two-spirited* (also known as LGBTQ2S) was proposed and affirmed by consensus (Lougheed, 2016; Balsam et al., 2004). The term could have also been seen as a potential solution for Indigenous scholars and activists regarding labels and an understanding of communities. Nevertheless, each nation's understanding of gender and sexual diversity is different and grounded in specific spiritual beliefs; thus, not all nations have a concept of two-spiritedness.

A brief look at history exposes discrimination toward Indigenous people and even more discrimination toward non-dichotomous gender-conforming Indigenous people who often face unique challenges since colonization related to their marginalized identities. The imposition of Western labels forced a semantic shift from their social roles to allegedly deviant and sexual behavior among those who did not fit into a dichotomous gender spectrum (Mongibello, 2018). Those familiar with labeling theory know the importance of understanding labels and the reaction of an individual(s) and their behavior through socially constructed labels that may determine or influence their behavior, self-concept, and social identity or identities, often associated with crime and deviance (Barmaki, 2019).

Historical Context of Indigenous and Indigenous Two-Spirit People

Colonization

According to existing research, Indigenous communities have endured a long history of violence and ethnic genocide (Gilbert, 2020; Kuokkanen, 2008; Weaver, 2009). Colonization—the removal and diminishment of another society, including their values, traditions, and culture—has been identified as a significant cause of violence against Indigenous people and within Indigenous communities (Gilbert, 2020; Weaver, 2009). Furthermore, colonization has lingering consequences that aid in understanding current Indigenous victimization.

Through colonization, Indigenous people have evolved from matriarchal societies to patriarchal ones, which created a societal shift in gender dynamics, thus promoting a continuous cycle of violence that places Indigenous women in danger (Gilbert, 2020; Kuokkanen, 2008). Furthermore, colonization has promoted stereotypes regarding Indigenous people, and Indigenous women specifically, as less deserving of respect and protection from violence. For example, Weaver (2009) contends that colonization has led non-Indigenous people to believe that Indigenous people are "savages" and "less than human."

Historical Trauma and Oppression

Two ways to understand the present-day existence of colonization are through *historical trauma* and *historical oppression*. Historical trauma refers to continuous, infinite, and persistent trauma imposed on a group(s) of people across generations (Burnette & Figley, 2016). Some examples of historical traumas include theft of tribal land, forced removal and relocation, assimilation, and genocide. Through these historical traumas, Indigenous people have experienced extreme loss of their traditions, culture, beliefs, language, people, and trust of outsiders (Burnette & Figley, 2016). Historical oppression expands historical trauma and refers to the constant, widespread, and intergenerational oppression experienced by Indigenous people (Burnette & Figley, 2016). After historical oppression is experienced for prolonged periods, it may become rationalized, forced, or adopted into the lives of those experiencing the oppression (Burnette & Figley, 2016). Additionally, historical oppression can include historical and contemporary traumas but focuses more on the proximal factors that maintain the oppression, such as discrimination, microaggression, poverty, and marginalization (Burnette & Figley, 2016).

Prevalence and Risk Factors of Violence and Victimization

Despite challenges, scholarly research focused on Indigenous people is growing and has identified this population as a high-risk group for victimization (Bachman et al., 2008; Rosay, 2016). For example, approximately 84% of Indigenous women and 82% of Indigenous men have experienced violence in their lifetime (Rosay, 2016). Additionally, it is also found that Indigenous women's victimization rates are ten times that of the national average on some Indian reservations (Bachman et al., 2008).

Research also suggests differences in violence against Indigenous people. For example, Indigenous people have higher rates of interracial victimization compared to other racial/ethnic groups. Specifically, 90% of Indigenous women experienced physical violence by an interracial perpetrator compared to 18% of Non-Hispanic White only women, and 85% of Indigenous men experienced physical violence by an interracial perpetrator compared to 17% of Non-Hispanic White only men (Rosay, 2016). Furthermore, Indigenous people are more likely to be assaulted with a weapon and suffer from medical injuries due to violence than non-Indigenous people (Bachman et al., 2008). Hence, it is crucial to understand that violence against Indigenous people is rooted in colonization, with the belief that Indigenous people do not belong and therefore should be punished (Weaver, 2009).

The limited existing research on LGBTQ2S suggests that compared with the general population and heterosexual Indigenous people, two-spirits may be at a notably higher risk for victimization. For example, one study found that 78% of Indigenous two-spirit women had been physically assaulted, and 85% were sexually assaulted (Grant et al., 2011). According to Grant and colleagues (2011), this is four times higher than the lifetime assault among non-two-spirit women in the general population. Additionally, LGBTQ2S men living in an urban environment are more likely to report being sexually and physically victimized than heterosexual men (Grant et al., 2011). Furthermore, it is not uncommon for two-spirit men and women to experience abuse by multiple perpetrators (e.g., family members, acquaintances, and strangers; Grant et al., 2011).

Substance Abuse

Compared with the US population in general, Indigenous people have the highest rates of alcohol, marijuana, cocaine, and hallucinogen use disorder and the second-highest methamphetamine abuse rates after Native Hawaiians (Bohn, 2003; Bryant-Davis et al., 2009; Substance Abuse and Mental Health Services Administration, 2019). The use and abuse of alcohol and other substances are often coping strategies for both Indigenous and Queer cultures (Garrett & Barret, 2003). While alcohol abuse and dependence among Indigenous people vary significantly by gender, tribe, and age, those living in urban environments are at an increased risk (Beauvais, 1998; May, 1996). For example, May (1996) found that urban Indigenous people have a higher consumption rate than those Indigenous people who live on an Indian reservation.

Poverty

Poverty is a widespread problem on Indian reservations (Bubar, 2009). Specifically, the poverty rate among Indigenous populations is twice that of the national rate (Sapra et al., 2014). Additionally, poverty is a risk factor for violence and victimization among Indigenous women and children (Bubar, 2009; Hamby, 2000). According to Hamby (2000), poverty has been linked to increased alcohol use, linked to victimization. Additionally, Malcoe and colleagues (2004) found that approximately 59% of Indigenous women had been physical or sexual victimization victims. Of those victimized, 49.2% were unemployed, 73.4% were living at or below the poverty line, and 30.1% were living in severe poverty.

Although there is some evidence that LGBT individuals are at an increased risk of poverty compared to cisgender heterosexual people (Wilson et al., 2020), there is an unfortunate lack of research on two-spirit individuals and poverty. Therefore, it is not safe to use broader literature to compare two-spirit individuals because of the lack of inclusivity; thus, more research is warranted.

It is essential to understand that prior to colonization, drugs (e.g., peyote and ayahuasca), alcohol (e.g., used for ceremonial purposes), and poverty did not exist in the same fashion, purpose, and magnitude that it does in the present day (Hamby, 2000). The continued trauma and oppression caused by the violence and constant victimization experienced by Indigenous people has forced them to rely on drugs and/or alcohol to cope. The larger population's lack of concern and recognition, including the federal government, has left Indigenous people to live in conditions (e.g., high poverty and high substance abuse rates) that are not conducive to surviving and thriving.

Identifying as Indigenous

As a result of colonization, many Indigenous people have been displaced and relocated from their tribes, attributing cultural and tribal affiliation as a risk factor for victimization. For example, Indigenous women who identify as Indigenous or are enrolled tribal members living off an Indian reservation have an increased risk of victimization compared to those who live on or near Indian reservations (Bryant-Davis et al., 2009). Similarly, Yuan and colleagues (2006) found that Indigenous women who lived on or near Indian reservations were less likely to be victimized; however, those who lived off an Indian reservation and identified as Indigenous were more likely to be victimized. Moreover, Indigenous men who speak the traditional language were less likely to be victimized than Indigenous women who speak the traditional language (Yuan et al., 2006).

Overall, these findings show that those who identify as Indigenous and LGBTQ2S are at an increased risk of violence and victimization while also identifying unique and shared risk factors necessary for exploring and understanding violence and victimization among this marginalized population. However, there is lacking research for identifying risk factors among LGBTQ2S individuals, which creates a gap in understanding the violence and victimization among this population, thus placing them at continued risk.

Identifying as LGBTQ and Two-Spirit

Historically two-spirited people have been revered; colonization shifted those ideals by alienating the two-spirit community from their Indigenous identity and establishing rigid binary gender roles (Wilson, 2011). As a result, two-spirited individuals are discriminated against and dehumanized by imposing Western heteronormative patriarchal roles. Thus, identifying as LGBTQ2S was shamed, forbidden, and punishable by some nations post-colonization (Wilson, 2011).

As Western cultural views shift, more LGBTQ2S are "re-storying" their experiences by decolonizing their identity in hopes of healing from the injustices and trauma. Nevertheless, not all tribes have accepted the rainbow that was once revered in their territory. However, federal and state laws that protect and guarantee rights to the LGBTQ community do not change things for LGBTQ2S residing in federally recognized Indian reservations as they are their sovereign nation.

Research has also identified a form of abuse that pertains specifically to the LGBTQ community: Identity abuse. Identity abuse is a set of victimization tactics that hetero-sexuals and cisgender individuals use against LGBTQ survivors (Woulfe & Goodman, 2021). Research has established four categories of abuse used in the LGBTQ community: (1) outing, (2) undermining and belittling identity, (3) using homophobic/transphobic language, and (4) isolating survivors from the LGBTQ community (Woulfe & Goodman, 2021). Each category is a unique way of victimizing those within the LGBTQ community and is experienced differently by those who identify as LGBTQ (Woulfe & Goodman, 2021).

Effects of Violence and Victimization

Mental Health

Indigenous people experience higher rates of personal trauma than Whites (Balsam et al., 2004). Prior research has found that Indigenous people have a higher degree of alcohol abuse, suicide, and mental health problems and have an occurrence of PTSD that is double that of the public (Bryant-Davis et al., 2009). For example, a study by Norton and Manson (1995) interviewed 16 Indigenous women and found that those women reported higher levels of depression, substance abuse, suicidal thoughts, and inadequate health since their first time being victimized. Similarly, Evans-Campbell and colleagues (2006) found that 64.5% (N=112) of the victims reported having depression compared to 44.7% who were not victims of violence.

A notable gap in the literature on Indigenous populations focuses on two-spirit people and mental health. However, the limited existing research identifies Indigenous two-spirit individuals as high risk for suicidality. For example, in a study done by the National Gay & Lesbian Task Force in 2011 with 6,404 participants, 75 identifying as two-spirited found that 56% of two-spirit transgender participants attempted suicide (Grant et al., 2011). Additionally, in general, two-spirit males and two-spirit women experience more suicidality than non-Indigenous people (Fieland et al., 2009). Furthermore, two-spirited individuals also experience higher levels of anxiety and depression compared to those who have not experienced bias-related victimization (Parker et al., 2017).

Discrimination

Indigenous LGBTQ2S individuals experience discrimination and oppression across multiple domains. For example, Indigenous LGBTQ2S confront stigma regarding their sexual orientation from the wider society and other Indigenous people, their families, and their tribal communities. Moreover, Indigenous LGBTQ2S experience racism from the wider society and other sexual minorities; and sexism from both Indigenous and LGBTQ communities (Grant et al., 2011). For example, Grant and colleagues (2011) found that 46% reported being rejected by family; 74% reported losing friendships due to being two-spirited; 19% of the participants reported having been refused a home or apartment; 11% reported being evicted because of their gender identity/expression, and 19% reported experiencing homelessness at some point in their lives because of being transgender.

Responding to Indigenous Victimization

When working with Indigenous populations, one must understand the effects of colonization and how that might impact those seeking out services and/or reporting victimization. The effects of colonization have created distrust of non-Indigenous people, as research has illustrated that Indigenous victims are less likely to seek out services than non-Indigenous people (Fiolet et al., 2019). Some reasons victims have expressed for not seeking agency support include not wanting to disgrace their family, they feel shame about being victimized, they do not want their children taken away, may not know that what happened to them is considered victimization, and they may not be aware of services available to them (Fiolet et al., 2019).

There is also a lack of culturally competent services for Indigenous populations. These services are vitally important for Indigenous people who have endured lasting historical racism, violence, oppression, and discrimination. Furthermore, the importance of understanding Indigenous culture, traditions, and beliefs cannot be overstated. Unfortunately, when seeking out services that are either off an Indian reservation or involve non-Indigenous professionals, some Indigenous people have experienced racist comments, substandard care, criticism, and mistreatment (Bubar, 2009; Finfgeld-Connett, 2015). Therefore, the lack of culturally competent services is a barrier to Indigenous victims' access to adequate support and can exacerbate their mistrust of victim service providers and continued victimization.

Given these barriers to Indigenous people's help-seeking, it is essential to identify solutions. For those who are non-Indigenous working in victim services, either on an Indian reservation or with a large Indigenous population, it is vital to not only consider the lasting effects of colonization but also to respect the long—and persistent—history of oppression by federal policies and the unique obstacles Indigenous victims face when they seek out support (Bubar, 2009; Finfgeld-Connett, 2015). Providers also need to be aware of internal biases or perceptions of Indigenous people that may hinder their ability to provide help and/or interact with them (Finfgeld-Connett, 2015). Furthermore, careful consideration of Western-style models for services, specifically mental health, should be taken because Indigenous victims may feel as though they are being further marginalized, and the technique may be seen as a continuation of institutional racism (Bubar, 2009).

Just as important as implementing traditional victim services in Indigenous communities, one must understand that many Indigenous communities have alternative methods for healing, such as traditional healers, sweat lodges, and talking circles (Bubar, 2009; Finfgeld-Connett, 2015). Therefore, it is crucial to collaborate with Indigenous community members to develop proper treatment methods (Bubar, 2009). Additionally, those working in victim services with Indigenous people should be trained in culturally appropriate ways and express cultural sensitivity when dealing with issues related to Indigenous victimization (Jones, 2008), including the use and understanding of Indigenous languages (Finfgeld-Connett, 2015). Furthermore, those in victim services can recognize and honor Indigenous values, culture, and traditions, which can help create trust and respect between the service provider and victim. Lastly, it is essential to note that those within the community, including tribal leadership, need to be educated about victimization, so they may be able to identify ways to end the victimization and can learn of ways to become involved (Finfgeld-Connett, 2015; Jones, 2008).

Conclusion and Future Research

Indigenous people and LGBTQ2S individuals have a history filled with trauma, discrimination, and oppression that still affects them today. Historically, Indigenous people have been ignored but are breaking their way into the forefront to make their voices heard. Their stories are necessary for understanding the dynamics of victimization, and we must listen and not respond to Indigenous issues with a savior mindset, thinking we can solve all their problems. Instead, it is our responsibility to listen and be willing to respond in culturally sensitive ways.

There are over 500 federally recognized tribes, each unique in their language, cultures, and traditions (Wahab & Olson, 2004). Thus, it is vital to research within individual tribes and at the national level. In addition, it is essential to understand the history of violence against Indigenous people and the role of colonization regarding the victimization of Indigenous people, including those who identify as LGBTQ2S. Finally, while research regarding Indigenous LGBTQ2S is scarce, it is vital to establish a rapport with Indigenous communities to understand their needs, determine where and how resources should be allocated, and develop the research needed and wanted to present opportunities for research and services, especially when there is a void of information and policy that would better help us cater to this population.

While it may be impossible to rectify the effects of colonization and the state of oppression, it is crucial to expand this conversation. Thus, defining gender by a Western binary spectrum proliferates the interpretation of Indigenous cultures and traditions into a Western worldview of gender roles. Therefore, when interpreting Indigenous teachings, conducting research, and/or advocating for LGBTQ2S, it is crucial not to foist Westernized policies, research methodologies, and/or suppress nonbinary gender identities. Hence, further research is needed to highlight the importance of addressing the effects of colonial labels at play in the LGBTQ2S community, the effects of residential schools (i.e., health, victimization, the cycle of violence), racism, homophobia, exile, and genocide to understand the interaction of the multiplicative effect when several risk factors are present.

In considering such efforts, future research should involve the knowledge and experiences of Indigenous people as their testimonies could provide further insight when creating tools that could potentially assess and/or identify risk, allocate resources, collect data, and advocate for their needs. In addition, the Indigenous communities are one of lore and tradition. Moreover, we encourage future research to stop subjecting them as objects of research but instead incorporate their knowledge and experiences to advance the field of criminology and criminal justice.

References

Bachman, R., Zaykowski, H., Kallymyer, R., Poteyeva, M., & Lanier, C. (2008). *Violence against American Indian and Alaska native women and the criminal justice response: What is known* (Report No. 223691). Retrieved from www.ncjrs.gov/pdffiles1/nij/grants/223691.pdf.

Balsam, K. F., Huang, B., Fieland, K. C., Simoni, J. M., & Walters, K. L. (2004). Culture, trauma, and wellness: A comparison of heterosexual and lesbian, gay, bisexual, and two-spirit native Americans. *Cultural Diversity and Ethnic Minority Psychology*, 10(3), 287. DOI: 10.1037/1099-9809.10.3.287.

Barmaki, R. (2019). On the origin of "labeling" theory in criminology: Frank Tannenbaum and the Chicago school of sociology. *Deviant Behavior*, 40(2), 256–271. https://doi.org/10.1080/0163962 5.2017.1420491.

Beauvais, F. (1998). American Indians and alcohol. *Alcohol Health and Research World*, 22(4), 253–259. Retrieved from www.ncbi.nlm.nih.gov/pmc/articles/PMC6761887/.

Bohn, D. K. (2003). Lifetime physical and sexual abuse, substance abuse, depression, and suicide attempts among native American women. *Issues in Mental Health Nursing*, 24(3), 333–352. DOI: 10.1080/01612840305277.

Bryant-Davis, T., Chung, H., & Tillman, S. (2009). From the margins to the center: Ethnic minority women and the mental health effects of sexual assault. *Trauma, Violence & Abuse*, 10(4), 330–357. DOI: 10.1177/1524838009339755.

Bubar, R. (2009). Cultural competence, justice, and supervision: Sexual assault against native women. *Women & Therapy*, 33(1–2), 55–72. DOI: 10.1080/02703140903404762.

Burnette, C. E., & Figley, C. R. (2016). Historical oppression, resilience, and transcendence: Can a holistic framework help explain violence experienced by Indigenous people? *Social Work*, 62(1), 37–44. DOI: 10.1093/sw/sww065.

Evans-Campbell, T., Lindhorst, T., Huang, B., & Walters, K. L. (2006). Interpersonal violence in the lives of urban American Indian and Alaska native women: Implications for health, mental health, and help-seeking. *American Journal of Public Health*, 96(8), 1416–1422. DOI: 10.2105/AJPH.2004.054213.

Fieland, K. C., Walters, K. L., & Simoni, J. M. (2009). Determinants of health among two-spirit American Indians and Alaska natives. In I. H. Meyer & M. E. Northridge (Eds.), *The health of sexual minorities* (pp. 268–300). Boston, MA: Springer. https://doi.org/10.1007/978-0-387-31334-4_11.

Finfgeld-Connett, D. (2015). Qualitative systematic review of intimate partner violence among native Americans. *Issues in Mental Health Nursing*, 36(10), 754–760. DOI: 10.3109/01612840. 2015.1047072.

Fiolet, R., Tarzia, L., Hameed, M., & Hegarty, K. (2019). Indigenous peoples' help seeking behaviors for family violence: A scoping review. *Trauma, Violence & Abuse*, XX(X), 1–11. DOI: 10.1177/1524838019852638.

Garnets, L., & Kimmel, D. (2003). *Psychological perspectives on lesbian, gay, and bisexual experiences*. New York: Columbia University Press.

Garrett, M. T., & Barret, B. (2003). Two spirit: Counseling native American gay, lesbian, and bisexual people. *Journal of Multicultural Counseling and Development*, 31(2), 131–142. https://doi.org/10.1002/j.2161-1912.2003.tb00538.x.

Gilbert, S. L. (2020). Intimate partner violence in a native American community: An exploratory study. *Boise State University Theses and Dissertations*. 1688. DOI: 10.18122/td/1688/boisestate.

Grant, J. M., Mottet, L. A., Tanis, J., Harrison, J., Herman, J. L., & Keisling, M. (2011). *Injustice at every turn: A report of the national transgender discrimination survey. Transgender Discrimination Survey*. Retrieved from www.transequality.org/sites/default/files/docs/resources/NTDS_Report.pdf.

Hamby, S. L. (2000). The importance of community in a feminist analysis of domestic violence among American Indians. *American Journal of Community Psychology*, 28(5), 649–669. DOI: 10.1023/A:1005145720371.

Indian Health Services. (2021). *Two spirit: Health resources*, February. Retrieved from www.ihs.gov/lgbt/health/twospirit/.

Jones, L. (2008). The distinctive characteristics and needs of domestic violence victims in a native American community. *Journal of Family Violence*, 23, 113–118. DOI: 10.1007/s10896-007-9132-9.

Kuokkanen, R. (2008). Globalization as racialized, sexualized violence. *International Feminist Journal of Politics*, 10(2), 216–233. https://doi.org/10.1080/14616740801957554.

Lougheed, B. (2016). Cool things in the collection: The two-spirited collection. *Manitoba History* (80), 59–61. Retrieved from www.mhs.mb.ca/docs/mb_history/80/twospirited.shtml.

Malcoe, L. H., Duran, B. M., & Montgomery, J. M. (2004). Socioeconomic disparities in intimate partner violence against native American women: A cross-sectional study. *BMC Medicine*, 2(20), 1–14. DOI: 10.1186/1741-7015-2-20.

May, P. A. (1996). Overview of alcohol abuse epidemiology for American Indian populations. In G. D. Sandefur, R. R. Rindfuss, & B. Cohen (Eds.), *Changing numbers, changing needs: American Indian demography and public health* (pp. 235–261). Washington, DC: National Academy Press.

Mongibello, A. (2018). From 'berdache' to 'two-spirit': Naming Indigenous women-men in Canada. In G. Balirano & O. Palusci (Eds.), *Miss man? Languaging gendered bodies* (pp. 156–167). New Castle upon Tyne, UK: Cambridge Scholars Publishing.

Norton, I. M., & Manson, S. M. (1995). A silent minority: Battered American Indian women. *Journal of Family Violence*, 10(3), 307–318. https://doi.org/10.1007/BF02110995.

Parker, M., Duran, B., & Walters, K. (2017). The relationship between bias-related victimization and generalized anxiety disorder among American Indian and Alaska Native lesbian, gay, bisexual, transgender, two-spirit, community members. *International Journal of Indigenous Health*, 12(2), 64–83. DOI: 10.18357/ijih122201717785.

Rosay, A. B. (2016). Violence against American Indian and Alaska native women and men: 2010 Findings from the national intimate partner and sexual violence survey. *U.S. Department of Justice, National Institute of Justice*, 1–79. Retrieved from http://hdl.handle.net/11122/7025.

Sapra, K. J., Jubinski, S. M., Tanaka, M. F., & Gershon, R. R. M. (2014). Family and partner interpersonal violence among American Indians/Alaska natives. *Injury Epidemiology*, 1(7), 1–14. Retrieved from www.injepijournal.com/content/1/1/7.

Substance Abuse and Mental Health Services Administration. (2019). *2018 national survey on drug use and health: Methodological summary and definitions*. Rockville, MD: Center for Behavioral Health Statistics and Quality, Substance Abuse and Mental Health Services Administration. Retrieved from www.samhsa.gov/data/.

Wahab, S., & Olson, L. (2004). Intimate partner violence and sexual assault in native American communities. *Trauma, Violence & Abuse*, 5(4), 353–366.

Weaver, H. N. (2009). The colonial context of violence: Reflections on violence in the lives of native American women. *Journal of Interpersonal Violence*, 24(9), 1552–1563. https://doi.org/10.1177%2F0886260508323665.

Wilson, T. (2011). Changed embraces, changes embraced-renouncing the heterosexist majority in favor of a return to traditional two-spirit culture. *American Indian Law Review*, 36(1), 161–188.

Wilson, B. D. M., Gomez, A. G. H., Sadat, M., Choi, S. K., & Badgett, M. V. L. (2020). *Pathways into poverty: Lived experiences among LGBTQ people*. Retrieved from https://escholarship.org/uc/item/3bp6b7dp.

Woulfe, J. M., & Goodman, L. A. (2021). Identity abuse as a tactic of violence in LGBTQ communities: Initial validation of the identity abuse measure. *Journal of Interpersonal Violence*, 36(5–6), 2656–2676. https://doi.org/10.1177%2F0886260518760018.

Yuan, N. P., Koss, M. P., Polacca, M., & Goldman, D. (2006). Risk factors for physical assault and rape among six Native American tribes. *Journal of Interpersonal Violence*, 21(12), 1566–1590. DOI: 10.1177/0886260506294239.

Framing Bi+ Experiences of Intimate Partner Violence

The Role of Monosexism and Bi+ Stigmas

Casey D. Xavier Hall, Jessie Miller, and Lauren Brittany Beach

Studies have revealed bi+ people are at heightened risk for intimate partner violence (IPV) compared to monosexual people (see Table 11.1 for definitions of key terms, Walters, 2011; Martin-Storey, 2015). IPV services, however, have largely been structured to provide support to survivors on the basis of presumed monosexuality. Many IPV services are targeted to straight women (Capaldi et al., 2012). IPV programs that do attempt to provide tailored services to sexual and gender minority (SGM) populations frequently are marketed as serving homogenized SGM populations without distinguishing the needs of bi+ vs. monosexual SGM survivors (Longobardi & Badenes-Ribera, 2017). These trends have largely resulted in the erasure of bi+ survivorship in research, services, and violence advocacy. This chapter summarizes the literature addressing bi+ experiences of IPV survivorship and presents a conceptual framework for understanding how monosexism contributes to the experience of IPV in bi+ population compared to monosexual people (see Table 11.1 for definitions of key terms, Walters, 2011; Martin-Storey, 2015). IPV services, however, have largely been structured to provide support to survivors on the basis of presumed monosexuality. Many IPV services are targeted to straight women (Capaldi et al., 2012). IPV programs that do attempt to provide tailored services to sexual and gender minority (SGM) populations frequently are marketed as serving homogenized SGM populations without distinguishing the needs of bi+ vs. monosexual SGM survivors (Longobardi & Badenes-Ribera, 2017). These trends have largely resulted in the erasure of bi+ survivorship in research, services, and violence advocacy. This chapter summarizes the literature addressing bi+ experiences of IPV survivorship and presents a conceptual framework for understanding how monosexism contributes to the experience of IPV in bi+ populations. In a 2020 Gallup poll, 54.6% of sexual minorities identified as bisexual, making bisexual the most common sexual identity among sexual minorities (Jones, 2021). Moreover, bi+ populations encompass a wide range of diversity by race and gender identity. For example, in the Youth Risk Behavior Survey (2005–2015) 9.6% of Black women and 9.8% of Hispanic/Latinx women identified as bisexual relative to 6.9% among White women (Phillips et al., 2019). In the US Transgender Survey at least 34% of transgender respondents identified as bi+ (James et al., 2016). Likewise, around 40% of respondents to the 2019 Asexual Community Survey also identified not only as asexual or on the asexual spectrum, but as having a bi+ identity (The Ace Community Survey, 2020). Dating patterns by gender vary among bi+ populations, as bi+ people may find themselves attracted to people of any combination of gender identities, including nonbinary and transgender partners (Xavier Hall et al., 2021). These data further underline the adage that bi+ advocates often cite: *There are as many ways to be bi+ as there are bi+ people*. In this chapter we focus on the specific axis of bi+ identity and its relation to

DOI: 10.4324/9781003400981-13

Table 11.1 Key Terms and Definitions

Term	Definition
Binegativity	Negative attitudes toward bisexual people
Biphobia	Dislike, fear, or prejudice against bisexual people
Bisexual Erasure	The denial of the existence of bisexual people due to monosexism
Monosexism	The multilevel and systematic oppression that bisexual people experience due to the belief that all people are attracted only to people of one gender
Heteronormativity	The belief and systematic promotion of heterosexuality as the preferred or normal sexual orientation in society
Homonormativity	The promotion of an assimilationist view adhering to heteronormative constructs in SGM communities
Heterosexism	The assumption that all people are heterosexual by default
Bi+	Bi+ is a community umbrella term that includes people who experience sexual and/or romantic attraction to people of more than one gender, including people who identify as bisexual, pansexual, fluid, Queer, or with no labels.
Bisexual	Attraction to people of two or more genders
Pansexual	Attraction to people of all genders or regardless of gender
Monosexual	People who have romantic and sexual attraction to a single gender (e.g., lesbian, gay, heterosexual)
Plurisexual	People who have romantic and sexual attraction to more than one gender (e.g., bi+)
Sexual and Gender Minorities	Refers to identities that represent a numeric minority in the US in reference to sexual identity (e.g., gay, lesbian, bisexual, pansexual, Queer, and more) and gender identity (e.g., transgender, nonbinary, and more)

IPV; however, it is important to recognize that bi+ experiences overlap and intersect across a range of identities.

A growing literature has identified elevated experience of IPV among bi+ populations relative to other sexual identities. The National Intimate Partner and Sexual Violence Survey (NISVS), a nationally representative sample, found that 61.1% of bisexual women experience IPV in their lifetime relative to 43.8% of lesbian women and 35% of heterosexual women (Walters, 2011). Additionally, 37.3% of bisexual men experience IPV relative to 26% of gay men and 29.0% of heterosexual men (Walters, 2011). Similar patterns have been observed in samples of cisgender and transgender college students (Whitfield et al., 2021), as well as cisgender youth (Martin-Storey, 2015). Despite the evidence of high rates of IPV among bi+ populations, very little research has endeavored to characterize unique factors contributing to IPV among bi+ populations.

Stigmas in Bi+ Communities

Bi+ populations face multiple overlapping forms of stigma, including monosexism and biphobia. At a basic level, monosexism can be defined as the belief that all people are attracted only to people of one gender (Roberts et al., 2015). As such, monosexism simultaneously legitimizes people who are attracted only to people of one gender, while erasing those who are attracted to people from a range of different gender identities. Thus, monosexism situates a power divide between monosexual people (e.g., heterosexual, gay, and lesbian people) and plurisexual people (e.g., bi+ people). Monosexism intersects with stigmas faced by bi+ populations, such as biphobia and bi-erasure, which specifically target bi+ populations. These stigmas manifest at the individual, interpersonal, organizational, and societal/policy levels (see Figure 12.1). The existence of bi+ stigma does not minimize or deny the existence of heterosexism or homophobia, as bi+ people are also impacted by these forms of systematic oppression tied to sexual identity. This chapter presents a conceptual framework for understanding how bi+ stigmas contribute to IPV in bi+ populations through multilevel socioecological pathways and reduce access to IPV support services for bi+ survivors. This discussion includes influences at the societal/policy, organizational, interpersonal, and intrapersonal levels. We conclude with a call to action.

The Multilevel Influence of Monosexism and Bi+ Stigma on the bi+ Experience of IPV

One model that has been used to describe multilevel influences on health behaviors is the social ecological model (SEM) which addresses mutually influencing factors along multiple levels of the social ecology. The model traditionally includes societal/public policy, community, organizational, interpersonal, and intrapersonal levels (McLeroy et al., 1988). The SEM has been extended and adapted in several ways, including applying the model to sexual violence outcomes in bisexual populations (Johnson & Grove, 2017). SEM offers a way of thinking about a behavioral health outcome, such as violence in a complex and multilevel way, pushing thinking away from exclusively considering individual-level influences and toward considering influences at different levels such as interpersonal (e.g., enacted stigma), organizational influences (e.g., cisgender heterosexual focus of violence services), community influences (e.g., stigma in LGBT spaces), societal (e.g., violence services policies). Factors may influence each other within levels (e.g., cisgender heterosexual focus of violence services and policing strategies at the organizational level) or between levels (e.g., monosexist societal norms and enacted stigma).

A second model, the minority stress framework, ties in multilevel influences of SGM stigma. Originally developed for lesbian populations (Brooks, 1981), and later applied to gay men (Meyer, 1995), the minority stress framework posits that SGM stigma (enacted, internalized, or anticipated) impacts cumulative stress and ultimately health outcomes. This framework has since been extended to violence outcomes (Balsam & Szymanski, 2005); however, it does not fully account for the unique stigmas faced by bi+ individuals. Nor does the model account for myriad pathways through which stigma impacts bi+ survivors beyond a stress pathway.

Informed by the frameworks, we address how stigmas faced by bi+ individuals occur on multiple levels of the social ecology to influence experiences of violence and survivorship. We focus on the societal (norms and policy), organizational (police, healthcare, and violence advocacy organizations), interpersonal, and intrapersonal levels. Compared to other applications of ecological models, we exclusively address bi+ populations and emphasize the relationship-based factors within interpersonal factors due to the focus on IPV, Extending the interpersonal level to focus on relationship-related factors.

Societal

Monosexism and bisexual erasure are deeply embedded into social norms in the US.

Bi+ people encounter a range of myths and stereotypes in their communities that reinforce these monosexist norms (Dobison et al., 2005). These include stereotypes that question the foundation of bi+ identity such as the idea that bi+ individuals are confused and that bi+ identities are invalid. Bi+ individuals experience these norms from both within and beyond SGM communities. In SGM communities some salient stereotypes relate to being traitors to Queer communities or enjoying comparable societal status as heterosexual individuals (Klesse, 2011). Many bi+ stereotypes relate to romantic or sexual relationships, such as assumptions about indiscriminate attraction, promiscuity, selfishness, and infidelity. Given the nature of these stereotypes and myths it is no surprise that they have impacts for the relationships of bi+ individuals including experience IPV. These norms may feed into issues at multiple levels, including partner jealousy (see section titled *Relationships*), bi+ patient interactions in healthcare settings (see section titled *Organizational*), and bi-erasure in multiple levels including policy (Marcus, 2018) to name a few. These implications are discussed in the sections that follow.

Monosexist social norms are broadly reflected in laws and policies (Marcus, 2015) and bi-erasure in state and national policies is common place, leaving bi+ individuals largely absent in discourse (Marcus, 2015; Maliepaard, 2015). When sexuality is mentioned in policies, they often address only gay and lesbian people without mention of bi+ identities (Maliepaard, 2015). However, even if bi+ identity is mentioned there may not be consideration of bi+ specific legal concerns (Maliepaard, 2015), which may include a range of legal considerations such as immigration, asylum, anti-discrimination laws, and parental custody (Marcus, 2018). Here we consider discrimination and custody as examples of such implications.

The legislative history of anti-discrimination laws seeking to prohibit discrimination against sexual minority individuals in the US often does not include any examples of anti-bi+ discrimination. Legislative histories are used by courts in cases of first impression to aid them in the interpretation of the scope and application of statutory law. Without examples of anti-bi+ discrimination in legislative histories, courts are left to decide for themselves whether patterns and stories of discrimination tied to mistreatment for having a history of relationships with people of more than one gender would really count as discrimination based on SGM status. Further, bi+ people are often not thought to make good plaintiffs in impact litigation cases seeking to advance SGM equality or to advance anti-discrimination protections on the basis of sexual identity (Marcus, 2015). The justification for exclusion of bisexual people as plaintiffs is often that courts would view bi+ identity as a choice and therefore as less deserving of protection under the law as compared to gay or lesbian people. In addition, when courts have issued favorable rulings recognizing the rights of SGM people, they often do not mention how the law specifically protects bi+ people (Marcus, 2015).

In addition, legal scholars have found that bi+ people may face discrimination in adoption (Strasser, 1996) and child custody hearings (Marcus, 2015), which can be relevant in the context of IPV. In divorce and child custody proceedings, a heterosexual parent may argue that a co-parent's bi+ identity should be viewed as a negative factor to obtain custody and visitation rights. Such arguments have been struck down as impermissible in many states (National Center for Lesbian Rights, 2009). However, if a heterosexual parent seeking custody does make such an argument the bi+ parent's attorney may have to make a legal counterargument, and possibly call expert witnesses to avoid discrimination. The ability to mount such a sophisticated legal defense may be beyond the financial reach of many bi+ parents seeking custody. In violent relationships involving a heterosexual abuser, threats to out the co-parent as bi+ may be yet another way to extend the abuser's power and control over their bi+ partner.

Legal recognition of some bi+ experiences in relationships may be further limited by discourse that focuses on legally recognized unions. While not all bi+ individuals pursue partnerships with multiple people simultaneously, polyamorous relationships are not recognized in the US (Klesse, 2011) and other contexts (Maliepaard, 2015). This could feasibly have implications for IPV that occurs in the context of polyamory for bi+ individuals.

Organizational

Police Systems

While research on policing has begun to address SGM populations, there are currently no US-based studies the authors are aware of that examine the relationship between bi+ IPV and arrest, specifically. The lack of disaggregated analyses by sexual identity in policing remains commonplace despite the fact that bi+ individuals maintain the highest rates of IPV in health surveillance data. SGM populations more broadly face a number of stigma-related issues in relation to policing. Research suggests that SGM perpetrators of IPV are ticketed and arrested less than straight perpetrators (Hirschel & McCormack, 2020). Arrests are less likely in same-sex IPV situations (Franklin, 2019); however, dual arrests, in which both members of a couple are arrested are significantly higher for same-sex couples than heterosexual couples, which may be increased by mandatory arrest laws (Hirschel & McCormack, 2020). In the absence of arrest, SGM experiences with the police in cases of IPV are often fraught with police misconduct, neglect, and bias. For example, in a 2013 report, 48% of SGM violence survivors reported police misconduct (National Coalition of Anti-violence Programs, 2013). Police have also been known to have homophobic responses to SGM individuals during the arrest process (Williams Institute, 2015), and some police consistently refuse to take reports or classify cases as SGM IPV (Mogul, 2011). Due to such negative experiences with the police, bisexual and gay men's perceptions of police helpfulness is diminished (Finneran & Stephenson, 2013).

While there is an apparent dearth of disaggregated data for bi+ individuals, this existing research raises several concerns regarding policing and bi+ experience of IPV. A 2011 study identified that bisexual men were 1.5 times more likely to report any type of recent arrest compared to gay men, though this is not IPV-specific (Lim et al., 2011). Given the aforementioned literature, bi+ individuals may experience increased arrests in the context of IPV for two different reasons: 1) They are more likely to be in different gender relationships than same-gendered relationships (Xavier Hall et al., 2021), which may contribute to increased arrests among bi+ individuals with different gender partners, 2) Bi+ individuals may be at higher risk for dual arrest when in same-gender relationships. Risk of arrest may be further elevated by racial bias when one or more individuals involved are people of color (Hirschel & McCormack, 2020), which may be particularly important as it was earlier established that the majority of bi+ individuals in the US are people of color. Unfortunately, due to a lack of disaggregated results on SGM IPV, researchers are still unsure of this relationship. It is critical to establish standards for disaggregation of SGM identities as well as bi-specific policing research.

Healthcare Organizations

Bi+ populations face limited access to culturally appropriate physical and mental healthcare (Choi & Israel, 2019). To illustrate, there is currently only one book chapter that focuses on evidence-based strategies for mental health treatment of bi+ individuals as separate from monosexual SGMs (Choi & Israel, 2019). Previous research has shown that bi+ people are less likely to have access to medical and mental health care nor a consistent site for healthcare or insurance (Macapagal et al., 2016). Besides this, bi+ individuals report being refused medical care, high rates of binegative comments, and being blamed for their health status by medical and mental health care providers (Dobinson et al., 2005; Lambda Legal, 2010). This prejudice and discrimination indicate that bi+ individuals are unable to access most therapeutic and healthcare services due to the internalized monosexism and binegativity of providers (Choi & Israel, 2019; Israel et al., 2019). It follows that bi+ patients are less likely to be out to their medical providers than other SGM patients (Macapagal et al., 2016), which may impact the quality of healthcare they receive.

There are no existing behavioral or social interventions for IPV in bi+ populations. However, online interventions have been shown to reduce binegativity following the Releasing Internalized Stigma for Empowerment (RISE) model (Israel et al., 2019). Moreover, bipositive experiences (Dyar & London, 2018), and high levels of community involvement have all been shown to reduce internalized binegativity and subsequently decrease rates of anxiety and depression (Lambe et al., 2017). These results are promising, as they may help reduce internalized stigma thus indirectly impacting IPV. For example, if internalized stigma increases risk for IPV and IPV-related risk factors (see section titled *Intrapersonal)*, then interventions that address internalized stigma may have an indirect impact on IPV. However, we cannot rely on indirect impact on this critical issue. Tailored, IPV-specific interventions may be needed to address IPV in bi+ populations. Considering the distinct and heightened needs of this population that are established in this chapter, further research should examine interventions specific to bi+ experience of IPV.

Violence Advocacy Organizations

IPV organizations are under-utilized by SGM populations (Brooks et al., 2021). This may be due to perceptions of IPV advocacy organizations as unhelpful and at times antagonistic to the needs of SGM populations (Freeland et al., 2018; Turell & Herrmann, 2008). Oftentimes, bi and gay men, as well as transgender individuals, have experienced further scrutiny and been excluded or refused care due to the domestic violence agency only providing gender-based services for cis women (Jordan et al., 2020; Freeland et al., 2018). Intersectional experiences of stigma have further implications for lack of culturally competent providers among Black and other SGM communities of color who experience racial bias (Brooks et al., 2021).

Additionally, violence service providers themselves often report not feeling able to serve SGM individuals (Furman et al., 2017). As seen in a quantitative study seeking input from Los Angeles based service providers, the majority of respondents had little to no training in SGM IPV, with a quarter never receiving any SGM IPV competency training (Ford et al.,

2013). This is despite the fact that almost 50% of providers reported serving SGM individuals in the past year. Service providers who did not work at SGM-focused organizations stated they feel only "minimally prepared" to serve SGM communities with disaggregated competency rating being highest for cis women followed by cis men then transgender individuals (Ford et al., 2013). Considering that violence providers feel unfit to work with SGM communities and have received very little training to do so, it follows that providers are likely ill-equipped to serve bi+ survivors.

Interpersonal

Previous research has identified stigma and the fear of consequences from disclosure of violence as major barriers to help seeking and disclosure among survivors of violence more broadly (Robinson et al., 2020). In addition to possible interpersonal consequences of disclosing violence, bi+ individuals' heterosexual and gay/lesbian peers (Feinstein & Dyar, 2017) and their most intimate social support networks (Hall & Girod, 2018) may also hold monosexist attitudes, thus posing additional consequences. This context of monosexism can lead to a form of *double jeopardy* for bi+ survivors of IPV, where they contend with stigma related to monosexism and to survivorship simultaneously (in addition to any other forms of stigma they encounter such as racism) (Pittman et al., 2020). Indeed, some existing research has described SGM populations as hesitant to disclose experiences of IPV due to fears of sexual identity and violence related stigma experiences (Pentaraki, 2017) because disclosure of violence within the context of an intimate relationship requires discussion of a partner including their gender (Øverlien, 2020). For bisexual individuals disclosing a same-gender partner may trigger stigma experiences but disclosing a different gender partner could also trigger stigma experiences if the recipient of the disclosure previously perceived the bi+ individual as gay or lesbian. This context may impact access to adequate informal social support and contribute to fear or stress over double disclosure as both bi+ and a survivor of IPV. Researchers have speculated that sexual identity disclosure may be associated with increased social support if bi+ individuals identify bi-affirming social support; however, sexual identity disclosure may also further isolate bi+ survivors if their communities or social networks ascribe to monosexist beliefs (Greene, 2007). Motivations to disclose or conceal bi+ identity and their implications for survivorship can be complex. Interpersonal motivations for bi+ identity avoiding disclosure (e.g., to avoid monosexist stigma) have been shown to be associated with increased anxiety and depression relative to intrapersonal motivations (e.g., one's bi+ identity not being salient) (Feinstein et al., 2020). Thus, fear of disclosure of bi+ identity due to anticipated stigma may further exacerbate stress and mental health status of bi+ survivors, compared to monosexual survivors.

Relationships

As this chapter discusses IPV, the relationship level further highlights interpersonal factors that occur in the context of interactions with romantic/sexual partners (e.g., at a dyadic level for couples or triadic, quadradic, etc., level for polyamorous relationships).

IPV may be related to monosexism within the context of relationships. A unique aspect of bi+ identities relative to monosexual ones is that bi+ identity is not typically made visible based on the gender of a partner. People may assume an individual is gay or lesbian if they have a partner that appears to be the same gender, or heterosexual if they have a partner that appears to be a different gender. Bi+ individuals may not share the same sexual identity with their partners. Bi+ individuals may have partners who are gay/lesbian or heterosexual (Xavier Hall et al., 2021). Thus, bi+ partners face the unique challenges of coming out to potential or existing partners, finding partners who are supportive of bi+ identity, and maintaining the visibility and salience of bi+ identity while in a relationship (Turell et al., 2018). Identity salience can be challenging for bi+ individuals in monogamous relationships because their partnership may lead to assumptions of homosexuality or heterosexuality even when a bi+ individual discloses their identity (Dyar et al., 2014). Bi+ people may find themselves in relationships with heterosexual or gay/lesbian partners who espouse monosexist ideas further exacerbating challenges to recognizing bi+ identity in context of relationships (Dyar et al., 2014). Past research shows that higher levels of partner biphobia are associated with an increased risk for IPV among bi+ people (Turell et al., 2018). Additionally, some qualitative research has found that violence tactics may be motivated by monosexist attitudes, such as emotional violence that invalidates the identity of a bi+ partner (Hall & Girod, 2018).

The monosexist stereotype that bi+ individuals are incapable of monogamy may lead to partner jealousy and misconceptions of what it means to be in a relationship with a bi+ partner. In an Australian-based study that followed-up seven years after an initial qualitative study on bisexual relationships, researchers found that only two out of 60 bisexual participants had engaged in infidelity (McLean, 2011). Some research suggests that bisexual people may be more open to polyamory, but it should be noted that this is often based on surveys that rely heavily on members of online bisexual organizations which may skew these samples (Turell et al., 2018). Moreover, openness to polyamory is not synonymous with inability to be monogamous. However, researchers have suggested that unclear relationship agreements may contribute to jealousy and perceptions of the threat of infidelity for relationships that include bi+ partners (Turell et al., 2018). On the other side of the spectrum, stereotypes of nonmonogamy among bi+ people may also contribute to other monosexist-motivated violence tactics such as non-bi+ partners coercing female bi+ partners into threesomes (Hall & Girod, 2018).

Partner gender may also play a role in IPV dynamics for bi+ populations. In the NISVS, 89.5% of bisexual women reported having only male perpetrators of IPV and 78.5% of bisexual men reported having only female perpetrators of IPV (Walters, 2011). This highlights one way that bi+ experiences of IPV may vary from lesbian and gay experiences. For example, based on previous research highlighting elevated IPV among gay men relative to heterosexual men, it may lead readers to assume that the majority of perpetrators for bi+ men may be male partners (Finneran & Stephenson, 2013). Patterns of partner gender over time may also be an influence unique to bi+ populations. In another example, SGM individuals assigned female at birth were at increased risk for IPV if they had both male and female sexual partners in their lifetime, relative to those with only male partners or who never had sex (Dyar et al., 2020). This was partially accounted for with partner jealousy (Dyar et al., 2020). Partner jealousy may result in controlling behaviors in particular (Turell et al., 2018). There may be a relationship between bi+ individuals past dating patterns with multiple genders and the activation of partner jealousy in their current relationship. As some qualitative research suggests, this may manifest in controlling behaviors motivated by stigma and jealousy such as when a non-bi+ partner attempts to limit who a bi+ partner may see regardless of gender or actively diminishing their access to bi+ community (Hall &

Girod, 2018). Thus, friends of multiple genders may be seen as a threat by jealous partners or partners that ascribe to biphobic stereotypes.

Intrapersonal

The intrapersonal level refers to factors that are internal to a bi+ individual, such as personal characteristics, mental health status, or individual behaviors. One such factor, internalized stigma, has been found to be associated with increased experience of IPV in gay or lesbian relationships (Longobardi & Badenes-Ribera, 2017), but the influence of internalized monosexism/biphobia has been examined in fewer studies. Internalized monosexism/biphobia can be disempowering (Greene, 2007). The external pressures of monosexism can even contribute to challenges in identity development and affirmation (Turell et al., 2018; Dobinson et al., 2005). Stereotypes exist that suggest bi+ identities are not a valid and that bi+ individuals are confused, experimenting, or on their way to identifying as lesbian or gay. While this is a stereotype among people in general, it is also often internalized for bi+ individuals as well. Among those in a relationship, internalized monosexism/biphobia may contribute to a sense of tension between self-actualized bi+ identity and a happy relationship. For example, some bi+ individuals avoid disclosing their identity due to fear of conflict with partners (DeCapua, 2017). For others, internalized stigma may prevent taking public pride in their identity due to a sense that it is a betrayal to their partner or relationship (Greene, 2007). Thus, internalized stigma may contribute to identity invalidation within the context of a relationship; however, the extent to which internalized monosexism/biphobia may influence power/control in relationships has not been fully characterized. It is plausible that internalized monosexism/biphobia contributes to power imbalances in relationships, which may put bi+ individuals at risk for IPV. Internalized monosexism may contribute to diminished self-esteem, diminished sense of self, and may increase the likelihood of belief in harmful bi+ stereotypes in bi+ individuals. These may be in combination with monosexual partners being falsely positioned as superior relative to bi+ partners within the context of monosexist norms and monosexual partners expressing these monosexist values. These combined factors may pose challenges to self-expression and self-advocacy within the context of a relationship for bi+ individuals who experience a high degree of internalized biphobia. Further qualitative and quantitative research is needed to characterize the impact of internalized monosexism on power dynamics in the context of relationships.

Monosexism may also contribute to other known individual-level risk factors for IPV. Research suggests that bi+ individuals experience high levels of health conditions such as substance use, stress, and other mental health concerns, in part due to monosexist stigma (Feinstein & Dyar, 2017). These conditions alone are known risk factors and comorbidities for IPV (Capaldi et al., 2012), so experiences of monosexist stigma and internalized monosexism may contribute to IPV indirectly by increasing these risk factors and comorbidities. For example, substance use and depression may be increased in bi+ populations due to monosexist stigma (Feinstein & Dyar, 2017), and these comorbid factors could put those affected at higher risk for IPV within the context of relationships (Capaldi et al., 2012). Thus, research and interventions addressing bi+ experience of IPV must incorporate an understanding of other known comorbid health disparities such as substance use.

Call to Action

We present a framework for understanding the multilevel influence of monosexism on the experience of IPV among bi+ populations based on the available research. This model is by no means exhaustive or definitive but is intended to be a call to action to better understand bi+ experiences of IPV among researchers, policymakers, and advocates.

Researchers

There is a critical need for in-depth research on unique factors that contribute to bi+ experiences of IPV, including (1) research to identify unique risk and protective factors, particularly at the interpersonal (including relationship), and societal levels; (2) research to identify ways of preventing violence such as through interventions that reduce monosexism; and (3) intervention research aimed at improving support for bi+ survivors of IPV. This call is at the intersection of two bodies of research that represent smaller proportions of SGM-specific funding dollars relative to other topics such as HIV. In a snapshot of the Bisexual Research Portfolio from the NIH in 2018, bi+ research comprised 12.7% of SGM-focused portfolio, and none of the projects were focused on IPV (Centers for Disease Control & Prevention, 2018). There has since been a call for research on bi+ experiences of IPV based on the NIH Bisexual Health Research Workshop in 2019 (National Institutes of Health, 2019); however, to our knowledge there has not been specific funding announcements allocated to this topic. Researchers who endeavor to address the bi+ experience of IPV should avoid contributing to epistemological violence (Teo, 2010) through the earnest incorporation of partnerships with bi+ community, and survivors through community-engaged approaches such as the Bi Us, For Us model (Beach & Xavier Hall, 2020). This model incorporates bi+ community members at every phase of research. Much like there is a lack of SGM research that disaggregates identity labels, there is a lack of research that disaggregates bi+ identities (e.g., bisexual, pansexual, and Queer). Future research should examine possible differences across different bi+ identity labels. Moreover, future research should endeavor to incorporate and center perspectives from people of color, transgender, nonbinary bi+ populations as well as bi+ populations in the Global South.

Policymakers

We call on policymakers to exercise a "Bi in All Policies" approach to eliminate the impact of monosexism in the response to address IPV (Beach & Xavier Hall, 2020). SGM policy advocates should ensure that when reforms to IPV-related laws are made, there are bi+ IPV survivors and IPV experts who testify before legislative bodies to ensure a bi-specific and bi-inclusive legislative history. Likewise, when administrative executive agencies issue guidance impacting the funding and operations of IPV shelters, they should expressly state that bi+ people should be welcomed into shelters for heterosexual and/or for SGM survivors. Any administrative rules, regulations, or guidance that is issued by federal or state agencies that require cultural responsiveness training for IPV providers should be sure to require not only training to provide inclusive services to SGM survivors, but also specifically to bi+ survivors; all such trainings should be delivered through the frame of intersectionality.

Advocates

We recommend the creation of bi-specific IPV resources and that organizations hold bi-specific IPV trainings aimed at increasing bi+ cultural competency of providers, particularly for monosexual providers who may need to address internal bias against bi+ people. Moreover, IPV programming and counseling need more bi+ representation. By moving to survivor-centered advocacy models and the use of inclusive language, providers can avoid making harmful assumptions of their bi+ clients and begin to extend their understandings of IPV outside of the female victim/male perpetrator binary. Ongoing evaluations are also needed to ensure quality care (Furman et al., 2017).

As this chapter establishes, bi+ individuals experience multiple forms of stigma, which have links to elevated experience of IPV in bi+ populations. In order for the well-being of bi+ individuals to improve, it is critical that change is aimed at the structural sources of their diminishment. This can be achieved through disaggregation of data by sexual identity and bi+ specific studies that emphasize influences at multiple levels of the social ecology as well as the development of bi+ specific intervention strategies.

References

The Ace Community Survey. (2020). Bi visibility day report: "Putting the Bin A." Retrieved January 8, 2021, from https://asexualcensus.wordpress.com/2020/09/22/bi-visibility-day-report-putting-the-b-in-a/.

Balsam, K. F., & Szymanski, D. M. (2005). Relationship quality and domestic violence in women's same-sex relationships: The role of minority stress. *Psychology of Women Quarterly*, 29(3), 258–269.

Beach, L. B., & Xavier Hall, C. D. (2020). Bi us, for us: Articulating foundational principles for research in partnership with bisexual communities. *Journal of Bisexuality*, 20(3), 251–272.

Brooks, D., Wirtz, A. L., Celentano, D., Beyrer, C., Hailey-Fair, K., & Arrington-Sanders, R. (2021). Gaps in science and evidence-based interventions to respond to intimate partner violence among Black gay and bisexual men in the U.S.: A call for an intersectional social justice approach. *Sexuality & Culture*, 25(1), 306–317. https://doi.org/10.1007/s12119-020-09769-7.

Brooks, V. R. (1981). *Minority stress and lesbian women*. Lexington, MA: Lexington Books.

Capaldi, D. M., Knoble, N. B., Shortt, J. W., & Kim, H. K. (2012). A systematic review of risk factors for intimate partner violence. *Partner Abuse*, 3(2), 231–280.

Centers for Disease Control & Prevention. (2018). *Bisexual research portfolio: A snapshot of the NIH FY 2018 SGM portfolio analysis*. Retrieved from https://dpcpsi.nih.gov/sites/default/files/SGMRO_SnapshotBisexualFactSheet02_508_FV.pdf.

Choi, A. Y., & Israel, T. (2019). Affirmative mental health practice with bisexual clients: Evidence-based strategies. In *Handbook of evidence-based mental health practice with sexual and gender minorities* (pp. 149–172). Oxford University Press. Retrieved July 28, 2021, from www.oxfordclinicalpsych.com/view/10.1093/med-psych/9780190669300.001.0001/med-9780190669300-chapter-7.

DeCapua, S. R. (2017). Bisexual women's experiences with binegativity in romantic relationships. *Journal of Bisexuality*, 17(4), 451–472.

Dobinson, C., MacDonnell, J., Hampson, E., Clipsham, J., & Chow, K. (2005). Improving the access and quality of public health services for bisexuals. *Journal of Bisexuality*, 5(1), 39–77.

Dyar, C., Feinstein, B. A., & London, B. (2014). Dimensions of sexual identity and minority stress among bisexual women: The role of partner gender. *Psychology of Sexual Orientation and Gender Diversity*, 1(4), 441.

Dyar, C., Feinstein, B. A., Zimmerman, A. R., Newcomb, M. E., Mustanski, B., & Whitton, S. W. (2020). Dimensions of sexual orientation and rates of intimate partner violence among young sexual minority individuals assigned female at birth: The role of perceived partner jealousy. *Psychology of Violence*, 10(4), 411.

Dyar, C., & London, B. (2018). Bipositive events: Associations with proximal stressors, bisexual identity, and mental health among bisexual cisgender women. *Psychology of Sexual Orientation and Gender Diversity*, 5(2), 204–219. http://dx.doi.org.proxy.cc.uic.edu/10.1037/sgd0000281.

Feinstein, B. A., & Dyar, C. (2017). Bisexuality, minority stress, and health. *Current Sexual Health Reports*, 9(1), 42–49.

Feinstein, B. A., Xavier Hall, C. D., Dyar, C., & Davila, J. (2020). Motivations for sexual identity concealment and their associations with mental health among bisexual, pansexual, Queer, and fluid (bi+) individuals. *Journal of Bisexuality*, 20(3), 324–341.

Finneran, C., & Stephenson, R. (2013). Gay and bisexual men's perceptions of police helpfulness in response to male—male intimate partner violence. *Western Journal of Emergency Medicine*, 14(4), 354–362. https://doi.org/10.5811/westjem.2013.3.15639.

Ford, C. L., Slavin, T., Hilton, K. L., & Holt, S. L. (2013). Intimate partner violence prevention services and resources in Los Angeles: Issues, needs, and challenges for assisting lesbian, gay, bisexual, and transgender clients. *Health Promotion Practice*, 14(6), 841–849. https://doi.org/10.1177/1524839912467645.

Franklin, C. A., Goodson, A., & Garza, A. D. (2019). Intimate partner violence among sexual minorities: Predicting police officer arrest decisions. *Criminal Justice and Behavior*, 46(8), 1181–1199. https://doi.org/10.1177/0093854819834722.

Freeland, R., Goldenberg, T., & Stephenson, R. (2018). Perceptions of informal and formal coping strategies for intimate partner violence among gay and bisexual men. *American Journal of Men's Health*, 12(2), 302–312. https://doi.org/10.1177/1557988316631965.

Furman, E., Barata, P., Wilson, C., & Fante-Coleman, T. (2017). "It's a gap in awareness": Exploring service provision for LGBTQ2S survivors of intimate partner violence in Ontario, Canada. *Journal of Gay & Lesbian Social Services*, 29(4), 362–377. https://doi.org/10.1080/10538720.2017.1365672.

Greene, B. (2007). *Becoming visible: Counseling bisexuals across the lifespan*. New York: Columbia University Press.

Hall, C. D., & Girod, C. (2018). *Minority stress and intimate partner violence among bisexual men and women in the U.S. South: A qualitative examination*. Denver, CO: Population Association of America Meeting, April.

Hirschel, D., & McCormack, P. D. (2020). Same-sex couples and the police: A 10-year study of arrest and dual arrest rates in responding to incidents of intimate partner violence. *Violence Against Women*, 1077801220920378. https://doi.org/10.1177/1077801220920378.

Israel, T., Choi, A. Y., Goodman, J. A., Matsuno, E., Lin, Y. J., Kary, K. G., & Merrill, C. R. S. (2019). Reducing internalized binegativity: Development and efficacy of an online intervention. *Psychology of Sexual Orientation and Gender Diversity*, 6(2), 149–159. http://dx.doi.org.proxy.cc.uic.edu/10.1037/sgd0000314.

James, S., Herman, J., Rankin, S., Keisling, M., Mottet, L., & Anafi, M. A. (2016). *The report of the 2015 US transgender survey*. Washington, DC: National Center for Transgender Equality.

Johnson, N. L., & Grove, M. (2017). Why us? Toward an understanding of bisexual women's vulnerability for and negative consequences of sexual violence. *Journal of Bisexuality*, 17(4), 435–450.

Jones, J. M. (2021). *LGBT identification rises to 5.6% in latest US estimate*. Gallup: Politics.

Jordan, S. P., Mehrotra, G. R., & Fujikawa, K. A. (2020). Mandating inclusion: Critical trans perspectives on domestic and sexual violence advocacy. *Violence Against Women*, 26(6–7), 531–554. https://doi.org/10.1177/1077801219836728.

Klesse, C. (2011). Shady characters, untrustworthy partners, and promiscuous sluts: Creating bisexual intimacies in the face of heteronormativity and biphobia. *Journal of Bisexuality*, 11(2–3), 227–244.

Lambe, J., Cerezo, A., & O'Shaughnessy, T. (2017). Minority stress, community involvement, and mental health among bisexual women. *Psychology of Sexual Orientation and Gender Diversity*, 4(2), 218–226. http://dx.doi.org.proxy.cc.uic.edu/10.1037/sgd0000222.

Legal, L. (2010). *When health care isn't caring: Lambda Legal's survey of discrimination against LGBT people and people with HIV*. New York: Lambda Legal.

Lim, J. R., Sullivan, P. S., Salazar, L., Spaulding, A. C., & DiNenno, E. A. (2011). History of arrest and associated factors among men who have sex with men. *Journal of Urban Health*, 88(4), 677–689. https://doi.org/10.1007/s11524-011-9566-5.

Longobardi, C., & Badenes-Ribera, L. (2017). Intimate partner violence in same-sex relationships and the role of sexual minority stressors: A systematic review of the past 10 years. *Journal of Child and Family Studies*, 26(8), 2039–2049.

Macapagal, K., Bhatia, R., & Greene, G. J. (2016). Differences in healthcare access, use, and experiences within a community sample of racially diverse lesbian, gay, bisexual, transgender, and questioning emerging adults. *LGBT Health*, 3(6), 434–442. https://doi.org/10.1089/lgbt.2015.0124.

Maliepaard, E. (2015). Bisexual citizenship in the Netherlands: On homo-emancipation and bisexual representations in national emancipation policies. *Sexualities*, 18(4), 377–393.

Marcus, N. C. (2015). Bridging bisexual erasure in LGBT-rights discourse and litigation. *Michigan Journal of Gender & Law*, 22(291), 291–344.

Marcus, N. C. (2018). The global problem of bisexual erasure in litigation and jurisprudence. *Journal of Bisexuality*, 18(1), 67–85.

Martin-Storey, A. (2015). Prevalence of dating violence among sexual minority youth: Variation across gender, sexual minority identity and gender of sexual partners. *Journal of Youth and Adolescence*, 44(1), 211–224.

McLean, K. (2011). Bisexuality and nonmonogamy: A reflection. *Journal of Bisexuality*, 11(4), 513–517.

McLeroy, K. R., Bibeau, D., Steckler, A., & Glanz, K. (1988). An ecological perspective on health promotion programs. *Health Education Quarterly*, 15(4), 351–377.

Meyer, I. H. (1995). Minority stress and mental health in gay men. *Journal of Health and Social Behavior*, 38–56.

Mogul, J. L. (2011). *Queer (in)justice: The criminalization of LGBT people in the United States*. Boston, MA: Beacon Press.

National Center for Lesbian Rights (NCLR). (2009). *Child custody and visitation issues for lesbian, gay, bisexual, and transgender parents in Florida*. San Francisco. Retrieved from www.nclrights. org/wp-content/uploads/2013/07/2007_10_02_FLCustodyPub.pdf.

National Coalition of Antiviolence Programs (NCAVP). (2013). *Lesbian, gay, bisexual, transgender, queer, and HIV affected intimate partner violence in 2013*. New York: Emily Waters.

National Institutes of Health. (2019). *Bisexual health research workshop September 23, 2019: Identifying research opportunities in bisexual health research*. Retrieved from https://dpcpsi.nih.gov/sites/default/files/Summary_BisexualHealthResearchWorkshopv2_508.pdf.

Øverlien, C. (2020). Young people's experiences of violence and abuse in same-sex relationships: Understandings and challenges. *Nordic Journal of Social Research*, 11(1), 109–128.

Pentaraki, M. (2017). Fear of double disclosure and other barriers to the help seeking behaviour of LGBT youth in Northern Ireland. In *Responding to domestic violence: Emerging challenges for policy, practice and research in Europe* (pp. 135–151). London: Jessica Kingsley Publishers.

Phillips, G., Beach, L. B., Turner, B., et al. (2019). Sexual identity and behavior among US high school students, 2005–2015. *Archives of Sexual Behavior*, 48, 1–17.

Pittman, D. M., Riedy Rush, C., Hurley, K. B., & Minges, M. L. (2020). Double jeopardy: Intimate partner violence vulnerability among emerging adult women through lenses of race and sexual orientation. *Journal of American College Health*, 1–9.

Roberts, T. S., Horne, S. G., & Hoyt, W. T. (2015). Between a gay and a straight place: Bisexual individuals' experiences with monosexism. *Journal of Bisexuality*, 15(4), 554–569. DOI: 10.1080/15299716.2015.1111183.

Robinson, S. R., Ravi, K., & Voth Schrag, R. J. (2020). A systematic review of barriers to formal help seeking for adult survivors of IPV in the United States, 2005–2019. *Trauma, Violence, & Abuse*, 1524838020916254.

Strasser, M. (1996). Legislative presumptions and judicial assumptions: On parenting, adoption, and the best interest of the child. *University of Kansas Law Review*, 45, 49.

Teo, T. (2010). What is epistemological violence in the empirical social sciences? *Social and Personality Psychology Compass*, 4(5), 295–303.

Turell, S. C., Brown, M., & Herrmann, M. (2018). Disproportionately high: An exploration of intimate partner violence prevalence rates for bisexual people. *Sexual and Relationship Therapy*, 33(1–2), 113–131.

Turell, S. C., & Herrmann, M. M. (2008). "Family" support for family violence: Exploring community support systems for lesbian and bisexual women who have experienced abuse. *Journal of Lesbian Studies*, 12(2–3), 211–224. https://doi.org/10.1080/10894160802161372.

Walters, M. L., Chen, J., & Breiding, M. J. (2011). The national intimate partner and sexual violence survey (NISVS). *2010 Findings on Victimization by Sexual Orientation*, 2013.

Whitfield, D. L., Coulter, R. W., Langenderfer-Magruder, L., & Jacobson, D. (2021). Experiences of intimate partner violence among lesbian, gay, bisexual, and transgender college students: The intersection of gender, race, and sexual orientation. *Journal of Interpersonal Violence*, 36(11–12), NP6040–NP6064.

Williams Institute. (2015). *Discrimination and harassment by law enforcement officers in the LGBT community*. Los Angeles, CA: Christy Mallory, Amira Hasenbush, & Brad Sears.

Xavier Hall, C. D., Feinstein, B. A., Sales, J. M., Girod, C., & Yount, K. M. (2021). Outness, discrimination, and depressive symptoms among Bi+ women: The roles of partner gender and sexual identity. *Journal of Bisexuality*, 21(1), 24–41.

Chapter 12

Queer Victims of Violence and Butch, Femme, Bear, and Twink Identities

An Empirical Test of Norm-Centered Stigma Theory

Meredith G. F. Worthen

Hetero-Cis-Normativity and Violence Against Queer, Butch, Femme, Bear, and Twink People

Hetero-cis-normativity is a system of norms, privilege, and oppression that situates hetero-sexual cisgender people above all others (Worthen, 2016). The desire to reinforce hetero-cis-normativity, especially when it comes to culturally "appropriate" norms about gender and sexuality, has been found to motivate violence against Queer people (Ball, 2013; Bedera & Nordmeyer, 2020; Franklin, 1998; Javaid, 2018; Meyer, 2015; Worthen, 2020). In particular, butch, femme, bear, and twink people can be targeted and attacked because of their transgressions against cultural gender expectations, particularly regarding femininity and masculinity. Yet there are important differences in the experiences of butch, femme, bear, and twink people that may inform their likelihood of enduring violence. These are discussed below.

Butch

Butch is a label that can be applied to a person's masculine gender presentation/performance and is often associated with the LGBTQ community. Indeed, one study found that 11% of Queer people identified as butch and that identifying as butch significantly increased the likelihood of also identifying as Queer (Worthen, 2021). A self-identified butch man likely adheres to many gender norms of masculinity and thus, may not be targeted for violence based on his gender presentation/performance while a self-identified butch woman likely transgresses gender norms by presenting/performing as masculine and thus, may be attacked as a result, especially in non-LGBTQ-dominated spaces/communities. Indeed, multiple studies have found that butches endure significantly more experiences with heterosexist discrimination as related to their gender expression than femmes do (Levitt & Horne, 2002; Levitt et al., 2012).

Butch identity may also be associated with relationship and sexual dynamics as in the case of the butch/femme duo (e.g., masculine/feminine or inserter/insertee) (Blair & Hoskin, 2015). In this type of relationship, the butch partner often plays the dominant role and thus, may be at less risk for certain types of violence, such as intimate partner violence. Furthermore, butch identity is often associated with masculine privilege and a generally higher social status/social power position than femme identity is, particularly in LGBTQ-dominated spaces/communities (Hoskin, 2019). Indeed, qualitative studies show that butch-identified people do not face the same level of discrimination as femme people do,

DOI: 10.4324/9781003400981-14

and they are more able to protect themselves from violence (Blair & Hoskin, 2015; Hoskin, 2020). Together, research demonstrates the importance of considering butch identity as it relates to violence.

Femme

Often a companion to butch, femme is a label that can be applied to a person's feminine gender presentation/performance that is also often associated with the LGBTQ community. In particular, some research suggests that Queer identification is an important component of femme identity (Blair & Hoskin, 2016). For example, nearly 1 in 5 (18%) Queer people identified as femme in one study and as similarly found among butches, identifying as femme significantly increased the likelihood of also identifying as Queer (Worthen, 2021). A self-identified femme man may be at risk for gender-based violence due to his feminine presentations/performances that transgress gender norms, particularly in spaces that are non-LGBTQ dominated. Indeed, one study found that both femme men and the partners of femme men felt the need to suppress their public displays of affection in efforts to thwart potential attacks against them (Matheson et al., 2021). Additional research finds that discomfort with male femininity can motivate acts of violence and aggression (Hoskin, 2020).

In addition, within LGBTQ spaces, femme women can experience femme negativity with some going so far as to look less feminine in order to fit in and/or to not be targeted/stigmatized for being too femme (Blair & Hoskin, 2015, 2016). Indeed, qualitative work with femme participants (N = 38) demonstrates evidence of femme-based gender policing and discrimination in LGBTQ spaces, with femmes of all genders being seen as generally weak and passive but more specifically, as sexually objectified targets who are "easy to prey on" (Hoskin, 2019, p. 691). This can be further enhanced by the butch/femme dynamic wherein the femme partner is expected to occupy the submissive/passive role[1] and the butch partner may embody the dominant role which can encompass a "masculine right of access" to the femme partner and the expectation that the femme should "accept sexual advances," which can be inclusive of harassment and violence (Hoskin, 2019, pp. 692–693; see also Hoskin, 2020). Indeed, one study found that femme identity was associated with more victimization as compared to butch identity (Balsam & Szymanski, 2005). Thus, it is important to consider the relationships between femme identity and violence.

Bear

Bear is a label linked to certain types of bodies (hairy and large but not muscular) and their sexual value that is also often associated with non-heterosexual men (Hennen, 2005, 2008; Ravenhill & de Visser, 2017; Wright, 1997, 2016). Bears can be part of a bear community, which is a more strongly integrated social network than, for example, butches and femmes occupy, and can include bear bars, societies, and conventions (Edmonds & Zieff, 2015; Maki, 2017). In addition, bears and more generally the bear community, have been embedded within a culture of hypermasculinity, masculine capital, and Queerness (Hennen, 2005, 2008; Ravenhill & de Visser, 2017). For example, Worthen (2021) found that 1 in 10 Queer people also reported a bear identity. Because bears' gender presentations/performances align with masculine expectations, they are likely not targeted for gender-based violence; however, their relationship/sexual dynamics that have been associated with aggression and hypermasculinity may relate to an increase in certain types of sexualized violence (Maki, 2017; Moskowitz et al., 2013; Schnarrs et al., 2016). Indeed, one study found that bears (n = 469) were more likely than other gay men to engage in risky sexual behaviors with a small but notable group reporting experiencing sexual assault (7%) or perpetrating sexual assault (3%) (Moskowitz et al., 2013). Such findings suggest that there may be a relationship between bear identity and certain types of violence.

Twink

Sometimes bears are presented in opposition to twinks (Ravenhill & de Visser, 2017). Often based on their thin/toned, hairless, and youthful body type, the twink is yet another group among non-heterosexual men that has been both feminized and Queered (Filiault & Drummond, 2007; Jones, 2015). Indeed, Worthen (2021) found that 9% of Queer people also identified as twink and that twink identity significantly increased the likelihood of identifying as Queer. Twink men often openly transgress gender roles by presenting/performing femininity which can put them at risk for gender-based violence (Filiault & Drummond, 2007; Maki, 2017). In addition, twinks have been found to be more likely to use alcohol and tobacco in comparison to other gay men, especially in public places such as gay bars, and these experiences can also be associated with an increase in violence (Lyons & Hosking, 2014; Mustanski et al., 2011). Within relationships, twinks often play the submissive role and are significantly more likely than other gay men to report engaging in receptive anal sex (Lyons & Hosking, 2014) and significantly less likely to report having a primary partner (Schnarrs et al., 2021). Twinks are also often fetishized and feminized in pornography as sexualized submissive objects (Brennan, 2016; Wang, 2021). Together, multiple studies suggest that twinks may be at risk for certain types of gender-based violence.

Overall, butch, femme, bear, and twink identities are associated with stereotypes and experiences that can impact the risk of violence. In addition, it is important to note that because sometimes butch, femme, bear, and twink identities are attractive to those who identify outside of the gender binary (e.g., genderQueer and/or nonbinary people), such identities can be a trigger for gender-based violence for these groups as well. Thus, butch, femme, bear, or twink can be identities that may represent social power *or* oppression depending on who is expressing them and what social circumstances they are in. Furthermore, when a person identifies as both Queer *and* butch, femme, bear, or twink, this intersectional identity experience may increase the likelihood of gender-based violence. However, no studies to date have examined these relationships, especially from a theoretically informed perspective. Thus, this is the first study to do so.

Norm-Centered Stigma Theory and Queer Stigma

Norm-Centered Stigma Theory (NCST) (Worthen, 2020) is a theoretical framework that focuses on the importance of norms/norm violations, social power, and interactions among these. It complements existing research about stigma that recognizes the significance of norms in conceptualizing stigma (especially Goffman, 1963; Link & Phelan, 2001; Stafford & Scott, 1986) and other established work that highlights how multiple axes of social power interact to impact varying life circumstances (e.g., Butler, 1993; Collins, 1999; Crenshaw, 1991; Davis, 2008). Together, NCST brings many of these concepts together and provides a theoretical model and accompanying testable hypotheses to engage further research.

NCST's Three Tenets

NCST Tenet 1: There is a Culturally Dependent and Reciprocal Relationship Between Norms and Stigma

Succinctly: stigma *depends* on norms, and there is no stigma without norms and norm violations. NCST defines this as *norm centrality*: the central element of identifying and understanding stigma *is* norms. There is a reciprocal relationship between norms and stigma because both stigma and norms are dependent on culturally bound established expectations and standards about beliefs, behaviors, identities, and life circumstances (see also Goffman, 1963; Stafford & Scott, 1986). For the purposes of this chapter, NCST Tenet 1 is as follows: There is a culturally dependent relationship between Queer identity and gender-based violence.

NCST Tenet 2: The Relationship Between Norms and Stigma is Organized by Social Power Dynamics Between the Stigmatized and the Stigmatizers

Under NCST, social power is defined as an organizational element among the links between norms and stigma. Put another way, established standards and expectations maintained by a particular group and/or society are embedded within and organized around existing culturally bound infrastructures that privilege some beliefs, behaviors, identities, and life circumstances while simultaneously oppressing others. Norm violators endure stigma and oppressive disadvantages while norm followers secure privileges that go along with the embodiment/adoption of certain social, familial, cultural, economic, and political norms. This creates a hierarchy of stigmatized norm violators and non-stigmatized norm followers that is organized by social power. Thus, NCST recognizes *social power as organizational* in the relationship between stigma and norms (see also, Jones, 1984; Link & Phelan, 2001; Schur, 1983). For the purposes of this chapter, NCST Tenet 2 is as follows: The relationship between Queer identity and gender-based violence is organized by the social power experiences of people who identify as butch, femme, bear, and twink.

NCST Tenet 3: Stigma is Inclusive of Negativity and Social Sanctions Directed Toward Norm Violations and Norm Violators Justified Through Social Power Dynamics

Because societies value upholding norms and rewarding norm followers, the stigma, social sanctions, and negativity norm violators endure become culturally validated. In other words, stigma (and its accompanying negativity) is justified by norms that reflect the oppression of those lacking social power and the simultaneous privilege of those with social power. Thus, NCST emphasizes *social power as justification* for the enduring negativity that stigmatized people experience (see also Link & Phelan, 2001). For the purposes of this chapter, NCST Tenet 3 is as follows: Queer stigma/gender-based violence is inclusive of negativity and social sanctions directed toward violations and violators of hetero-cis-normativity justified through social power dynamics of Queer, butch, femme, bear, and twink identities.

NCST Theoretical Model and Hypotheses

According to NCST, social power organizes the lens from which the relationship between norm violations and stigma should be examined. Specifically, NCST identifies two lenses: the *stigmatizer lens*[2] and the *stigmatized lens*. This chapter utilizes the *stigmatized lens*

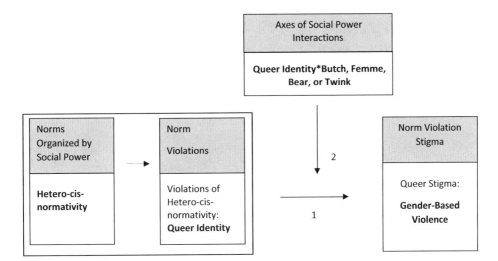

Figure 12.1 Theoretical Model of NCST and Queer, Butch, Femme, Bear, and Twink Stigma with Model Numbers to be Examined in Table 12.2

which examines how the target of stigma's (i.e., the stigmatized) own axes of social power impact their own experiences with negativity, prejudice, and stigma. There are two important relationships that NCST outlines (see Figure 12.1). First, there is a direct relationship between norm violations and stigma. For example, stigma increases as norm violations become more numerous and/or more threatening. Second, the relationship between norm violations and stigma is moderated by social power: social power impacts the relationship between norm violations and stigma. Together, this leads to the following hypotheses that guide this chapter.

- *Hypothesis 1*: Queer identity (violating hetero-cis-normativity) increases the likelihood of experiencing gender-based violence (Queer stigma).
- *Hypothesis 2*: The relationship between Queer identity and gender-based violence is moderated by interactions among Queer identity and butch, femme, bear, and twink identities.

Methods

Data and Sample Characteristics

The data come from the 2018 LGBTQ and Hetero-cis Population Study (Worthen, 2020). The data collection process was reviewed and approved by the University of Oklahoma Institutional Review Board for compliance with standards for the ethical treatment of human participants. The data were collected using panelists recruited from Survey Sampling International (SSI), an international survey research and survey sample provider with over 5 million US online panel participants. SSI panel members are recruited from online communities, social networks, and the web. SSI profiles, authenticates, and verifies each panel member as a reliable respondent for rigorous research participation. SSI awards incentives to respondents upon survey completion.

A sample of adults aged 18–64 stratified by US census categories of age, gender, race/ethnicity, and census region was obtained by SSI. For the first sampling frame, a total of 63,466 email invites were sent out by SSI to *only* heterosexual cisgender potential respondents. A quota of 1,500 respondents (750 hetero-cis men and 750 hetero-cis women) was requested and met (*n* = 1500). For the second sampling frame, a total of 103,001 email invites were sent out by SSI to *only* LGBT potential respondents. A quota of 1,520 respondents (330 each of lesbian women, gay men, bisexual women, bisexual men; 100 each of trans women and trans men) was requested, met, and exceeded for lesbian women, gay men, and bisexual women; however, quotas were not met for bisexual men (*n* = 314), trans women (*n* = 74), nor trans men (*n* = 55). A total of 4,994 individuals accessed the survey by clicking the survey invite link, 4,583 began the survey by answering one or more survey items, and 3,104 respondents completed all items in the survey for a survey start to completion rate of 68%. Missing data were handled by listwise deletion. All hetero-cis respondents were excluded (n = 1,500), and the current study sample consists of only LGBTQ respondents (N = 1,604). See Table 12.1 for more details.

Table 12.1 LGBTQ Sample Characteristics (N = 1,604)

	n	%
Queer	313	19.5%
Butch	125	7.8%
Femme	229	14.3%
Bear	94	5.9%
Twink	55	3.4%
Social Power Axes Interactions		
Queer*Butch	30	1.9%
Queer*Femme	53	3.3%
Queer*Bear	20	1.2%
Queer*Twink	17	1.1%
Sociodemographics		
Cis Man[R]	669	41.7%
Cis Woman	711	44.3%
Trans Woman	74	4.6%
Trans Man	55	3.4%
Nonbinary	95	5.9%
Caucasian/White[R]	1,267	79.0%
African American/Black	146	9.1%
Asian American/Pacific Islander	75	4.7%
Native American/Alaskan Native	32	2.0%
Multiracial	53	3.3%
Other Race	16	1.0%
Latinx Race	12	0.8%
Latinx Ethnicity	209	13.0%
	Mean	*(SD)*
Education	3.78	(1.46)
Town Type (Rural—Large City)	2.65	(1.01)
Age	40.85	(14.34)

[R]reference category in regression models

Survey Design and Implementation

The author created the survey instrument via Qualtrics (an online survey platform). The survey was live on the internet from November 5, 2018, to November 23, 2018, in efforts to meet the quotas for the LGBT groups described above. Through the link provided in the invitation email from SSI, panelists could access the survey via PCs, laptops, tablets, and mobile phones. The survey included 184 closed-ended questions with both multiple- and single-response items with about 77% of the survey items in matrix format. The average time to complete the survey was 25.8 minutes.

Description of Variables

Gender-Based Violence

Respondents were asked to respond to the following statement, "I have experienced violence because of my gender." Those who indicated gender were coded as (1) for gender-based violence and (0) for others. As seen in Figure 12.2 among Queer-identified people (n = 313), twinks experienced the most gender-based violence (53%), followed by femmes (49%), butches (43%), and bears (30%). Among non-Queer-identified people (n = 1,291), femmes experienced the most gender-based violence (16%), followed by butches (9%), bears (3%), and twinks (3%).

Queer, Butch, Femme, Bear, and Twink Identities

Survey respondents were provided with the following statement: "I identify as (select all that apply)" with the following to select from: Queer, butch, femme, bear, and twink. If a

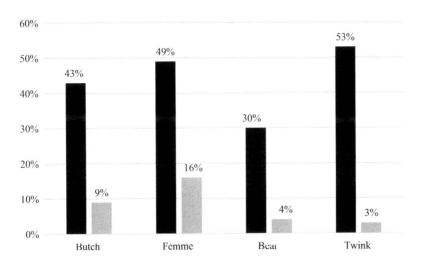

Figure 12.2 Percentage of Butch, Femme, Bear, and Twink Queer, and Non-Queer People Reporting Gender-Based Violence (N = 1,604)

respondent selected an option, they were coded as (1) for that option. If a respondent did not select an option, they were coded as (0) for that option.

Gender

Respondents were asked "What best describes your gender?" with responses that were coded as cis men (those who indicated "I identify as a man, and my sex assigned at birth was male"), cis women (those who indicated: "I identify as a woman, and my sex assigned at birth was female"), trans men (those who indicated "I identify as a man, and my sex assigned at birth was female"), trans women (those who indicated "I identify as a woman, and my sex assigned at birth was male"), and nonbinary/genderQueer (those that selected the statement "I am gender-nonbinary, gender fluid, or genderQueer").

Racial and Ethnic Identity

For racial identity, response options were, Caucasian/White, African American/Black, Asian American/Pacific Islander, Native American/Alaskan Native, Multiracial, and Other Race: Please Specify. For Other Race, $n = 25$ respondents wrote in responses (e.g., "Hispanic," $n = 12$; "Mexican," $n = 6$) that were recoded into a new category of Latinx Race. The final Other Race category ($n = 24$) was comprised of about half (46%, $n = 11$) Middle Eastern individuals. In a separate question for Latinx ethnicity, respondents were also asked "Are you Hispanic or Latino/a/x? (A person of Cuban, Mexican, Puerto Rican, South or Central American or other Spanish culture of origin regardless of race)."

Education response options were, (1) less than high school, (2) high school/GED, (3) some college, (4) Associate's, (5) Bachelor's, or (6) greater than Bachelor's.
Town type (where the majority of life was spent) response options were coded into four dummy variables: rural, small town, suburb, and large city.
Age was measured in years (18–64).

Method of Analysis

Table 12.2 uses logistic regression to explore NCST and gender-based violence as related to Queer, butch, femme, bear, and twink identities as described in Figure 12.1. Multicollinearity was examined using STATA command "collin" (Ender, 2010), which provides collinearity diagnostics for all variables utilized in each model. The Mean VIF values were 1.13, suggesting no issues with multicollinearity (Allison, 2012).

Results

Logistic Regression

In Table 12.2 Model 1, being Queer was significantly related to .86 times increase in the likelihood of gender-based violence ($p < .05$). Thus, *Hypothesis 1* is fully supported. In addition, being femme was associated with a .39 times increase in the likelihood of gender-based violence but only approached significance at $p = .08$. However, neither butch, bear, nor twink were statistically significant in Model 1.

Table 12.2 Logistic Regression Results with Odds Ratios and (Standard Errors) Estimating NCST and Gender-Based Violence as Related to Queer, Butch, Femme, Bear, and Twink Identities with Social Power Axes Interactions (N = 1,604)

	Model 1	Model 2
Queer	1.86 (.34)*	1.06 (.24)
Butch	1.21 (.32)	.60 (.23)
Femme	1.39 (.26)†	.87 (.20)
Bear	1.29 (.53)	.56 (.35)
Twink	1.88 (.78)	.28 (.29)
Social Power Axes Interactions		
Queer*Butch		4.74 (2.92)*
Queer*Femme		3.48 (1.47)*
Queer*Bear		2.31 (2.36)
Queer*Twink		12.88 (15.60)*
Sociodemographic Controls		
Cis Woman	4.67 (1.10)*	4.81 (1.15)*
Trans Woman	4.31 (1.67)*	5.40 (2.13)*
Trans Man	4.74 (1.89)*	5.87 (2.42)*
Nonbinary	4.84 (1.58)*	4.95 (1.66)*
African American/Black	1.23 (.30)	1.13 (.29)
Asian American/Pacific Islander	.33 (.18)*	.39 (.21)†
Native American/Alaskan Native	.90 (.47)	1.03 (.55)
Multiracial	1.57 (.57)	1.54 (.57)
Other Race	.43 (.46)	.42 (.47)
Latinx Race	1.27 (1.07)	1.24 (1.04)
Latinx Ethnicity	.92 (.21)	1.00 (.23)
Education	1.00 (.06)	1.02 (.06)
Town Type (Rural—Large City)	.99 (.08)	.96 (.08)
Age	.90 (.01)*	.90 (.01)*
Mean VIF	1.13	1.13
Pseudo R²	.11	.13

*p <.05; †p <.10

In Model 2, neither Queer, butch, femme, bear, nor twink were significantly significant. However, three of the interaction terms were significant. Specifically, being Queer and butch was significantly related to a 3.74 times increase in the likelihood of gender-based violence (p <.05); being Queer and femme was significantly related to a 2.48 times increase in the likelihood of gender-based violence (p <.05); and being Queer and twink was significantly related to a 11.88 times increase in the likelihood of gender-based violence (p <.05). However, being Queer and bear was not statistically significant. Thus, *Hypothesis 2* is partially supported.

Controls and Goodness of Fit

Among the controls, in comparison to being a cis man (reference category), being a cis woman, trans woman, trans man, or nonbinary person all increased the likelihood of gender-based violence in both models. In contrast, in comparison to being Caucasian/White (reference category), being Asian American/Pacific Islander decreased the likelihood of gender-based violence in both models, and age was also negatively related to gender-based violence in both models. No other sociodemographic controls were significant in any models. The pseudo R^2 values ranged from .11 to .13.

Discussion

This chapter utilized the theoretical lens of Norm-Centered Stigma Theory (NCST) (Worthen, 2020) to offer insight into the intersecting ways that being Queer *and* being butch, femme, bear, or twink relate to experiences with victimization. In line with NCST, both hypotheses were supported, and findings demonstrated that Queer butch, femme, bear, and twink people are at particular risk for gender-based violence, which may be related to the ways that they can transgress various gender norms and violate hetero-cis-normativity; yet there were important differences found across the groups.

First, looking at Queer identity, the prevalence of gender-based violence among Queer butch, femme, bear, and twink people was notably higher than non-Queer butch, femme, bear, and twink people's gender-based violence (see Figure 12.2). In addition, logistic regression results demonstrated that Queer identity was significantly related to an increase in the likelihood of experiencing gender-based violence (see Model 1 in 12.2) as were the intersections among Queer identity and butch, femme, and twink identities (Model 2). Such findings are consistent with previous work that has found that Queer identity is related to an increased risk for violence (Meyer, 2015; Worthen, 2020) but also demonstrate that the overlapping, intersectional experiences of being Queer and butch, femme, and twink are especially significant in understanding gender-based violence among these groups.

Looking next at butch identity, gender-based violence was quite high among Queer butches with close to half reporting such instances (43%), though this was slightly less in comparison to Queer femmes (49%) and Queer twinks (53%) but notably more than Queer bears (30%) (see Figure 12.2). In addition, being butch was not significantly related to an increase in the likelihood of experiencing gender-based violence (see Model 1 in Table 12.2); however, the intersectional experience of being butch and Queer was related to a more than three-fold increase in the odds of gender-based violence (Model 2). Such results demonstrate that gender-based violence against butches is likely entwined with other transgressions of hetero-cis-normativity that are associated with Queerness, as found in other research focusing on butch women's experiences with heterosexist discrimination (Levitt & Horne, 2002; Levitt et al., 2012).

Among femmes, gender-based violence was high (49% among Queer femmes; 16% among non-Queer femmes), being femme approached a significant relationship with gender-based violence (p = .08; see Model 1 in Table 12.2), and the intersectional experience of being femme, and Queer was related to a more than twofold increase in the odds of gender-based violence (Model 2). Thus, violence may be exacerbated among Queer femmes perhaps due to perceptions that they deserve punishment for being too femme (Blair & Hoskin, 2015, 2016), for being weak sexual objects/prey (Hoskin, 2019, 2020), and/or for their transgressions of gender norms, especially in the case of Queer femme men (Hoskin, 2020; Matheson et al., 2021).

Bears were unlike the other groups in three distinct ways: (1) Queer bears reported the least gender-based violence (30%), (2) bear identity was not significantly related to the likelihood of experiencing gender-based violence (see Model 1 in Table 12.2), and (3) the intersectional experience of being bear and Queer was also not statistically significant (see Model 2). Such findings suggest that that bear (hyper)masculinity may operate as a protective factor against gender-based violence and may even serve as a form of masculine social capital, as others have found (Edmonds & Zieff, 2015; Hennen, 2005, 2008; Maki, 2017; Ravenhill & de Visser, 2017; Wright, 1997, 2016).

Twinks were found to be at an especially high risk for gender-based violence with more than half of Queer twinks (53%) reporting such experiences. In addition, although being twink was not significantly related to the likelihood of experiencing gender-based violence (see Model 1 in Table 12.2), the intersectional experience of being twink and Queer was related to a nearly twelve-fold increase in the odds of gender-based violence (Model 2). Thus, Queer twinks may be the most vulnerable group explored in this study perhaps due to their feminization (Filiault & Drummond, 2007; Maki, 2017), their subordination into a submissive/sexualized role (Brennan, 2016; Lyons & Hosking, 2014), as well as other social experiences which may amplify their experiences of violence that have been found in previous research such as twinks' higher use of drugs/alcohol and greater prevalence of multiple partners in comparison to other gay men (Mustanski et al., 2011; Schnarrs et al., 2021).

Overall, the three tenets of NCST were supported in this exploration. First, in line with NCST's Tenet 1: There is a culturally dependent relationship between <u>Queer identity</u> and <u>gender-based violence</u>. By examining the importance of norms (*norm centrality*) as related to stigma, NCST provides a framework with violations of hetero-cis-normativity as central to understanding the victimization of Queer butch, femme, bear, and twink people. Second, in line with NCST's Tenet 2: the relationship between <u>Queer identity</u> and <u>gender-based violence</u> is organized by the social power experiences of <u>people who identify as Queer butch, femme, and twink</u>. In this way, *social power is organizational* in these relationships because these identities interact with one another and are significantly related to gender-based violence. Third, results are in line with NCST's Tenet 3: <u>Queer stigma/gender-based violence</u> is inclusive of negativity and social sanctions directed toward violations and violators of <u>hetero-cis-normativity</u> justified through social power dynamics of <u>Queer, butch, femme, bear, and twink identities</u>. The overlapping stereotypes and deeply embedded cultural concerns/preoccupations with the ways that Queer butch, femme, bear, and twink people violate hetero-cis-normativity, especially femininity and masculinity, contribute to a cultural *justification* for their victimization (Blair & Hoskin, 2016; Hennen, 2008; Hoskin, 2019; Levitt & Horne, 2002; Lyons & Hosking, 2014; Matheson et al., 2021; Meyer, 2015; Ravenhill & de Visser, 2017; Worthen, 2020).

To summarize, between 30% and 53% of Queer butch, femme, bear, and twink people reported gender-based violence and the intersectional experiences of being Queer and being butch, femme, twink (but not bear) were significantly related to an increase in the likelihood of gender-based violence. Together, these results show that although there are some important similarities across these groups, there are also notable differences in prevalence and patterns of victimization. Such findings highlight the importance of future examinations of LGBTQ violence. with careful attention to cultural responses to the hetero-cis-normativity/ femininity/masculinity violations of Queer butch, femme, bear, and twink people, as some previous work has done (Hoskin, 2019; Levitt & Horne, 2002; Lyons & Hosking, 2014; Meyer, 2015; Moskowitz et al., 2013; Worthen, 2020).

Policy and Practice Implications

The results from the current study show that those working with survivors of gender-based violence, including social workers, criminal justice personnel, and mental health care professionals, should be careful to understand how people with intersecting Queer, butch, femme, bear, and twink identities may be vulnerable to gender-based violence. In addition, the findings presented here demonstrate the significance of a more nuanced and expanded investigation of gender-based violence beyond those provided in, for example, the FBI hate crimes definitions which are limited to "anti-male," "anti-female," "anti-transgender," and "anti-gender nonconforming" (FBI, 2019). In particular, victimologists should continue to examine intersecting Queer, butch, femme, bear, and twink identities in future studies.

Future Research

Overall, the current study's findings demonstrate the importance of considering the intersecting complexities of multiple layers of social power/marginalization, including Queer, butch, femme, bear, and twink identities but also call attention to future work that can better highlight the significance of race, ethnicity, class, gender, and sexuality, as previous scholars of intersectionality have established (Collins, 1999; Crenshaw, 1991; Davis, 2008). Indeed, we must continue to center Queer people and their various intersecting identities into discussions of victimization and violence. In particular, a norm-centered focus is essential in future work because, as I have demonstrated elsewhere (Worthen, 2020), cultural responses to violations of hetero-cis-normativity, especially in regards to femininity and masculinity, are often at the crux of LGBTQ negativity. Specifically, Norm-Centered Stigma Theory emphasizes the need for continued nuanced and intersectional explorations that highlight the lived experiences of LGBTQ people and provides a theoretical framework with which to understand LGBTQ violence.

Notes

1 For example, one study found that partners of femme women earn higher incomes and that femme-identified women are perceived by their partners as doing more housework (Rothblum et al., 2018).
2 The *stigmatizer lens* examines how the stigmatizer's (i.e., the individual who is potentially expressing negativity or passing judgement on another) own axes of social power impact their feelings about the target of stigma.

References

Allison, P. D. (2012, April). Handling missing data by maximum likelihood. *SAS Global Forum*, 2012(312), 1038–1021.

Ball, M. (2013). Heteronormativity, homonormativity and violence. In K. Carrington, M. Ball, E. O'Brien, & J. M. Tauri (Eds.), *Crime, justice and social democracy: International perspectives* (pp. 186–199). London: Palgrave Macmillan UK. DOI: 10.1057/9781137008695_13.

Balsam, K. F., & Szymanski, D. M. (2005). Relationship quality and domestic violence in women's same-sex relationships: The role of minority stress. *Psychology of Women Quarterly*, 29(3), 258–269. DOI: 10.1111/j.1471-6402.2005.00220.x.

Bedera, N., & Nordmeyer, K. (2020). An inherently masculine practice: Understanding the sexual victimization of queer women. *Journal of Interpersonal Violence*, 0886260519898439. DOI: 10.1177/0886260519898439.

Blair, K. L., & Hoskin, R. A. (2015). Experiences of femme identity: Coming out, invisibility and femmephobia. *Psychology & Sexuality*, 6(3), 229–244. DOI: 10.1080/19419899.2014.921860.

Blair, K. L., & Hoskin, R. A. (2016). Contemporary understandings of femme identities and related experiences of discrimination. *Psychology & Sexuality*, 7(2), 101–115. DOI: 10.1080/19419899.2015.1053824.

Brennan, J. (2016). 'Bare-backing spoils everything. He's spoiled goods': Disposal and disgust, a study of retired power bottom Twink Jake Lyons. *Porn Studies*, 3(1), 20–33. DOI: 10.1080/23268743.2015.1074867.

Brontsema, R. (2004). A queer revolution: Reconceptualizing the debate over linguistic reclamation. *Colorado Research in Linguistics*, 17(1), 1–17. DOI: 10.25810/dky3-zq57.

Butler, J. (1993). Critically queer. *GLQ: A Journal of Lesbian and Gay Studies*, 1(1), 17–32.

Callis, A. S. (2014). Bisexual, pansexual, queer: Non-binary identities and the sexual borderlands. *Sexualities*, 17(1–2), 63–80. DOI: 10.1177/1363460713511094.

Collins, P. H. (1999). *Black feminist thought: Knowledge, consciousness, and the politics of empowerment*, Revised, 10th Anniversary, 2nd edition. New York: Routledge.

Crenshaw, K. (1991). Mapping the margins: Intersectionality, identity politics, and violence against women of color. *Stanford Law Review*, 43(6), 1241–1299. JSTOR. DOI: 10.2307/1229039.

Davis, K. (2008). Intersectionality as buzzword: A sociology of science perspective on what makes a feminist theory successful. *Feminist Theory*, 9(1), 67–85. DOI: 10.1177/1464700108086364.

Edmonds, S. E., & Zieff, S. G. (2015). Bearing bodies: Physical activity, obesity stigma, and sexuality in the bear community. *Sociology of Sport Journal*, 32(4), 415–435. DOI: 10.1123/ssj.2014-0166.

Ender, P. (2010). *Collinearity issues*. Retrieved January 7, 2010, http://www.philender.com/courses/categorical/notes2/collin.html.

FBI. (2019). *2019 hate crimes statistics*. Retrieved October 4, 2021, from FBI website: https://ucr.fbi.gov/hate-crime/2019.

Filiault, S., & Drummond, M. (2007). The hegemonic asethetic. *Gay & Lesbian Issues and Psychology Review*, 3(3), 1–11.

Franklin, K. (1998). Unassuming motivations: Contextualizing the narratives of antigay assailants. In G. M. Herek (Ed.), *Stigma and sexual orientation: Understanding prejudice against lesbians, gay men, and bisexuals* (pp. 1–23). Thousand Oaks, CA: Sage Publications.

Gamson, J. (1995). Must identity movements self-destruct? A queer dilemma. *Social Problems*, 42(3), 390–407. DOI: 10.2307/3096854.

Goffman, E. (1963). *Stigma. Notes on the management of spoiled identity*. Englewood Cliffs, NJ: Prentice-Hall.

Hennen, P. (2005). Bear bodies, bear masculinity: Recuperation, resistance, or retreat? *Gender & Society*, 19(1), 25–43. DOI: 10.1177/0891243204269408.

Hennen, P. (2008). *Faeries, bears, and Leatherman: Men in community queering the masculine*. Chicago, IL: University of Chicago Press.

Hoskin, R. A. (2019). Femmephobia: The role of anti-femininity and gender policing in LGBTQ+ people's experiences of discrimination. *Sex Roles*, 81(11), 686–703. DOI: 10.1007/s11199-019-01021-3.

Hoskin, R. A. (2020). "Femininity? It's the aesthetic of subordination": Examining femmephobia, the gender binary, and experiences of oppression among sexual and gender minorities. *Archives of Sexual Behavior*. DOI: 10.1007/s10508-020-01641-x.

Javaid, A. (2018). Out of place: Sexualities, sexual violence, and heteronormativity. *Aggression and Violent Behavior*, 39, 83–89. DOI: 10.1016/j.avb.2018.02.007.

Jones, E. E. (1984). *Social stigma: The psychology of marked relationships*. New York: W.H. Freeman.

Jones, R. G. (2015). Queering the body politic: Intersectional reflexivity in the body narratives of queer men. *Qualitative Inquiry*, 21(9), 766–775. DOI: 10.1177/1077800415569782.

Khayatt, D. (2002). Toward a queer identity. *Sexualities*, 5(4), 487–501. DOI: 10.1177/1363460702005004006.

Levitt, H. M., & Horne, S. G. (2002). Explorations of lesbian-queer genders: Butch, femme, androgynous or "other." *Journal of Lesbian Studies*, 6(2), 25–39. DOI: 10.1300/J155v06n02_05.

Levitt, H. M., Puckett, J. A., Ippolito, M. R., & Horne, S. G. (2012). Sexual minority women's gender identity and expression: Challenges and supports. *Journal of Lesbian Studies*, 16(2), 153–176. DOI: 10.1080/10894160.2011.605009.

Link, B. G., & Phelan, J. C. (2001). Conceptualizing stigma. *Annual Review of Sociology*, 27(1), 363–385. DOI: 10.1146/annurev.soc.27.1.363.

Lyons, A., & Hosking, W. (2014). Health disparities among common subcultural identities of young gay men: Physical, mental, and sexual health. *Archives of Sexual Behavior*, 43(8), 1621–1635. DOI: 10.1007/s10508-014-0315-1.

Maki, J. L. (2017). Gay subculture identification: Training counselors to work with gay men. *Vistas Online*, 22, 1–12.

Matheson, L., Ortiz, D., Hoskin, R. A., Holmberg, D., & Blair, K. L. (2021). The feminine target: Gender expression in same-sex relationships as a predictor of experiences with public displays of affection. *The Canadian Journal of Human Sexuality*. Retrieved from https://muse.jhu.edu/article/796809/summary.

Meyer, D. (2015). *Violence against queer people: Race, class, gender, and the persistence of anti-LGBT discrimination*. New Brunswick, NJ: Rutgers University Press.

Moskowitz, D. A., Turrubiates, J., Lozano, H., & Hajek, C. (2013). Physical, behavioral, and psychological traits of gay men identifying as bears. *Archives of Sexual Behavior*, 42(5), 775–784.

Mustanski, B. S., Newcomb, M. E., Bois, S. N. D., Garcia, S. C., & Grov, C. (2011). HIV in young men who have sex with men: A review of epidemiology, risk and protective factors, and interventions. *The Journal of Sex Research*, 48(2–3), 218–253. DOI: 10.1080/00224499.2011.558645.

Ravenhill, J. P., & de Visser, R. O. (2017). "There are too many gay categories now": Discursive constructions of gay masculinity. *Psychology of Men & Masculinities*, 18(4), 321–330. http://dx.doi.org.ezproxy.lib.ou.edu/10.1037/men0000057.

Rothblum, E. D., Balsam, K. F., & Wickham, R. E. (2018). Butch, femme, and androgynous gender identities within female same-sex couples: An actor-partner analysis. *Psychology of Sexual Orientation and Gender Diversity*, 5(1), 72–81. DOI: 10.1037/sgd0000258.

Schnarrs, P., Jones, S. S., Parsons, J. T., Baldwin, A., Rosenberger, J. G., Lunn, M. R., & Rendina, H. J. (2021). Sexual subcultures and HIV prevention methods: An assessment of condom use, PrEP, and TasP among gay, bisexual, and other men who have sex with men using a social and sexual networking smartphone application. *Archives of Sexual Behavior*, 50(4), 1781–1792. DOI: 10.1007/s10508-020-01784-x.

Schnarrs, P., Rosenberger, J., Schick, V., Delgado, A., Briggs, L., Dodge, B., & Reece, M. (2016). Difference in condom use between bear concordant and discordant dyads during the last anal sex event. *Journal of Homosexuality*, 64. DOI: 10.1080/00918369.2016.1174024.

Schur, E. M. (1983). *Labeling women deviant: Gender, stigma, and social control*. Philadelphia: Temple University Press.

Stafford, M. C., & Scott, R. R. (1986). Stigma, deviance, and social control. In S. C. Ainlay, G. Becker, & L. M. Coleman (Eds.), *The dilemma of difference: A multidisciplinary view of stigma* (pp. 77–91). Boston, MA: Springer US. DOI: 10.1007/978-1-4684-7568-5_5.

Wang, Y. (2021). The twink next door, who also does porn: Networked intimacy in gay porn performers' self-presentation on social media. *Porn Studies*, 8(2), 224–238. DOI: 10.1080/23268743.2020.1841019.

Worthen, M. G. F. (2016). Hetero-cis—normativity and the gendering of transphobia. *International Journal of Transgenderism*, 17(1), 31–57.

Worthen, M. G. F. (2020). *Queers, bis, and straight lies: An investigation of LGBTQ stigma*. New York: Routledge.

Worthen, M. G. F. (2021). Categorically queer? An exploratory study of identifying queer in the USA. *Sexuality Research and Social Policy*. DOI: 10.1007/s13178-021-00606-6.

Wright, L. (1997). *The bear book: Readings in the history and evolution of a gay male subculture*, 1st edition. New York: Routledge.

Wright, L. (2016). *The bear book II: Further readings in the history and evolution of a gay male subculture*. New York: Routledge.

Chapter 13

Police Do Not Protect Us, and Other Lessons I learned As a Queer Victim

Allyn Walker

In the spring of 2010, I went clubbing with Caitlyn, a friend I had known since high school. I had just moved to New York City to start my master's program in social work. Caitlyn, who by this time was an experienced New Yorker with three years there under her belt, already knew all the best ways for Queers to meet other Queers in the city. At the time, I had identified as a woman, and a lesbian, and I was thrilled to have a lesbian friend to show me around and explore the gay parts of the city with.

Caitlyn and I took the 1 train from our dorms in Morningside Heights down to the Village to go to Henrietta Hudson. Henrietta's was my favorite lesbian bar in the city at that time. I loved the vibe there: low lighting, loud music, teeny, overpriced drinks. That night, I was feeling confident. I had a couple of drinks with Caitlyn. I locked eyes with Jones, a mysterious someone I had never met before. They were shooting pool, looking dashing in a fedora. We danced together, then talked outside while Jones and Caitlyn shared a cigarette. It could have been the perfect night out for a new New Yorker.

I left with Caitlyn around 2:00 am. We were walking from Henrietta's to the 1 train at Christopher Street when two girls approached us. They looked to be a bit younger than my 21 years—probably teenagers. They asked me for a dollar for the train. I unzipped my small clutch, which I was already carrying in my hand, and gave one of the girls a dollar.

Then they asked me if I like girls. I've thought about this question, and my response, so often since. I'm not sure if I thought they were hitting on me or if I thought they were asking surreptitiously for directions to Henrietta's, or if I didn't think about it at all, but I smiled and answered, "Yeah, I like girls."

Abruptly, I felt myself being slammed against a wall, and I saw about six of their friends, who had been almost an entire block away, running toward us. Caitlyn and I were both held against a building, as this group groped at my breasts and groin. At first, I froze—I can't remember how long I was held there. Fifteen seconds? A minute? But then I pushed my way out and started running for the train. Moments later I realized I was alone. Terrified, I screamed for Caitlyn. Then, somehow, she was out too, and we ran to the 1 train together, without looking back.

It took us some time to process what happened, but the ride on the 1 from Christopher Street to 116th gave us a while. At first, I was just shocked. "What the fuck just happened? Did that really just happen?" And then I was embarrassed. And ashamed. That I had disclosed my sexuality to a stranger at 2:00 am on the street, that I had been drinking and maybe had poor judgement as a result, that I had given a stranger money (to this day I no longer carry cash—it feels too unsafe). And then I was angry. I gave them the dollar they asked for, and then they pushed us against a wall and grabbed our parts! Caitlyn joked that

DOI: 10.4324/9781003400981-15

I should be glad I hadn't given them more. "At least it was a cheap assault!" It wasn't funny, but we laughed at that until our train ride ended.

By the time I had arrived home, it occurred to me that what happened to us would likely be considered a hate crime. Only a few months prior, President Barack Obama had signed into law The Matthew Shepard and James Byrd Jr. Hate Crimes Prevention Act, which, in part, expanded hate crimes definitions to include crimes motivated by the victim's status as a member of LGBT communities. The legislation had felt so important to me at the time—an acknowledgement that we existed, that we should not be the targets of violence based on our genders and the genders of those we loved. An acknowledgement that we deserved some kind of protection. I wanted to feel protected, too. And knowing from my prior experiences as a victim's counselor that so many crimes go unreported, I felt a responsibility to report this to 911. So I called.

A woman picked up, and I explained to her what had happened. "This happened on Christopher Street?" she asked. I confirmed. "You should have stayed there to call 911. Now you're in a different precinct." Despite her lecture about how crime victims should apparently stay in the place they were attacked to make a report, she wanted to make sure I was okay. She asked if I was hurt at all, and if she should send emergency medical services. I said no. I was physically okay. I just wanted to report what had happened. She told me the police would be arriving at my dorm soon.

Shortly thereafter, a bevy of police officers was congregating in and just outside of my dorm room. EMS arrived as well, even though I had already said I didn't need them. I sat on my bed to recount what had happened. Two or three male police officers entered my small room, with one female officer and multiple other male officers waiting in the hall. The officers crowding my room asked a number of questions, while standing. All I could think about was how their junk was at eye level, and how that would have been even more traumatizing had I experienced worse just before. I never asked them to sit down. I wish I had.

The officers asked questions in an even tone, almost seeming bored as I explained what happened. Then I recounted that those who joined in—the girls' friends—included a boy, and at that point, the officers began jumping over each other with questions. "A boy? How old? Did *he* touch you? Where?" I couldn't recall seeing who had touched me, specifically. I was annoyed. Why should that have been when they started to care? Why should the gender of the people who sexually assaulted me matter? "Forcible touch," the police officers corrected me. "Not sexual assault." In insisting on this language, these officers communicated to me that my experience of being sexually violated was unimportant. It was clear to me that their own definitions—of both gender and law—were all that mattered to them.

As the week wore on, I continued processing the assault, and I brought it up at dinner with "B." B was a White, gay man several years older than me, whom I knew through a friend. He had a well-paying job in the medical industry, and knowing I had little disposable income as a graduate student, he frequently invited me out to dinner at fancy restaurants and paid, just to be nice. I told him about what had happened. The first words out of his mouth in response were, "Were they Black?" I wanted to scream at him or at least to challenge him: "Why in the fuck would you assume that? Why in the fuck would that matter?" But I didn't. I no longer talk to B.

A couple of weeks later, I received a call from police in the precinct where I was attacked. They asked me to come to their office to look at photos and potentially identify who had attacked us. I made an appointment for an upcoming date, but I felt conflicted about doing so. What would happen if I couldn't identify anyone? If I couldn't remember their faces? What would happen if I *could*?

The question, "What would happen if I could?" was the one I agonized over. Ultimately, I didn't want them to be charged. I didn't know why they had done what they had done, but as far as I could tell, they were likely teenagers who thought they were playing a game. Yes, I had been terrified, ashamed, and angry, and this event would continue to affect how I behaved in and thought about my city for many years to come. But what was justice here? I wanted them to know what they did was wrong. I wanted to know why they did what they did. I wanted them to know how it had affected me. I didn't want them to do it to anyone ever again. And I also didn't wish them any harm. Involvement in the justice system would have been unequivocally harmful. I was working at the Correctional Association of New York at the time, as an intern with their Prison Visiting Project. I spent my days hearing from incarcerated people about their terrible experiences in jails and prisons, and I knew the harms of the system more than most. But I didn't know what my options were in this situation, and as far as I could tell, the only two were to do nothing, or to look through photos of potential suspects.

So I went to the police station, still unsure of what I was going to do, still unsure of what the right thing to do was. A police officer sat me down with a binder full of mugshots. They had no leads on who had done this to me, and as far as I could tell, they had done no investigating up until this point. The best they could offer was to look through photos of people who had been previously arrested in the area. Looking through the photos, I never saw one that rang any bells. I couldn't bring anyone's faces to mind in the first place—I had just been thinking that one of the photos might jog my memory. But it didn't. I was almost relieved.

I never heard back from the police after that day. As far as I know, they went no further into my case than having me look through those photos.

When we talk about the need for police in our society, we often talk about the need for protection. But the police did not protect me from harm. They weren't there to keep this from happening. A few months later I moved further north in Harlem. Police were on every block of that neighborhood. Why were they out there standing on every single block north of 125th Street, where the residents were mostly Black? Why were they nowhere to be found when I was being pushed against a wall in Greenwich Village, a majority White neighborhood? Why were they nowhere to be found in the neighborhood I was still living in as a White graduate student surrounded mostly by other White students? (I'm not really asking. We know why.)

Beyond the police not protecting me from initial harm, they did not make me feel protected when I asked for help. Upon responding to my initial call, I was scolded for keeping myself safe by leaving. I did not feel safeguarded by the officers in my dorm room, towering over me, their focus only on the boy in the group, and their correction in the language I used to refer to my experience. I did not feel defended by the police asking me to look through some random photos, and never calling me back.

And I would not have felt supported by the options provided to me as a victim if these teens had been found. Justice would not be a year in jail (the maximum sentence for forcible touch in New York). It would not be extra penalties for the hate crimes that may have been attached. It would not have been probation or community service. Justice to me could be restorative: a conversation between myself and these teens, so they could know the harm they had caused, and I could know that they recognized the wrongness of their actions, that they would never want to do this to another person. Justice could look like societal transformation: it could involve these teens being educated by their parents and communities about LGBTQ people's accomplishments, so they would not have thought in the first place that attacking people for being Queer would be fun. Maybe justice would involve having late-night hours for community centers so teens can drop in and hang out in a supportive atmosphere, or financial help for families so that parents can be around at night. Justice could look like this volume, a collective sharing of experiences by us, for us, to know we are not alone.

There is more I could say here. There are connections I could make about a system that criminalizes Black people and other people of color and points to their arrests and imprisonment as measures of safety for White people like me. There are connections I could make about a system that has historically vilified Queer people that continues to vilify Queer people of color, Queer migrants, Queer sex workers, and other Queer people just trying to survive. There are connections I could make about the potential in transformative justice practices, and how we should look to individuals and community outside of oppressive systems to keep us safe. I've said these things elsewhere, and I'll keep saying them. For now, I'll just say this; these direct lessons I learned as a victim myself:

Police do not protect us. Queer people are not made safe by hate crime laws. The criminal processing system cannot save us from harm.

We need support. We need community. We need each other.

Queer Victimology and Queer Victimization in the System

Chapter 14

Queer Invisibility

LGBTQA+ Victimization in Carceral Settings

Susana Avalos and Breanna Boppre

Introduction

Pathways to incarceration often start during youth for LGBTQA+ people. Throughout their life course, LGBTQA+ people experience higher rates of victimization than cis or hetero individuals, and racially and sexually marginalized people face increased risks (Conover-Willaims & Teal, 2019). LGBTQA+ people also suffer higher poverty rates, homelessness, and lack of access to services compared to their cis and hetero counterparts. Further, LGBTQA+ people are systematically criminalized and mistreated within the criminal legal system in comparison to cis and hetero people (Braunstein, 2017; Carpenter & Marshall, 2017; Hodge & Sexton, 2020; Nadal, 2020; Owen et al., 2018; Serpe & Nadal, 2017; Sexton et al., 2010; Stotzer, 2014; Walker et al., 2018). Their pathways to system involvement are distinct from cis and hetereo people and are often characterized by abuse, discrimination, exclusion, and trauma (Schmitz et al., 2020).

This chapter examines LGBTQA+ victimization to broaden the understanding of Queer issues within the US carceral system and the complexities of multiplicative marginalization. First, we provide an overview of the link between victimization and system involvement among LGBTQA+ people, often beginning with contact in the juvenile justice system. Next, we discuss contexts of incarceration and supervision that cause increased vulnerability and secondary victimization among LGBTQA+ individuals. Finally, we provide research and policy recommendations to improve conditions for LGBTQA+ individuals and reduce unnecessary systemic trauma.

Victimization and Pathways to System Involvement

LGBTQA+ people face varied risks and experiences of victimization (Conover-Williams & Teal, 2019; Langenderfer-Magruder et al., 2016). For example, one study found that LGB participants reported more childhood psychological and physical abuse by parents or caretakers, more childhood sexual abuse, more partner psychological and physical victimization in adulthood, and more sexual assault experiences in adulthood in comparison to hetero participants (Balsam et al., 2005). Within their families, LGBTQA+ youth face increased victimization and exclusion due to their identities and sexuality (Conover-Williams & Teal, 2019). When LGBTQA+ people are of color, the likelihood of victimization in general is even higher (Hodge & Sexton, 2020; Hunt & Moodie-Mills, 2012; Woods et al., 2013).

LGBTQA+ people tend to have fewer protective safeguards (e.g., family, school, work support) than cis and hetero peers (Conover-Williams & Teal, 2019). LGBTQA+ youth'

DOI: 10.4324/9781003400981-17

experiences in schools create particularly discriminatory and challenging conditions. LGBTQA+ youth, especially racially marginalized, are more likely to be expelled or harshly disciplined than their heterosexual counterparts despite committing similar infractions (Snapp et al., 2015). Likewise, LGBTQA+ youth are often punished harshly for public displays of affection and dress code violations (Garnette et al., 2011). LGBTQA+ youth also experience increased rates of victimization and bullying (physical and online) by peers (Clark et al., 2020; Horn et al., 2009; Kosciw et al., 2013) and are discriminated against by administrators, educators, and staff (Snapp et al., 2015). Adverse school experiences with peers and school staff contribute to LGBTQA+ youths' social exclusion and isolation, interpersonal problems, low academic performance, discipline and truancy problems, and mental health issues that can result in death (i.e., suicide; Clark et al., 2020; Poteat et al., 2011). These circumstances place LGBTQA+ youth at increased risk for involvement in the juvenile justice system (Mountz, 2020).

LGBTQA+ youth are often underserved within child welfare systems, acting as a funnel to system involvement (Mountz, 2020). Although underexplored among LGBTQA+ populations, the gendered pathways perspective indicates that victimization, abuse, and trauma are major pathways to system involvement among girls and women (Boppre et al., 2018) but may also apply to LGBTQA+ populations. LGBTQA+ youth may run away from home to escape abuse, sexual violence, discrimination, and rejection within the home (Holsinger & Hodge, 2016; Kosciw et al., 2013; Mountz, 2020; Robinson, 2020). They may resort to criminalized and vulnerable acts (i.e., sex work/exploitation, drug sales) in order to survive on the streets (Conover-Williams & Teal, 2019; Nazaretian, 2019; Sexton et al., 2010). These circumstances place LGBTQA+ individuals at further risk for victimization. Victimization has direct links to mental health concerns, including anxiety, depression, post-traumatic stress disorder (PTSD), and self-harm (Steinberg & Lassiter, 2018). Research indicates that generally LGBTQA+ people have higher rates of mental health issues than their cis and hetero counterparts (Nazaretian, 2019). Untreated mental health issues can lead to adverse impacts, including engagement in criminalized substance use to medicate underlying symptoms of trauma (e.g., Boppre & Boyer, 2021).

LGBTQA+ people also face distinct circumstances for reporting or seeking help for victimization. Services for victimization, especially IPV, are lacking for sexually marginalized individuals. LGBTQA+ people face increased barriers to seeking help due to valid concerns over homophobia and transphobia (Bornstein et al., 2006). LGBTQA+ people may also be hesitant to seek assistance from police as responding officers may victim blame or respond with force (Buist & Stone, 2014). Multiple recent studies indicate that the interactions trans people have with law enforcement are related to discomfort in reporting victimization, whether that is due to mistrust, fear of retribution, or personal safety, and failure of police to believe them, despite changes in legislation (Dario et al., 2020; Grant et al., 2011; Hodge & Sexton, 2020; James et al., 2016; Owen et al., 2018; Serpe & Nadal, 2017; Woods et al., 2013). Accordingly, secondary victimization by law enforcement prevents LGBTQA+ people from seeking help when victimized.

Incarceration and Supervision

LGBTQA+ youth face distinct and increased risks for system involvement, beginning during childhood/adolescence and extending into adulthood (Snapp et al., 2015; Russel & Fish, 2016; Meyer & Frost, 2013). Within the US Juvenile Justice System, LGBTQA+ youths constitute roughly 13 to 15% of the population (Irvine, 2010; Holsinger & Hodge, 2016). Among those arrested and detained every year, it is estimated that 300,000 are trans, gay, or gender nonconforming, 60% of whom are Latino or Black (Hunt & Moodie-Mills, 2012).

Relative to the general population, LGBTQA+ adults are three times more likely to experience incarceration (Meyer et al., 2017). Within LGBTQA+ communities, certain members are mistreated and discriminated against at higher rates, namely trans and gender nonconforming individuals (Buist & Stone, 2014; Jenness & Fenstermaker, 2016; Nadal, 2020; Reisner et al., 2014; Rosenberg & Oswin, 2015; Sexton et al., 2010). According to the Vera Institute of Justice, 16% of trans adults have been incarcerated compared to cis adults at 2.7% (Zavidow, 2016). The likelihood of incarceration is compounded when a trans person is also racially marginalized. Specifically, when a trans person is Black, there is a higher chance of being incarcerated than non-Black trans and cis people (Grant et al., 2011). Accordingly, among the two million incarcerated individuals in the US, LGBTQA+ people are disproportionately visible (Braunstein, 2017; Pattillo et al., 2004).

Despite their overrepresentation, the US carceral system continues to enact policies and procedures that are harmful to LGBTQ+ clients (Boppre, 2019). As discussed, the link between victimization and system involvement is particularly strong among LGBTQA+ people as they are more likely to experience victimization relative to cis and hetero people (Conover-Williams & Teal, 2019). Yet, symptoms of trauma may be exacerbated due to a lack of trauma-responsive care, and culturally-responsive care (Boppre, 2019). Correctional facilities are gendered and sexualized environments, where incarcerated individuals are housed based on binary and biological sex (Sumner & Sexton, 2015). Invasive protocols (i.e., strip searches) oftentimes traumatize LGBTQA+ people, which can retraumatize those who have been victims of sexual violence. LGBTQ+ clients also face discriminatory interpersonal interactions with staff (Boppre, 2018; Kerrison, 2018) and other clients as well, shaped by homophobia and transphobia (Mountz, 2020).

Additionally, LGBTQA+ people are more likely to be placed in solitary confinement (Meyer et al., 2017). Their placement in solitary is justified as a measure of protection from actual or potential victimization from other clients, through administrative segregation or protective custody. Yet, solitary confinement is the same response to disciplinary infractions and is used as punishment (Boppre, 2019). Placement in solitary confinement, especially long-term, has been shown to lead to significant adverse mental and physical effects, including anxiety, depression, psychosis, heart palpitations, weight loss, and suicide (Shalev, 2014). Such impacts are especially concerning for LGBTQA+ people as they already face higher rates of mental health symptoms that can be worsened by solitary confinement (Nazaretian, 2019).

Beyond a lack of inclusive services and interactions, LGBTQA+ individuals face increased risks of victimization while incarcerated (Meyer et al., 2017; Mogul et al., 2011). According to the Bureau of Justice Statistics, LGBQ people are ten times as likely to be sexually victimized by another incarcerated person and 2.6 times as likely to be victimized by staff as hetero incarcerated people (Beck et al., 2013). Further, more than one-third of incarcerated trans people were sexually assaulted in comparison to 4% of all incarcerated people (Beck et al., 2013). In a recent study, James et al. (2016) found that trans people are five times as likely to be sexually assaulted by staff. In Californian male prisons, sexual assault was 13 times more prevalent among trans women then trans men (Jenness et al., 2007).

In 2003, the Prison Rape Elimination Act (PREA) was enacted following a recurring call for regulations against sexual victimization within carceral spaces. Under PREA, there is a zero-tolerance policy toward sexual abuse and harassment, where staff must undergo training on how to investigate allegations properly. Before intake, all people must be screened for heightened vulnerability to sexual abuse where LGBTQA+ status is a factor to be addressed. Further, if a person is victimized, they are to receive medical and mental health care and have access to victim support services.

All incarcerated people are at risk of sexual victimization. However, as LGBTQA+ people are at heightened risk, PREA is significant to the LGBTQA+ population (Shay, 2013). In 2012, incarcerated trans people were amended to PREA as evidence demonstrated they were at higher risk of sexual victimization by both staff and incarcerated people (Malkin & DeJong, 2019; Jenness et al., 2007; Jenness & Fenstermaker, 2016). To date, it is unknown whether PREA reduces sexual victimization or increases reporting among LGBTQA+ people. Conflicting policies and disregard for PREA regulations by staff reverting to former policies place LGBTQA+ people at continual risk of sexual victimization in carceral settings (Malkin & DeJong, 2019).

Since the federal implementation of PREA, there is evidence of inconsistent policy implementation across state and local governments, namely related to protective custody and segregated housing policies (Malkin & DeJong, 2019). For example, under PREA, LGBTQA+ people are barred from being placed in solitary confinement indefinitely for their protection, and they should not be segregated unless there is a consent decree. Nonetheless, there is evidence that staff and administrators continue to place LGBTQA+ people, particularly trans people, in long-term solitary confinement at increased rates despite PREA regulations (Andasheva, 2016; James & Venko, 2021; Malkin & DeJong, 2019; Martin, 2018; Trimble, 2019).

To summarize, LGBTQA+ individuals face higher risks for victimization in the community and within the carceral system. Despite their overrepresentation in US carceral spaces, LGBTQA+ people's distinct experiences and needs are ignored or dismissed. Oppressive and punitive environments do not address the complex underlying trauma experienced by LGBTQA+ people. Instead, LGBTQA+ people face secondary victimization and systemic trauma once involved with the carceral state.

Research and Policy Recommendations

This chapter demonstrates the distinct circumstances of victimization within LGBTQA+ persons' lives that persist through system involvement. Several steps must be taken to prevent their system involvement to begin with, as disrupting such pathways will reduce the systemic harm faced once in juvenile and adult carceral systems. For LGBTQA+ youth, navigating their identities when living in unaccepting and unsupportive family environments poses serious mental health challenges, including suicidality. In addition, most traumas that likely create pathways to system involvement for LGBTQA+ youth stem from the family unit. Therefore, family involvement in preventive mental health treatment is necessary, whether through individual or group activities that focus on trauma and maltreatment. Maintaining family connectedness through inclusive trauma-informed practices is critical for shaping self-esteem and life outcomes, reducing stressors, and fostering resilience.

For decades community-based services have been shown to be crucial for positive youth development, well-being, and mental health outcomes of at-risk youth (Eccles & Gootman, 2002; Erdem et al., 2016; Iachini et al., 2016). As LGBTQA+ youth become increasingly visible in society, they have expressed a desire for resources and support (Belknap et al., 2014; Kahle & Rosenbaum, 2021). LGBTQA+ community-based services provide identity development tools, aid in overcoming family issues, and provide safe spaces that alleviate feelings of isolation (Allen et al., 2012; Fish et al., 2019; Herdt & Boxer, 1996; Lerner et al., 2009; Paceley, 2016). Further, LGBTQA+ community-based services foster positive relationships with peers and adults as well as play a critical role in the prevention of substance use and abuse. Yet, despite the role of LGBTQA+ community-based services, financial support from stakeholders is found to be lacking (Fish et al., 2019). More efforts must support community-based services as they have long-lasting positive effects on the LGBTQA+ population, which can help prevent their system involvement. A possible way to increase visibility is through service providers integrating issues faced by LGBTQA+ people into discussions of support services.

School acts as a protective factor for many youth, yet for LGBTQA+ youth, the exclusion and disciplinary practices can lead directly to the juvenile justice system (Toomey et al., 2011). Despite the prevalence of abuse for LGBTQA+ youth in school settings, 26 states and one territory do not have anti-bullying laws that protect these youths (Movement Advancement Project, 2021). Accordingly, policymakers must push for anti-bullying laws that include sexual orientation and gender identity as protected categories on a state level. Further, LGBTQA+ inclusive curriculum and school-based supports are the most promising in improving school climates and educational outcomes for LGBTQA+ youth (Kosciw et al., 2013; Kosciw et al., 2015; Russel & Fish, 2016). Training school staff on LGBTQA+ youth identities, issues, and risk factors can increase school performance and engagement, increase feelings of safety, and lower absenteeism which could potentially halt pathways into juvenile and adult carceral systems. In training school staff on LGBTQA+ youth identities, issues, and risk factors, school staff is more likely to intervene if abuse, harassment, and discrimination occur.

While substantially reducing the nation's reliance on punishment and incarceration should be the goal, reforms should also be made to the carceral system itself. As LGBTQA+ people face significant victimization, abuse, and trauma, trauma-responsive care must be prioritized (Steinberg & Lassiter, 2018). Trauma-responsive care takes a universal approach to providing services and treatment that assumes every client has experienced traumatizing events (Steinberg & Lassiter, 2018). Staff are therefore better able to identify and treat symptoms of trauma.

Yet, experiences of trauma are intersectional and must also be addressed through a culturally-responsive approach (De La Rue & Ortega, 2019). LGBTQA+ people, especially those racially marginalized, have faced discrimination and exclusion in the community, as insidious and systemic trauma shaped by homophobia and transphobia (Goldsmith et al., 2014; Mountz, 2020). Therefore, staff must also be trained in intersectionality-responsive approaches, to address the complex realities of LGBTQA+ people in the carceral system (Boppre, 2019). This includes treatment and services specifically for LGBTQA+ people, similarly situated staff, and addressing oppression and marginalization faced in the carceral system and community (Boppre, 2019). Confirmation of search and consent before a search, respect requested name, and pronouns, neutral non-confrontational tones are recommended to increase inclusivity and avoid exacerbating symptoms of trauma.

Given the multitude of adverse mental and physical consequences, placement in solitary confinement, an approach used to punish within carceral settings, is not advised as a protective measure (Boppre, 2019). Such practices serve to further exclude and harm LGBTQA+ people. Additionally, more efforts must be made to prevent and address the victimization of LGBTQA+ people within carceral settings, including accountability and safe reporting practices under PREA. For example, placing someone in solitary confinement who reports sexual violence may deter individuals from reporting.

We hope our chapter sparks increased awareness, research, and activism toward LGBTQA+ victimization, both within carceral settings and the community. Of note, we found significant gaps in the literature related to LGBTQA+ people's pathways into system involvement and their experiences in carceral settings. Future LGBTQA+ scholars must be supported to engage in such research with those directly impacted. Similar to Mountz (2020), we especially advise community-based participatory action research to engage *with* LGBTQA+ people on developing resources and policy changes.

References

Allen, K. D., Hammack, P. L., & Himes, H. L. (2012). Analysis of GLBTQ youth community-based programs in the United States. *Journal of Homosexuality*, 59, 1289–1306.

Andasheva, F. (2016). Aren't I a woman: Deconstructing sex discrimination and freeing transgender women from solitary confinement. *Florida International University Law Review*, 12, 117–150.

Balsam, K. F., Rothblum, E. D., & Beauchaine, T. P. (2005). Victimization over the life span: A comparison of lesbian, gay, bisexual, and heterosexual siblings. *Journal of Consulting and Clinical Psychology*, 73(3), 477.

Beck, A., Berzofsky, M., Caspar, R., & Krebs, C. (2013). *Sexual victimization in prisons and Jails reported by inmates, 2011–12 (Report No. NCJ 241399)*. Retrieved from www.bjs.gov/content/pub/pdf/svpjri1112.pdf.

Belknap, J., Holsinger, K., & Little, J. S. (2014). Lesbian, gay, and bisexual youth incarcerated in delinquent facilities. In *Handbook of LGBT communities, crime, and justice* (pp. 207–228). New York: Springer.

Braunstein, M. D. (2017). The five stages of LGBTQ discrimination and its effects on mass incarceration. *Miami Race and Social Justice Law Review*, 217–246.

Boppre, B. (2018). *Intersections between gender, race, and justice-involvement: A mixed methods analysis of women's experiences in the Oregon criminal justice system* (Unpublished doctoral dissertation). Las Vegas: University of Nevada.

Boppre, B. (2019). Improving correctional strategies for women at the margins: Recommendations for an intersectionally-responsive approach. *Corrections*, 4(3), 195–221.

Boppre, B., & Boyer, C. (2021). "The traps started during my childhood": The role of substance abuse in women's responses to adverse childhood experiences (ACEs). *Journal of Aggression, Maltreatment & Trauma*, 30(4), 429–449.

Boppre, B., Salisbury, E. J., & Parker, J. (2018). Pathways to crime. In H. Pontell & K. Holtfreter (Eds.), *Oxford research encyclopedia of criminology and criminal justice*. Oxford: Oxford University Press.

Bornstein, D. R., Fawcett, J., Sullivan, M., Senturia, K. D., & Shiu-Thornton, S. (2006). Understanding the experiences of lesbian, bisexual and trans survivors of domestic violence: A qualitative study. *Journal of Homosexuality*, 51(1), 159–181.

Buist, C. L., & Stone, C. (2014). Transgender victims and offenders: Failures of the United States criminal justice system and the necessity of queer criminology. *Critical Criminology*, 22(1), 35–47.

Carpenter, L. F., & Marshall, R. B. (2017). Walking while trans: Profiling of transgender women by law enforcement, and the problem of proof. *William & Mary Journal of Women and the Law*, 24(1), 5–38.

Clark, K. A., Cochran, S. D., Maiolatesi, A. J., & Pachankis, J. E. (2020). Prevalence of bullying among youth classified as LGBTQ who died by suicide as reported in the national violent death reporting system, 2003–2017. *JAMA Pediatrics*, 174(12), 1211–1213.

Conover-Williams, M., & Teal, J. (2019). LGBTQ, criminal offending, and victimization. In F. Bernat (Ed.), *The encyclopedia of women and crime* (pp. 659–660). Hoboken, NJ: Wiley.

Dario, L. M., Fradella, H. F., Verhagen, M., & Parry, M. M. (2020). Assessing LGBT people's perceptions of police legitimacy. *Journal of Homosexuality*, 67(7), 885–915.

De La Rue, L., & Ortega, L. (2019). Intersectional trauma-responsive care: A framework for humanizing care for justice involved girls and women of color. *Journal of Aggression, Maltreatment & Trauma*, 28(4), 502–517.

Eccles, J., & Gootman, J. A. (2002). *Community programs to promote youth development Committee on community-level programs for youth. Board on children, youth, and families. Commission on behavioral and social sciences education, national research council and institute of medicine.* Washington, DC: National Academies of Science.

Erdem, G., DuBois, D. L., Larose, S., De Wit, D., & Lipman, E. L. (2016). Mentoring relationships, positive development, youth emotional and behavioral problems: Investigation of a mediational model. *Journal of Community Psychology*, 44, 464–483.

Fish, J. N., Moody, R. L., Grossman, A. H., & Russell, S. T. (2019). LGBTQ youth-serving community-based organizations: Who participates and what difference does it make? *Journal of Youth and Adolescence*, 48(12), 2418–2431.

Garnette, L., Irvine, A., Reyes, C., & Wilber, S. (2011). Lesbian, gay, bisexual, and transgender (LGBT) youth and the juvenile justice system. In F. T. Sherman & F. H. Jacobs (Eds.), *Juvenile justice: Advancing research, policy, and practice* (pp. 156–173). Hoboken, NJ: Wiley.

Goldsmith, R. E., Martin, C. G., & Smith, C. P. (2014). Systemic trauma. *Journal of Trauma & Dissociation*, 15(2), 117–132.

Grant, J. M., Mottet, L. A., Tanis, J., Harrison, J., Herman, J. L., & Keisling, M. (2011). *Injustice at every turn: A report of the national transgender discrimination survey.* Washington, DC: National Center for Transgender Equality and National Gay and Lesbian Task Force.

Herdt, G., & Boxer, A. (1996). *Children of horizons.* Boston, MA: Beacon Press.

Hodge, J. P., & Sexton, L. (2020). Examining the blue line in the rainbow: The interactions and perceptions of law enforcement among lesbian, gay, bisexual, transgender and queer communities. *Police Practice and Research*, 21(3), 246–263.

Holsinger, K., & Hodge, J. (2016). The experiences of lesbian, gay, bisexual, and transgender girls in juvenile justice systems. *Feminist Criminology*, 11(1), 23–47.

Horn, S. S., Kosciw, J. G., & Russell, S. T. (2009). Special issue introduction: New research on lesbian, gay, bisexual, and transgender youth: Studying lives in context. *Journal of Youth Adolescence*, 38, 863–866.

Hunt, J., & Moodie-Mills, A. (2012). The unfair criminalization of gay and transgender youth: An overview of the experiences of LGBT youth in the juvenile justice system. *Center for American Progress*, 29, 1–12.

Iachini, A. L., Bell, B. A., Lohman, M., Beets, M. W., & Reynolds, J. F. (2016). Maximizing the contribution of after-school programs to positive youth development: Exploring leadership and implementation within girls on the run. *Children & Schools*, 39, 43–52.

Irvine, A. (2010). We've had three of them: Addressing the invisibility of lesbian, gay, bisexual, and gender nonconforming youths in the juvenile justice system. *Columbia Journal of Gender & Law*, 19, 675–701.

James, K., & Vanko, E. (2021). *The impacts of solitary confinement. Evidence brief: Vera institute of justice*, April. Retrieved from www.vera.org/downloads/publications/the-impacts-of-solitary-confinement.pdf.

James, S. E., Herman, J. L., Rankin, S., Keisling, M., Mottet, L., & Anafi, M. (2016). *The report of the 2015 U.S. Transgender survey.* National Center for Transgender Equality. Retrieved from https://transequality.org/sites/default/files/docs/usts/USTS-Executive-Summary-Dec17.pdf.

Jenness, V., & Fenstermaker, S. (2016). Forty years after Brownmiller: Prisons for men, transgender inmates, and the rape of the feminine. *Gender & Society*, 30(1), 14–29.

Jenness, V., Maxson, C. L., Matsuda, K. N., & Sumner, J. M. (2007). Violence in California correctional facilities: An empirical examination of sexual assault. *Bulletin*, 2(2), 1–4.

Kahle, L. L., & Rosenbaum, J. (2021). What staff need to know: Using elements of gender-responsive programming to create safer environments for system-involved LGBTQ girls and women. *Criminal Justice Studies*, 34(1), 1–15.

Kerrison, E. M. (2018). Risky business, risk assessment, and other heteronormative misnomers in women's community corrections and reentry planning. *Punishment & Society*, 20(1), 134–151.

Kosciw, J. G., Palmer, N. A., & Kull, R. M. (2015). Reflecting resiliency: Openness about sexual orientation and/or gender identity and its relationship to well-being and educational outcomes for LGBT students. *American Journal of Community Psychology*, 55(1–2), 167–178.

Kosciw, J. G., Palmer, N. A., Kull, R. M., & Greytak, E. A. (2013). The effect of negative school climate on academic outcomes for LGBT youth and the role of in-school supports. *Journal of School Violence*, 12(1), 45–63.

Langenderfer-Magruder, L., Walls, N. E., Whitfield, D. L., Brown, S. M., & Barrett, C. M. (2016). Partner violence victimization among lesbian, gay, bisexual, transgender, and Queer youth: Associations among risk factors. *Child and Adolescent Social Work Journal*, 33(1), 55–68.

Lerner, J. V., Phelps, E., Forman, Y., & Bowers, E. P. (2009). Positive youth development. In R. M. Lerner & L. Steinberg (Eds.), *Handbook of adolescent psychology: Individual bases of adolescent development* (pp. 524–558). Hoboken, NJ: Wiley.

Malkin, M. L., & Dejong, C. (2019). Protections for transgender inmates under PREA: A comparative study of correctional policies in the United States. *Sexuality Research and Social Policy*, 16, 393–407.

Martin, A. (2018). *Challenging corrections: Empowering LGBTQ folx* (Unpublished undergraduate thesis). University of Iowa.

Meyer, I. H., Flores, A. R., Stemple, L., Romero, A. P., Wilson, B. D. M., & Herman, J. L. (2017). Incarceration rates and traits of sexual minorities in the United States: National inmate survey, 2011–2012. *American Journal of Public Health*, 107(2), 234–240.

Meyer, I. H., & Frost, D. M. (2013). Minority stress and the health of sexual minorities. In C. J. Patterson & A. R. D'Augelli (Eds.), *Handbook of psychology and sexual orientation* (pp. 252–266). Oxford: Oxford University Press.

Mogul, J. L., Ritchie, A. J., & Whitlock, K. (2011). *Queer (In)justice: The criminalization of LGBT people in the United States*. Boston, MA: Beacon.

Mountz, S., Capous-Desyllas, M., & Sevillano, L. (2020). Educational trajectories of youth formerly in foster care who are LGBTQ: Before, during, and after emancipation. *Child Welfare*, 97(6), 77–99.

Movement Advancement Project. *Equality maps: Safe schools laws*. Retrieved May 25, 2021, from www.lgbtmap.org/equality-maps/safe_school_laws.

Nadal, K. L. Y. (2020). *Queering law and order: LGBTQ communities and the criminal justice system*. Blue Ridge Summit, PA: Lexington Books.

Nazaretian, A. (2019). LGBTQ offenders and imprisonment. In F. Bernat (Ed.), *The Encyclopedia of women and crime* (pp. 660–661). Hoboken, NJ: Wiley.

Owen, S. S., Burke, T. W., Few-Demo, A. L., & Natwick, J. (2018). Perceptions of the police by LGBT communities. *American Journal of Criminal Justice*, 43, 668–693.

Paceley, M. S. (2016). Gender and sexual minority youth in nonmetropolitan communities: Individual- and community-level needs for support. *Families in Society: The Journal of Contemporary Social Services*, 97, 77–85.

Pattillo, M., Western, B., & Weiman, D. (Eds.). (2004). *Imprisoning America: The social effects of mass incarceration*. New York: Russell Sage Foundation.

Poteat, V. P., Mereish, E. H., DiGiovanni, C. D., & Koenig, B. W. (2011). The effects of general and homophobic victimization on adolescents' psychosocial and educational concerns: The importance of intersecting identities and parent support. *Journal of Counseling Psychology*, 58, 597–609.

Reisner, S. L., Bailey, Z., & Sevelius, J. (2014). Racial/ethnic disparities in history of incarceration, experiences of victimization, and associated health indicators among transgender women in the US. *Women & Health*, 54(8), 750–767.

Robinson, B. A. (2020). The lavender scare in homonormative times: Policing, hyper-incarceration, and LGBTQ youth homelessness. *Gender & Society*, 34(2), 210–232.

Rosenberg, R., & Oswin, N. (2015). Trans embodiment in carceral space: Hypermasculinity and the US prison industrial complex. *Gender, Place & Culture*, 22(9), 1269–1286.

Russel, S. T., & Fish, J. N. (2016). Mental health in lesbian, gay, bisexual, and transgender (LGBT) youth. *Annual Review of Clinical Psychology*, 12, 465–487.

Schmitz, R. M., Robinson, B. A., & Sanchez, J. (2020). Intersectional family systems approach: LGBTQ+ Latino/a youth, family dynamics, and stressors. *Family Relations*, 69(4), 832–848.

Serpe, C. R., & Nadal, K. L. (2017). Perceptions of police: Experiences in the trans* community. *Journal of Gay & Lesbian Social Services*, 29(3), 280–299.

Sexton, L., Jenness, V., & Sumner, J. M. (2010). Where the margins meet: A demographic assessment of transgender inmates in men's prisons. *Justice Quarterly*, 27(6), 835–866.

Shalev, S. (2014). *Solitary confinement as a prison health issue*. World Health Organisation, Prisons, and Health. Retrieved from www.euro.who.int/en/health-topics/health-determinants/prisons-and-health/publications/2014/prisons-and-health/report-by-chapters/chapter-5.-solitary-confinement-as-a-prison-health-issue.

Shay, G. (2013). PREA's elusive promise: Can DOJ regulations protect LGBT incarcerated people? *Loyola Journal of Public Interest Law*, 15, 343–356.

Snapp, S. D., Hoenig, J. M., Fields, A., & Russell, S. T. (2015). Messy, butch, and Queer: LGBTQ youth and the school-to-prison pipeline. *Journal of Adolescent Research*, 30(1), 57–82.

Snapp, S. D., McGuire, J. K., Sinclair, K. O., Gabrion, K., & Russel, S. T. (2015). LGBTQ-inclusive curricula: Why supportive curricula matter. *Sex Education*, 15(6), 580–596.

Steinberg, J. L., & Lassiter, W. L. (2018). Toward a trauma-responsive juvenile justice system. *North Carolina Medical Journal*, 79(2), 115–118.

Stotzer, R. L. (2014). Law enforcement and criminal justice personnel interactions with transgender people in the United States: A literature review. *Aggression and Violent Behavior*, 19(3), 263–277.

Sumner, J., & Sexton, L. (2015). Lost in translation: Looking for transgender identity in women's prisons and locating aggressors in prisoner culture. *Critical Criminology*, 23(1), 1–20.

Toomey, R. B., Ryan, C., Diaz, R. M., & Russell, S. T. (2011). High school gay—straight alliances (GSAs) and young adult well-being: An examination of GSA presence, participation, and perceived effectiveness. *Applied Developmental Science*, 15(4), 175–185.

Trimble, P. E. (2019). Ignored LGBTQ prisoners: Discrimination, rehabilitation, and mental health services during incarceration. *LGBTQ Policy Journal*, 9, 31–38.

Walker, A., Sexton, L., Valcore, J., Sumner, J., & Wodda, J. (2018). Transgender and non-binary individuals. In C. Roberson (Ed.), *Routledge handbook of social, economic, and criminal justice* (pp. 220–233). New York: Routledge.

Woods, J. B., Galvan, F. H., Bazargan, M., Herman, J. L., & Chen, Y. T. (2013). Latina transgender women's interactions with law enforcement in Los Angeles county. *Policing*, 7(4), 379–391.

Zavidow, E. (2016). Vera institute of justice. In *Transgender people at higher risk for justice system involvement*, May 10. Retrieved from www.vera.org/blog/gender-and-justice-in-america/transgender-people-at-higher-risk-for-justice-system-involvement.

Chapter 15

What About Us?

The Omission of Queer Experiences in Criminology and Criminal Justice Curricula

Alessandra Early and Brian E. Rainey

During their second semester teaching, one of the authors was invited to guest lecture about Queer criminology and their importance to a group of predominantly undergraduate criminology and criminal justice majors. While discussing the violence that many Queer, trans, nonbinary, and gender diverse people experience at the hands of the state, a student promptly raised her hand. Although the author *had* told the students to interrupt with questions, the anger in this person's eyes, coupled with the large scowl on her face, told the author that they were in for a treat. After the student was called on, they whipped out their phone and the author recalls them reading the following scripture from their Bible app:

> Genesis 2:20–24: So the man gave names to all the livestock, the birds in the sky and all the wild animals. But for Adam no suitable helper was found. So the Lord God caused the man to fall into a deep sleep; and while he was sleeping, he took one of the man's ribs and then closed up the place with flesh. Then the Lord God made a woman from the rib he had taken out of the man, and he brought her to the man. The man said, "This is now bone of my bones and flesh of my flesh; she shall be called 'woman,' for she was taken out of man." That is why a man leaves his father and mother and is united to his wife, and they become one flesh.

The silence, save for the chairs creaking under the other students' uncomfortable fidgeting, was thundering—or perhaps that was the sound of the author's own heartbeat pounding in their ears. The student finished reading and proceeded to hurl an onslaught of statements, masqueraded as questions that were centered around the general homophobic and transphobic idea that "since all this Queerness is a choice or a phase, these people are choosing to be treated this way."

Another one of our authors experienced a similarly problematic—albeit less confrontational—instance of transphobia while attending a lecture on contemporary issues in correctional settings as a teaching assistant during their first year as a Ph.D. student. Considering the pervasiveness of sexual assault within prison, the professor, whom the author was assisting, began speaking about how trans people within these settings "further complicate" the issue. According to this professor, trans women in men's prisons ought to be kept separate from the men or in solitary confinement "for their own protection." Although the professor seemed to recognize the increased risk of victimization that many trans people face while surviving incarceration, they repeatedly presented trans people as a "complication" and blamed them for their own victimization. Moreover, the professor never even acknowledged how forcibly placing trans people within these gendered

DOI: 10.4324/9781003400981-18

institutions (Britton, 1997) that do not match their gender is highly violent in itself. To make matters worse, on at least one occasion, the professor uttered a transphobic slur, which he surreptitiously attempted to shroud under the guise of "playing devil's advocate" and speaking from the perspective of an incarcerated person. With a single word, many in the lecture hall squirmed with discomfort, including a trans student who had previously come out to the author.

While these experiences might be considered out of the ordinary, the hostility and heckling that can manifest around discussing Queerness[1] in the classroom is something with which many educators, and Queer students like the authors, are all too familiar. Supplemented by personal experiences, this chapter will discuss the scarce and haphazard incorporation of inclusive conversations about gender and sexuality within criminology/criminal justice courses. We argue that the subversive erasure of Queerness within criminology and criminal justice classrooms can function as a form of symbolic erasure and violence for Queer students and communities. As such, we advocate for further respectful inclusion of Queerness and Queer topics within criminology and criminal justice classrooms. We also discuss how the ways that educators teach these topics can traumatize and trigger Queer students in addition to reinforcing prejudicial beliefs. We conclude with a brief discussion of best and sensitizing practices for criminology and criminal justice educators when covering Queerness within the classroom.

The Exclusion of Gender and Sexuality in Criminology and Criminal Justice Courses

Between the two authors, we have taken over 16 years of sociology, criminology, and criminal justice courses at the high school, undergraduate, and graduate level. Out of all of these, one author has taken only two courses explicitly dedicated to conversations about gender and sexuality, which were solely offered in sociology and women's, gender, and sexuality studies departments at the graduate level.[2] The other author was only offered one course during their undergraduate career that focused on violence against women; however, this course narrowly focused on cisgender and heterosexual people. Similarly, in our other classes, many of them designated core courses (e.g., theory and corrections), discussions of gender or sexuality, *if* included, were primarily centered on the experiences of cisgender heterosexual women. As young Queer students, both as undergraduates and graduates, we learned two valuable lessons from the exclusion of any material beyond cisheteronormativity: 1) That the perpetual and insidious violence that our communities face was deemed unworthy of criminological and pedagogical attention, and 2) That we could expect to be tasked with doing the emotional labor of bringing up and defending Queer issues and the contributions of Queer scholars.

The exclusion of Queer experiences within criminology and criminal justice in American curricula is similar to the initial (and ongoing) omissions of explicit conversations about racialized inequalities. However, there has been a recent uptick in the creation of courses dedicated to the intersection of race/ethnicity and the criminal justice system (Cannon & Dirks-Linhorst, 2006). As Fradella et al. (2009) explained, "While criminal justice education has strived to become less racist and less sexist (important goals, both), corresponding efforts to combat anti-GLBT bias have been lacking" (p. 129). Similarly, analyses of criminal justice textbooks have found sparse engagement with and inclusion of Queer issues or experiences (Olivero & Murataya, 2001).

A survey exploring the state of Queer inclusion within US criminal justice undergraduate programs found that while some departments offered courses focused on race/ethnicity or gender, single-discipline criminal justice departments—meaning criminal justice only departments—were significantly less likely to offer courses dedicated to Queer issues and content outside of cisgender and heterosexual conceptualizations of gender. In fact, out of the 188 participating departments, including those outside of criminal justice only departments—such as combined and other social science departments—there was only one reported course that focused on sexual orientation and the law; this course was also cross-listed with a women's studies department (Cannon & Dirks-Linhorst, 2006).

This disparity might be reflective of a perception of Queer issues as an invasion of liberal propaganda within the classroom or that some faculty may not believe that they could incorporate Queerness since they have not been trained in the area (Fradella et al., 2009). However, both justifications (and any justification for that matter) for the omission of Queerness in the classroom are extremely troubling to us. By excluding Queerness, unintentionally or not, educators wordlessly declare that the very real violence that many Queer people and communities experience is inconsequential. This wilful neglect transforms classrooms into homophobic and transphobic spaces.

Literature has shown that criminal justice undergraduate students, particularly cisgender male students (Hayes & Ball, 2010) and those preparing for a career in law enforcement (Miller, 2001; Olivero & Murataya, 2001), are more homophobic than students in other fields of study (Hayes & Ball, 2009). Similarly, criminal justice majors are often less accepting—and have negative views—of Queer communities (Cannon, 2005; Ventura et al., 2004).[3] Consider the snide comment heard by one of the authors in a foundational class. After presenting on the experiences of violence that some trans people who are incarcerated face and the implications of embedding federal protections for them within the Prison Rape Elimination Act, the author overheard one of their classmates say to their friend, "Don't drop the soap." Both proceeded to quietly chuckle amongst themselves. For some, it may be tempting to excuse this behavior and consider it a crude joke. However, the lack of response by the professor and other students in the class is reflective of heteronormative pop-culture depictions of sexual assault as comedic (Levan et al., 2011), the perpetuation of Queer labeled behavior (e.g., stereotypes that consider anal sex to be only for gay men) as inherently "rapey," and "the belief that gay[4] prisoners deserve or enjoy rape" (Cahill, 2017, p. 8).

While no research, to our knowledge, has explored cis-heterosexist views among criminology or criminal justice graduate students, some have considered the resistance of heterosexual undergraduate law and justice students to engage with Queer topics (Hayes & Ball, 2010), the experiences of their Queer colleagues in law school (Austin et al., 1998; Ihrig, 1995), and the commonality of homophobic attitudes and sentiments among criminal justice undergraduates (Cannon, 2005; Cannon & Dirks-Linhorst, 2006; Miller, 2001; Ventura et al., 2004). Cannon and Dirks-Linhorst's (2006) work found that Queer identities are less likely to be included in hate crime courses compared to other identities. Encouraging discourses on gender and sexuality within a core first-year law and justice course at an Australian university, Hayes and Ball (2010) found that while some students were willing to reflect on and deconstruct their beliefs about Queerness, others with more deep-seated negative attitudes were unwilling to engage with such discussions. In fact, the students with negative attitudes viewed any engagement with Queerness as a personal threat to their heterosexuality (Hayes & Ball, 2010).[5]

Investigating the experiences of gay, lesbian, and bisexual law students, Ihrig (1995) described how these students are often silenced when they raise Queer issues, told that they need to separate their personal politics from their academic studies, forced to navigate linguistic violence and social ostracization, and rendered invisible in legal curricula and discussions (p. 558). Similarly, although 87% of students in Austin et al.'s (1998) study reported discussing Queer issues in one of their courses, the manner in which these issues were discussed was careless, given inadequate attention, and considered a joke. Consequentially, the classroom environment led some Queer students to feel discouraged to bring up Queer issues for fear of having to be "the voice" of their communities and forced to linguistically "come out" simply because of the heterosexist assumption that only Queer people will talk about Queer issues (Austin et al., 1998).

The stories of the students above remind us of our own traumas as Queer students navigating pervasive cis-heteronormative curricula and situations within criminology and criminal justice classrooms. In fact, we have grown almost comfortable with the awkward silence that inevitably follows when we challenge cis-heteronormative conceptualizations of gender and sexuality. While we have found some power within educating ourselves (and others) within Queer criminological traditions, we are concerned with the lack of intentional and institutional inclusion which can produce rippling layers of victimization that can extend outside of our classroom and into our communities.

If institutions and curricula do not include serious and meaningful discussions about the intersections of Queerness and the criminal justice system, then they can produce future educators who do not feel comfortable incorporating Queer topics within their classrooms and who do not "see the value of doing so in major courses" (Fradella et al., 2009, p. 133). Consequently, their students, who may be future educators themselves, may be forced to take our approach: self-education outside of regular graduate responsibilities. Or they may read their professors' omissions as indications that neither Queerness nor their Queer identities have a place in the classroom.

Additionally, students who are future practitioners are similarly disadvantaged, in a very precarious positions since they will spend a lot of time knowingly, or unknowingly, engaging with Queer communities and Queer colleagues. A considerable amount of research has underscored the heightened violence and vulnerability Queer communities face at the hands of criminal justice actors and how Queer criminal justice actors, themselves, can simultaneously perpetuate and be subjected to homophobia and transphobia (Bloomberg Law, 2020; Dwyer, 2008). Dwyer (2014), for example, explains how policing has, historically and contemporarily, been used as a tool of surveillance and violence against Queer communities. As a result, many Queer communities are afraid to report crimes to the police for fear of victimization by law enforcement officials (Cannon & Dirks-Linhorst, 2006). Similarly, some Queer police officers and lawyers have experienced homophobic harassment from their own colleagues (Bloomberg Law, 2020; Leinen, 1993), and some are afraid to be out at work for fear of subsequent victimization (Colvin, 2009).

In this regard, when we as educators omit Queerness in the classroom, intentionally or unintentionally, we perpetuate an insidious cycle that: 1) victimizes Queer students who are unable to see themselves, their experiences, and their communities taken seriously; 2) victimizes Queer communities through the future practitioners we fail to educate on these issues; and 3) does a great disservice to our cisgender heterosexual students who have not been pushed to consider identities outside of normative conceptualizations of gender and sexuality. As such, we agree with Cannon and Dirks-Linhorst's (2006) statement that, "criminal justice professionals are only as proficient in these community interactions as their education, training and personal attitudes permit" (p. 265).

The Inclusion of (Queer) Gender and Sexuality in Criminal Justice Courses

While we have illustrated how omitting discussions about Queer identities in the classroom can have significant and rippling consequences, it should also be noted that the inclusion of Queer topics in classroom discussions can have further implications. Remember that outspoken and religious student who hurled biblical quotes at one of the authors? You may be surprised to learn that the same student enrolled in the author's course the following semester. Each class became a battle between the author, who was attempting to transform the classroom into a Queer-friendly space to encourage discussions on LGBTQIA+ experiences within the criminal justice system, and the student, who met every conversation with contempt and occasionally made linguistically violent comments. For example, the student would make comments like, "Transsexuals[6] bring all this police violence on themselves because they choose to dress and behave that way" and "it's a sinful world—people just make up who they are . . . the Queers are following the devil straight down to hell." When the author approached a senior faculty member to alert them to the issue and seek advice early on, they were met with apathy. The faculty member said that the author was "kinda" bringing this on themselves for including inflammatory topics and that they should probably just remove it to "make it easier" on themselves; the author quickly and painfully realized that they were heading into uncharted waters. Furthermore, the author was already aware that the student's comments existed in a gray area of some legal protection offered by the United States Supreme Court via the First Amendment (Murray, 2016) and that institutions generally only label such behavior as hate speech if 1) it is a violation of the law; 2) it is in relation to prohibited "harassment"—a term often up for debate—of a protected class; and 3) it is a threat hurled at specific people. As a young educator, the author felt hamstrung. They could do little but meet each comment with responses such as, "One of our classroom agreements that we all decided on was to treat people and communities different from us with respect and compassion"; "Please be respectful of the course materials"; "That terminology is offensive for [X, Y, and Z reasons]. Please do not use that again in this classroom, but if you would like to discuss your feelings related to the course materials, feel free to see me after class."

Now, let's really test your memory. Remember when one of the authors encountered a professor who made some deeply troubling and transphobic comments about trans people in prison? Good. We know that the rights of trans people in prisons, and more broadly, are undoubtedly a crucial issue that deserve extensive discussion and attention within criminology and criminal justice classrooms. Yet, while that professor did include conversations about how trans people are forced to navigate carceral settings that are not affirming of their gender—which is, unfortunately, a topic quite rare in criminology and criminal justice classrooms—the ways in which the professor discussed trans people and their potential victimization within these settings completely missed the mark and further perpetuated transphobic sentiments. Had the professor included this topic in a respectful manner, where they refused to use transphobic and prejudicial language and shifted the blame and responsibility from trans people to the perpetrators of violence, then this would, perhaps, be an entirely different story. However, what the author found most disturbing was the trauma suffered by the one trans student in the classroom. That student later told the author that the whole situation had made them feel extremely uncomfortable.

Approaches to including Queer identities in criminological research—and social scientific work more generally—have historically been, for lack of a better term, "messy." From its very origin, criminology has demonized Queer people and, as Woods (2014) points out, the apparent "father of criminology"—whom we cheekily like to call "Daddy Lombroso"—developed criminal typologies that categorized cisgender gay men as a distinct type of criminal. Although many contemporary criminologists may dismiss Lombroso's views as antiquated, his early theories have inevitably shaped the field by embedding an association of Queerness with immorality and deviance (Woods, 2014; see also Cohen, 1955).[7]

Certain hegemonic methods for teaching Queer topics in the criminal justice classroom may also potentially limit students' understandings of the heightened interactions between Queerness and the criminal justice system, particularly in regard to victimization(s). Miller's (2001) finding that Queer people are less likely to be considered victims of hate crime by criminal justice students may highlight both society's penchant for cisheteronormativity and the discipline's lack of overall inclusivity. Thus, it seems that there is a very limited understanding of Queer identities and criminal justice—on the part of both students and departments—particularly when it comes to Queer victimization.

As briefly described in the previous section, the ways in which Queer topics are taught in criminal justice classrooms can have lasting implications for how students interact with Queer people when they enter the criminal justice field and how negative interactions with criminal justice professionals impact the ways in which Queer people interact with different criminal justice contexts. As Daigle (2017) explains, Queer people who are victims of a crime may fear that police officers will insult or harm them. Similarly, and depending on the nature of the victimization, some Queer people may assume that police officers may use derisive and belittling language when referring to their victimization and/or insinuate that their victimization is less valid or real (e.g., such as with intimate partner violence cases; see Guadalupe-Diaz, 2019). Moreover, Queer people experiencing victimization may fear that their victimization will be shared between law enforcement and others within their communities, which may be particularly problematic if the person is not out or openly Queer. Ultimately these experiences stem from what Tjaden et al. (1999) describe as a general lack of recognition by society and law enforcement that many instances of Queer victimization—such as intimate partner violence—are just as valid as cis-heteronormative victimizations.

Conclusion

At this point, you might be wondering, "What does a positive inclusion of Queerness within a criminology and criminal justice classroom look like in practice?" Before we answer that question, we'd like to share a potential and affirming result of the inclusion of Queerness within the classroom. At the end of teaching a class which intentionally utilized a Queer criminological lens, the author agreed to meet with a senior criminology and criminal justice student who, over the course of the semester, had transformed from a quiet student to one who spoke almost every class. After the class cleared the room, the student's eyes began to well up with tears which immediately concerned the author. The student wiped their tears on their sleeve and the author recalls them saying,

> I just wanted to let you know that I'm gay, and this class really meant a lot to me. I've never talked about gay people in any of my other criminal justice classes, and I think what you're doing is brave. It's really important. Thank you and please continue doing this.

This interaction, which deeply moved the author, reaffirmed and underscored just how important it is to Queer criminology and criminal justice classrooms.

During the first week of class, the author made several decisions that we believe were crucial in integrating Queerness into their criminology and criminal justice classroom. First, they facilitated classroom or community agreements, a strategy often used in advocacy and diversity and inclusion spheres, that were designed by and for the students; essentially, the author asked the students to create ground rules (e.g., active listening and no interrupting) for everyone to follow to make the classroom feel safe and comfortable. Although a lot of the students were initially unimpressed and thought the idea seemed silly—it took a few weeks for them to truly understand why the guidelines were so important—by the end of the semester, the majority of them were holding each other accountable and actively participating within their crafted guidelines. Next, the author spent the remainder of the class, and some of the following classes,[8] collectively defining Queer terminology[9] (e.g., What does the acronym, "LGBTQIA+" stand for? What does "Queer" mean?). This approach can help prime students for a semester's worth of unlearning stereotypes and assumptions about Queer communities. The author also encouraged their students to approach every topic with an open mind and heart, reminding them that some of the topics or ideas might, at some point, make them feel uncomfortable. The author would explain, "Lean into that discomfort and really ask yourself, 'Where is this discomfort coming from? Why do I feel this way about X topic?'" From parenting during and after incarceration to the social organization of crime to substance use, *every single topic* was discussed the same way. The author approached each with the understanding that the social construction of gender, sex as defined by biology, and sexuality does indeed shape pathways to and desistance from behavior(s) labeled as criminal.

We hope that this chapter will not be read as an indictment of either of our previous, current, or future institutions. Rather, we hope that through our own personal experiences, we have made a clear case for the inclusion of Queer topics, issues, and identities in criminology and criminal justice classrooms. We cannot emphasize it enough: The exclusion of Queer identities from criminal justice curricula not only symbolically victimizes Queer people, by suggesting the inconsequentiality of Queer experiences, it also leaves future criminal justice practitioners ill-prepared to interact with Queer communities, which leads to violent and lasting ramifications. We also hope that we have offered ample support to evince that we must not simply include Queer identities via an "add Queer and stir" method (Ball, 2014; as cited in Buist & Lenning, 2015, p. 7). That is, to put plainly, simply not enough because the ways in which these topics are discussed matter immensely as well.

Now you might ask, "How do I *actually* include Queer experiences in my curricula? Where do I get started?" While we want to emphasize that there isn't a one-size fits all method, we will conclude with a number of suggestions and best practices for criminal justice instructors—indeed, instructors in any discipline—as they aim to be more inclusive of Queer topics and experiences. In fact, many of these are practices that we wish had been adopted for the courses we took as students. We hope that these recommendations will make for a more inclusive and Queer-friendly criminal justice classroom.

- **Start with basic LGBTQIA+ terminology and common assumptions with the goal of unpacking cisheteronormativity and privilege.** Lenning (2014) has a terrific outline of the myriad ways that one might approach these topics and describes how difficult it may be for some students to recognize the embeddedness of cisheteronormativity within American society and how they themselves may perpetuate it.
- **Facilitate classroom or community agreements to develop a list of guidelines by and for your students.** While some students, and even faculty, may think this approach is childish, we believe that 1) there is nothing wrong with teaching students how to be vulnerable and considerate of the feelings of their peers; and 2) helping students craft some ground rules gives them a sense of agency and accountability within the classroom, which can encourage more participation. For more information and some examples of implementation, see the Teaching Guide for Graduate Student Instructor within the Teaching & Resource Center at Berkeley under the heading, "Creating Community Agreements" (https://gsi.berkeley.edu/gsi-guide-contents/discussion-intro/discussion-guidelines/) and the fact sheet designed by UMassAmherst's Center for Teaching & Learning entitled, "Developing Class Participation Agreements" (www.umass.edu/ctl/sites/default/files/Handout-Developing%20Class%20Participation%20Agreements.pdf).
- **As such, create brave(r) spaces.** Many of us are familiar with the concept of a "safe space," which is a place where one is assured that they will not be discriminated against for their identities. However, Arao and Clemens (2013) argue for moving beyond this conceptualization to create brave(r) spaces which act as places in which "all participants have the opportunity to shape the group norms and expectations" (p. 143). Within these spaces, painful life experiences and complex topics, rather than being given a cursory and apathetic acknowledgement—or worse yet, avoiding them altogether—are acknowledged, explored, and supported (Cook-Sather, 2016). Therefore, brave(r) spaces can act as communities where instructors and students alike can work through these tough, complex issues together (Atiya et al., 2013).
- **Encourage students to lean into discomfort and to ask questions.** Pereira (2012) describes teaching through "didactic discomfort," meaning, "intellectual and/or emotional discomfort felt by students, which is triggered directly or indirectly by the material covered and/or methods deployed in a course and is perceived by teachers (and often also by the students themselves) as an experience that can enable or generate learning" (p. 129). The author notes that encouraging students to step outside of their comfort zones takes a lot of time, emotional labor, and energy which can only be accomplished through trust; students have to trust each other and their teachers in order to feel comfortable leaning in. As such, didactic discomfort can "transform students' experiences of discomfort into generative learning tools" (Pereira, 2012, p. 133).
- **It's okay to not have all the answers. Simply tell the student(s) that you'll get back to them.** While it may be tempting to make up an answer on the spot, we want to encourage *you* to lean into *your own* discomfort. Be vulnerable and take the time to go and research the question, speak with your colleagues (those who work within the area rather than asking someone just because they are Queer) who may have the answer(s), and then bring the answer(s) to your student(s).

- **Avoid the use of othering language and <u>never</u> use offensive epithets.** For some, this may be controversial as it may feel like we're asking them to restrict their freedom of speech. Firstly, and as described in the second bullet point, we see no issue in shaping personal discourse in an effort to make others feel more comfortable. Secondly, we believe that there is never an appropriate reason or excuse (e.g., "It's written in the text") to use any kind of offensive epithet in the classroom. Now, we understand that terminology is fluid, constantly updating, and that acceptable terminology for some may be offensive to others. However, as educators, it is our responsibility to keep ourselves updated as best as we can with *current*, *appropriate*, and *respectful* terminology. Again, lean into *your* vulnerability and do not take offense if a student corrects or attempts to update you. For additional information, the GLAAD Media Reference Guide—Terms to Avoid (www.glaad.org/reference/offensive) offers several examples of offensive and othering language that have historically been used when referring to Queer communities; this guide also offers preferred alternatives (GLAAD, 2016).
- **Finally, to avoid discussing Queerness as a form of deviance, use contemporary, widely accepted terminology when referring to Queer identities and strive to use language that is inclusive of a wide array of identities and experiences.** Although, historically, Queerness has been associated with deviant behavior, a significant amount of research (Foucault, 1978; Snorton, 2017) has illustrated that Queerness has always existed and should be considered normative. In continuing to associate Queerness with a form of deviance, educators perpetuate violent stereotypes and stigmatizations that label Queer people as inherently abnormal. Similarly, terms like "homosexual," while used historically, are no longer appropriate due to their historical use in pathologizing Queer people in addition to their co-optation by homophobic and transphobic radicals. *Take the time* to transform your classroom into Queer-friendly spaces that are both affirming to Queer students (and communities) and offer opportunities for other students to unpack their assumptions. We repeat, there is absolutely nothing wrong with *taking the time* to make others feel comfortable and safe around you and in your classroom. In fact, we believe every classroom should be Queered, making it a welcoming and inclusive space, which we hope will ultimately help Queer communities within classrooms and beyond.

Notes

1 Throughout this chapter, while we use the terms "Queer" and "LGBTQIA+" interchangeably, we primarily use the former as an umbrella term, as "it allows for those with shared experiences by virtue of their existing outside of heteronormativity to be represented in research" and "it also allows researchers and others to bring criminological attention to bear on issues of injustice, or to important silences in these discourses, and open up a space for these injustices to be remedied, or these silences to be broken" (Ball, 2013, p. 5).

2 It is important to note here that while there may have been other departments (e.g., women's studies) that probably offered courses explicitly focused on gender and sexuality, no such courses within the field of criminology or criminal justice have been offered to us at the undergraduate or graduate level.

3 Although some may reasonably question whether this is an instance of selection bias, the prejudicial inclusion of Queer topics, like the one mentioned above, may further promote these sentiments, regardless of methodological biases.

4 We want to make it clear that in using the above quote we are not stating that all trans people are gay or that all gay people are trans. Rather, it further highlights the essentialization of LGBTQIA+ identities such as a classmate's use of a stereotype commonly associated with gay cisgender men and "gay sex" in a conversation regarding trans people.

5 Hayes and Ball (2010) also advise readers not to automatically categorize these resistant students as homophobic, "as this term does not necessarily account for the complexity of the discourses that inform students' reactions in this context. This "homophobia" may simply be related to a way of performing gender and sexual identity as opposed to overt discrimination and fear" (p. 1).

6 Although some transgender communities have reclaimed the word, this term has historically been used as a slur, which made us very hesitant to write it in its entirety. We decided to include it, however, as it is a direct quote that illustrates linguistic violence.

7 We'd like to emphasize that criminology's complicity in the vilification of Queer people is shared with other disciplines. Woods (2014) does a fantastic job in outlining how psychology has moved away from Sigmund Freud's (1905, 1911) analysis of Queerness as normative to Queerness as a diagnosable (e.g., the American Psychiatric Association's Diagnostic and Statistical Manual of Mental Disorders) pathology through the works of Bergler (1956) and Bieber et al. (1962).

8 Please keep in mind that this may take several classes! It is also extremely helpful to ask students if there are any terms within the readings that they found confusing or needed further clarification.

9 Lenning (2014) describes how important it is to spend a significant amount of time "unpacking" the differences between sexuality, sex as defined by biology, and gender, which can ultimately help students understand how heterosexual privilege manifests in the criminal justice system and society more broadly (p. 85).

References

Arao, B., & Clemens, K. (2013). From safe spaces to brave spaces. In *The art of effective facilitation: Reflections from social justice educators* (pp. 135–150). Sterling, VA: Stylus Publishing, LLC.

Atiya, S., Davis, S. W., Green, K., Howley, E., Pollack, S., Roswell, B. S., Turenne, E., Werts, T., & Wilson, L. (2013). From safe space to brave space: Strategies for the anti-oppression classroom. In *Turning teaching inside out* (pp. 105–112). New York: Palgrave Macmillan.

Austin, J. L., Cain, P. A., Mack, A., & Strader, J. K. (1998). Results from a survey: Gay, lesbian, and bisexual students' attitudes about law school. *Journal of Legal Education*, 48, 157–175.

Ball, M. (2014). What's queer about queer criminology? In *Handbook of LGBT communities, crime, and justice* (pp. 531–555). New York: Springer.

Bergler, E. (1956). *Homosexuality: Disease or way of life*. New York: Hill and Wang.

Bieber, I., Dain, H. J., Dince, P. R., Drellich, M. G., Grand, H. G., & Gundlach, R. H., et al. (1962). *Homosexuality: A psychoanalytic study of male homosexuals*. New York: Basic Books.

Bloomberg Law. It's Gotten Better to Be LGBTQ in Big Law, but Struggles Remain, June 29, 2020. Retrieved September 24, 2021, from https://news.bloomberglaw.com/us-law-week/its-gotten-better-to-be-lgbtq-in-big-law-but-struggles-remain

Britton, D. M. (1997). Gendered organizational logic: Policy and practice in men's and women's prisons. *Gender & Society*, 11(6), 796–818.

Buist, C. L., & Lenning, E. (2015). *Queer criminology*, 1st edition. London: Routledge.

Cahill, S. (2017). From "don't drop the soap" to PREA standards reducing sexual victimization of LGBT people in the juvenile and criminal justice systems. *LGBTQ Politics: A Critical Reader*, 3, 134–152.

Cannon, K. D. (2005). "Ain't no faggot gonna rob me!": Anti-gay attitudes of criminal justice undergraduate majors. *Journal of Criminal Justice Education*, 16(2), 226–243.

Cannon, K. D., & Dirks-Linhorst, P. A. (2006). How will they understand if we don't teach them? The status of criminal justice education on gay and lesbian issues. *Journal of Criminal Justice Education*, 17(2), 262–278.

Cohen, A. K. (1955). *Delinquent boys: The culture of the gang*. New York: The Free Press.

Colvin, R. (2009). Shared perceptions among lesbian and gay police officers: Barriers and opportunities in the law enforcement work environment. *Police Quarterly*, 12(1), 86–101.

Cook-Sather, A. (2016). Creating brave spaces within and through student-faculty pedagogical partnerships. *Teaching and Learning Together in Higher Education*, 1(18), 1.

Daigle, L. E. (2017). *Victimology: A text/reader*. Los Angeles, CA: SAGE Publications.

Dwyer, A. (2008). Policing queer bodies: Focusing on queer embodiment in policing research as an ethical question. *Law and Justice Journal*, 8(2), 414–428.

Dwyer, A. (2014). Pleasures, perversities, and partnerships: The historical emergence of LGBT-police relationships. In *Handbook of LGBT communities, crime, and justice* (pp. 149–164). New York: Springer.

Foucault, M. (1978). *The history of sexuality: The use of pleasure*. New York: Vintage Books, Random House.

Fradella, H. F., Owen, S. S., & Burke, T. W. (2009). Integrating gay, lesbian, bisexual, and transgender issues into the undergraduate criminal justice curriculum. *Journal of Criminal Justice Education*, 20(2), 127–156.

Freud, S. (1905). *Three essays on the theory of sexuality*, Standard edition (Vol. 7, pp. 125–245). London: Hogarth Press.

Freud, S. (1911). *Psychoanalytical notes on the autobiographical account of a case of paranoia (Dementia Paranoides)*, Standard edition (Vol. 12, pp. 1–82). London, UK: White Press.

GLAAD Media Reference Guide—Terms to Avoid. (2016). GLAAD, October 25. Retrieved from www.glaad.org/reference/offensive.

Guadalupe-Diaz, X. L. (2019). *Transgressed: Intimate partner violence in transgender lives*. New York: NYU Press.

Hayes, S., & Ball, M. (2009). Sexuality in a criminal justice curriculum: A study of student conceptualisations of gay identity. *Journal of Australian Studies*, 33(3), 273–287.

Hayes, S., & Ball, M. (2010). Homophobia in the University classroom: Law and justice students' conceptualisations of queer identity. In B. Scherer (Ed.), *Queering paradigms* (pp. 181–196). Peter Lang Publishing. Retrieved from www.peterlang.com/index.cfm?vID=11970&vLang=E&vHR=1&vUR=2&vUUR=1.

Ihrig, S. N. (1995). Sexual orientation in law school: Experiences of gay, lesbian, and bisexual law students. *Law & Inequality*, 14, 555–591.

Leinen, S. H. (1993). *Gay cops*. New Brunswick, NJ: Rutgers University Press.

Lenning, E. (2014). The invisible minority: Making the LGBT community visible in the criminal justice classroom. In *Teaching criminology at the intersection*. New York: Routledge.

Levan, K., Polzer, K., & Downing, S. (2011). Media and prison sexual assault: How we got to the "don't drop the soap" culture. *International Journal of Criminology and Sociological Theory*, 4(2), 674–682.

Miller, A. J. (2001). Student perceptions of hate crimes. *American Journal of Criminal Justice*, 25(2), 293–307.

Murray, B. (2016). Words that wound, bodies that shield: Corporeal responses to Westboro Baptist church's hate speech. *First Amendment Studies*, 50(1), 32–47.

Olivero, J. M., & Murataya, R. (2001). Homophobia and university law enforcement students. *Journal of Criminal Justice Education*, 12(2), 271–281.

Pereira, M. D. M. (2012). Uncomfortable classrooms: Rethinking the role of student discomfort in feminist teaching. *European Journal of Women's Studies*, 19(1), 128–135.

Snorton, C. R. (2017). *Black on both sides: A racial history of trans identity*. Minnesota: University of Minnesota Press.

Tjaden, P., Thoennes, N., & Allison, C. J. (1999). Comparing violence over the life span in samples of same-sex and opposite-sex cohabitants. *Violence and Victims*, 14(4), 413–425.

Ventura, L. A., Lambert, E. G., Bryant, M., & Pasupuleti, S. (2004). Differences in attitudes toward gays and lesbians among criminal justice and non-criminal justice majors. *American Journal of Criminal Justice*, 28(2), 165–180.

Woods, J. B. (2014). "Queering criminology": Overview of the state of the field. In *Handbook of LGBT communities, crime, and justice* (pp. 15–41). New York: Springer.

Chapter 16

Bad Blood

Media's Role in Blaming the Queer Community for HIV/AIDS

Jack M. Mills, Caroline A. Mooney, and Kyle G. Knapp

The impact of the human immunodeficiency virus (HIV) and its subsequent acquired immune deficiency syndrome (AIDS) was catastrophic. Claiming the lives of over 40 million people in just the last five decades, HIV/AIDS[1] was, and in many regards still is, one of the worst sociomedical events in human history (Mann, 1992, 1996; Parker, 2002; Pratt, 1992; Way et al., 1994). While the impact of HIV/AIDS has been felt globally, special attention should be given to the sociomedical effect this disease has on sexual and gender minoritized people (Gossett, 2020; Raimondo, 2010; Rollins, 1996; Rosenfeld, 2019; Spurlin, 2019). Specifically, news framing of HIV/AIDS has played a critical role in shaping societal attitudes toward the Queer community by exhibiting homophobic prejudice and stigma toward HIV/AIDS sufferers (Brennan et al., 2020; Huebner et al., 2002; Reddy, 2010; Ruel & Campbell, 2006). The framing of Queer people's[2] role in spreading HIV/AIDS has varied greatly across the world; however, the underlying tone was clear: Queer communities were at fault for the advent and spread of HIV/AIDS (Clift & Memon, 1990; Goh, 2008; Lima et al., 1993; Petros et al., 2006).

Our chapter explores the phenomenon of HIV/AIDS news framing and its impact on both Queer and non-Queer communities. Derived from an ethnographic content analysis (Altheide, 1987), we examined 1,313 news articles portraying the intersection of the Queer community and HIV/AIDS in the US between 1981 and 2000. To effectively capture the social responses to HIV/AIDS, our chapter will discuss past literature and qualitative findings from our content analysis to highlight the false perceived threat of Queer people, harmful discourse of homophobic perceptions that are integrated into oppressive policies, and finally recommendations for overcoming stigmatized policies.

Method

The current study examines media representation of Queer people and HIV/AIDS through an ethnographic content analysis across the 1,313 sampled front-of-page print news clippings which were sampled from Newspaper Archive, a digital repository of scanned newspapers. In line with Altheide's (1987) ethnographic content analysis, systematic sampling could not possibly convey the full reporting themes found in media representations of Queer people and HIV/AIDS. Therefore, our analysis contains every sampled article. Our analysis consisted of three phases: (i) collection and exploration of raw data, (ii) thematic development and coding, and (iii) data interpretation and discussion. To ensure reliability and validity, our study underwent rigid reliability checks that mandated unanimous support from each researcher after the study's second phase was completed. The larger study

DOI: 10.4324/9781003400981-19

consists of several additional measures, such as framing, spatial, and temporal analyses. For this chapter, we selected structural and thematic content variables. Structural variables include publication date, census region, and newspaper outlet. Thematic content variables include several measures, among them characterization, article's tone, social vilification and criminalization, and victimization. This chapter aims to explore media representations of Queer people at the height of the HIV/AIDS epidemic through a mixed-method analysis.

Perceived Threat of Queer People

For as long as sensationalized news has dominated our channels of disseminating information, media representation of Queer people in the US has been largely negative (Lupton, 1999; Gillett, 2003; Labra, 2015). Past literature has found that these negative attitudes toward Queer communities have largely been the result of stigmatized and prejudiced media framing and other social responses (Brennan et al., 2020; Huebner et al., 2002; Reddy, 2010; Ruel & Campbell, 2006). Fear is a driving force for discrimination, homophobia, and social vilification against Queer communities (see also, Bouton et al., 1987; Goh, 2008; Sjöstedt, 2010; Young et al., 1991). Our analysis corroborates these findings through our tonal measure which categorizes media representation of Queer people and HIV/AIDS in a positive, neutral, or negative manner:

> Jamie Springer is gay, but unlike many gay or lesbian teenagers who "closet" their sexual orientation, Jamie has "come out." The San Clemente High School senior is hoping his willingness to accept his gay lifestyle will encourage other teenagers to come out and accept their gay or lesbian needs.
>
> (San Clemente Sun Post News, October 1995)

From our 1,313 sampled articles, 21.3% of news clippings were categorized as positive. Positive depictions of Queer communities were often discussed through policy and civil rights advancements for sexual minorities, sympathy, and respect from heterosexual communities, and initiatives to end stigma against Queer HIV/AIDS sufferers. Trends of positive depictions fluctuated over our sample's time frame, with a noticeable decline in positive depictions of Queer people and HIV/AIDS between 1994 and 2000. Notably, in the first two years of our analysis there were zero clippings with positive depictions and the highest rate of these depictions was in 1987. While positive depictions decreased over time, they were often replaced with neutral depictions, showing that the growing social capital of Queer people, as well as education and awareness about HIV/AIDS had a positive, or at least neutral, impact in newspaper representation.

> People who receive transfusions face a one in 40,000 chance of receiving AIDS-tainted blood despite screening intended to keep the blood supply clean, according to a federal study published today. The researchers emphasize that despite this "remote but real risk," people who need transfusions should not be deterred from receiving them.
>
> (Annapolis Capital, February 1988)

In our sample, 60.8% of news clippings conveyed neutral representations of Queer people and HIV/AIDS. These depictions often conveyed statistics in case trends of HIV/AIDS over time or in a given community. Certain objective discussions of policy, victim statements, and medical responses to HIV/AIDS were also coded as neutral. Trends of neutral depictions were much more evenly dispersed across our sample's time frame, experiencing their maximum in 1987 and minimum in 1981 and 1982. Many clippings were also found to avoid any direct representations of Queer identity. While not inherently negative, many of these instances did not omit Queer labels for anonymity, and instead, clearly focused on removing Queer identity from the conversation of HIV/AIDS even when vilifying Queer people for their alleged role in contaminating society. Negative representations of Queer people and HIV/AIDS were the least conveyed tone, consisting of 17.8% of our sample. These depictions ranged considerably; certain clippings denied the existence of Queer people while others called for social vilification, criminalization, and even the killing of all sexual minorities:

"Kill 'em," [Texas State Senator Carl] Parker said, immediately adding that he was only joking. Almost every news report carried throughout the state said Parker made the comment in jest but the senator felt the circumstances of the situation weren't adequately conveyed.

(Port Arthur News, March 1989)

Often, negative representations were influenced by conservative policies and religious intolerance to homosexuality and Queerness in general. Trends of negative depictions fell over time and specifically after 1987. Unlike the other two tonal depictions, negative depictions remained the same between 1995 and 1996 as well as 1998 and 1999. The frequency of negative depictions experienced its maximum in 1985, and similar to both positive and neutral depictions, experienced its minimum in 1981 and 1982:

Crucial to the study of media, correlational and causal language is rarely used for many reasons. For instance, though a news clipping may be negative in nature, the reporting outlet may have been largely quoting another viewpoint on the topic of Queer communities and HIV/AIDS. It is important for the reader to understand our findings as descriptive without the constraint of causal language. Instead, our qualitative illustrations corroborate previous studies that have examined media framing of Queer-related social issues (e.g., Gillett, 2003; Labra, 2015; Lupton, 1999; Mykhalovski & Rosengarten, 2009). Beyond literature that has analyzed the intersection of media and HIV/AIDS, other studies have examined several factors that create negative attitudes toward sexual minorities, including masculinity (Davies, 2004; Herek & Capitanio, 1995), contact with Queer people (Lingiardi et al., 2016), racial factors (Lemelle & Battle, 2004), religious values (Gilad & Stepanova, 2015; Herek & Capitanio, 1995; Roggemans et al., 2015), conservative values (Olatunji, 2008; Whitehead & Baker, 2012), internalized homophobia (Lingiardi & Nardelli, 2014), and other factors (e.g., Steffens et al., 2015).

Translating Stigma to Policy

While there is currently a growing consensus regarding media's influence on public policy (Seib, 2012), it is undoubtedly true that the media has impacted public policy since its inception. Media, especially in the sense of uprooting oppressive attitudes toward Queer people, has always been tremendously impactful in maintaining the status quo of Queerphobia

(Chalk, 2014; Madiba, 2013). Despite this foundational understanding, this field has not yet been studied in a manner which contextualizes the power that media has in influencing public policy related to HIV/AIDS and Queer communities. Cadwell (1991) outlined several factors in media mismanagement of HIV/AIDS, such as victim blaming, labeling AIDS as a gay-only disease, correlating homosexuality with immorality, and other stigmatization. Our study corroborated this finding, as 21.01% of our sample contained some form of stigmatization (i.e., social distancing, social vilification, discrimination, anti-Queer campaigns, violence, and criminalization):

> Wearing gloves and armed with brushes, rags and a bucket of bleach, the restaurant crew scrubs every inch of the booth where (an AIDS infected person) sat. Anything he might have touched—plates, silverware, glasses, napkins, even the tip on the table—is dumped into a pan of bleach-water and meticulously cleaned.
>
> (Sandusky Register, December 1987)

In comparison to other forms of social vilification, (mis)representations of Queer people in US media have been more widely studied. Several content analyses have found that media representation of HIV/AIDS and Queer people impacted the government response to ending the HIV/AIDS pandemic and to creating anti-Queer policies (e.g., Carson, 2010; DeJong et al., 2001; Groves et al., 2021; Johnson, 2005; Stevens & Jull, 2013; Wagner & Van Volkenburg, 2011). Our analysis corroborates that social vilification was enhanced by negative political, social, and media representation of Queer people with HIV/AIDS.

> Now a healthcare worker in his 40s, (a gay man) worries about discrimination of gays and lesbians. "It's more than just AIDS," he says. "It's the mentality of the country. It's Ronald Reagan and George Bush and fundamentalist religions that are down on anyone who isn't white, Anglo-Saxon Protestant. I believe—maybe I was living in a fantasy land—but in the '60s and '70s people accepted people for what they were."
>
> (0067; Jacksonville Journal Courier, 1992)

> "It's only going to be a matter of time before a student or teacher is going to have AIDS," Superintendent Dennis Murray told his Citizens' Advisory Committee Thursday afternoon . . . A small group of Altoona Area High School students brought the issue of AIDS to the public's attention when they refused on Nov. 22 to go to classes. These students were among the 200-plus who signed a petition against having homosexual students in school.
>
> (Altoona Mirror, 1986)

Additionally, Herek et al. (2003) surveyed US adults regarding HIV surveillance policies and its relation to negative attitudes toward AIDS sufferers and other Queer groups, finding anonymous reporting styles to be favored across the US (see also, Cadwell, 1991; Card et al., 2019; Chalk, 2014; Purcell, 2021). While surveillance programs have been generally supported in the US, calls for criminalization have also been accounted for in prior literature (Breslow & Brewster, 2020). In line with past studies, we often observed anti-Queer attitudes that attempted to exclude Queer people from society, especially if the Queer people in question are racial minorities. Overall, 51.58% of our sample exhibited stigma and/or social vilification, dispersed between eight measures: verbal stigma, political stigma, barred from traveling, barred from social activities, evictions, hiring exclusions, employment termination, and social distancing:

> [Dr. Paul] Cameron, introduced as "an educational guest lecturer," said he wanted to emphasize the public health aspect of homosexuality as well as summarize its history. In an hour-long lecture laced with generalizations about history, patriotism, religion, and morality, he said through the ages all major religions have considered homosexuality as "somewhere between an abomination or a great misfortune," and that homosexuals had been imprisoned or put to death in "most cultures."
> (Fayetteville Northwest Arkansas Times, April 1985)

> Florida is the only state in the country proposing special wards for AIDS carriers who knowingly risk infecting others, a Washington research group says.
> (Key West Citizen, January 1988)

Much of the literature in this area has discussed interpersonal and gender-based violence (e.g., Barker & Ricardo, 2005; Jansen van Rensburg, 2007; Sowell et al., 1999; Strebel et al., 2006; Voisin, 2003). While these factors of violence have been thoroughly examined at the individual level, community-level violence has been understudied. Like other studies, our analysis examined intimidation, fearmongering, and violence as indicators to socially vilify and criminalize Queer people (Breslow & Brewster, 2020; King et al., 2013), finding similar associations with these factors:

> AIDS, fueled by indifference or hostility from police, is increasing violence against homosexuals, gay activists have told Congress. . . . "We're not talking about name-calling. We're talking about physical abuse- stabbings, beatings, broken bones, slashed faces. In some cases we're talking about murder," said Diana Christensen, executive director of Community United Against Violence.
> (Corbin Times Tribune, 1986)

A trademark of the HIV/AIDS response was pervasive victim blaming of positive Queer people for community contagion rates. When considering the perceived role that Queer people and especially gay men had in spreading the disease, studies have suggested that stigma has fluctuated over time; however, there is a clear association between continuous anti-Queer stigma and victim blaming and generalized homophobia (Clarke, 2006).

Disrupting Stigmatized Policy

Countless policy discussions have taken place in the US since the first recorded case of HIV in 1981. Several studies have examined the negative effects of HIV/AIDS public policy on Queer people (Herek et al., 2002; Herek et al., 2003) and specifically Queer Black men (Arnold et al., 2014; Epprecht, 2005; Jeffries et al., 2013). Many of these contributions have also offered insight to promote more equitable sociomedical policy. For instance, Robinson (2010) discussed the impact of Queer voices educating heterosexual communities about Queer-related topics and HIV/AIDS. Additionally, removing gender-based differences in HIV/AIDS care is another solution, one which has been studied from the viewpoint of countries with oppressive laws in place for homosexuality (White & Carr, 2005). Other studies have more plainly outlined the government's inability or unwillingness to legalize homosexuality negatively contributes to the rising problem of HIV/AIDS (Rodríguez et al., 2013; Saavedra et al., 2008; Varas-Díaz et al., 2008). Gates and Mitchell (2013) provided several nongovernmental factors to stigmatized policy, such as the support of progressive corporations, social programs, and other employment protections for Queer people.

During the late 1980s and early 1990s, several celebrities became infected. Rock Hudson, Freddie Mercury, Magic Johnson, Ryan White, Alexis Arquette, and Liberace were a few of many well-known and well-respected celebrities that fell victim to HIV/AIDS. Our analysis found that the awareness generated by celebrities with HIV/AIDS caused a—relatively large and instantaneous—ripple effect of sympathetic support toward HIV/AIDS sufferers and the Queer community. Importantly, many of these celebrities (particularly Rock Hudson and Magic Johnson) banded with non-infected celebrities and politicians, like Elizabeth Taylor and Ronald Reagan, to fundraise for HIV/AIDS related research:

> President [Reagan] and Mrs. Reagan, longtime friends of [Rock] Hudson from their Hollywood days, said in a statement, "Nancy and I are saddened by the news of Rock Hudson's death. He will always be remembered for his dynamic impact on the film industry, and fans all over the world will certainly mourn his loss. . . . Last week Hudson announced he was giving $250,000 to a new national foundation to battle AIDS. The week before, at a star-studded fund-raiser, he brought tears to the eyes of many with a statement."
>
> (Sandusky Register, October 1985)

Awareness of HIV/AIDS greatly benefited Queer people in any given community and has begun deconstructing the false idea that HIV/AIDS was, or is, a homosexual disease. The influx of news stories about celebrities with HIV/AIDS enabled those without personal connections to see familiar faces among the victims they may have previously othered. Celebrities quickly made fundraising and red-ribbon awareness a staple at Hollywood events, in turn mainstreaming the display of public empathy and interest in vocal support for those fighting HIV/AIDS. However, awareness alone has yet to create enough progressive force to overpower stigma.

Conclusion

Queer representation in media has proven to be particularly impactful in shaping public policy, discrimination, homophobia, and stigmatization against gender and sexual minorities. Past literature has discussed several implications of HIV/AIDS and Queer-related policy, emphasizing the role of destigmatization in removing sociopolitical homophobic and anti-Queer sentiment. Our study is supported by previous literature that reviewed media representation of Queer people during the formidable period of HIV/AIDS. Through our content analysis, we found several factors of positive, neutral, and negative reporting, such as social vilification, stigma, homophobia, political bias, HIV/AIDS impact and victimization, as well as religious intolerance to Queer communities. As these factors have been exacerbated by the media, researchers, and policymakers should take note of its expansive ability to influence public opinion, policy, and attitude forming on marginalized groups.

Finally, we would be remiss not to acknowledge the immense help from two research assistants to our larger HIV/AIDS Media Representations database, Joshua Warren and

Laura Marguriet. Our chapter concludes with a dedication for all HIV/AIDS sufferers, including my great uncle Ted (Teddy) Fenton. May they all rest in peace and our policies amplify their voices.

Notes

1 When referring to collective impact or social responses, this chapter will use the term HIV/AIDS unless referring specifically to HIV or AIDS.
2 Queer people refers to all sexual and gender minorities.

References

Altheide, D. L. (1987). Reflections: Ethnographic content analysis. *Qualitative Sociology*, 10(1), 65–77.

Arnold, E. A., Rebchook, G. M., & Kegeles, S. M. (2014). 'Triply cursed': Racism, homophobia and HIV-related stigma are barriers to regular HIV testing, treatment adherence and disclosure among young Black gay men. *Culture, Health & Sexuality*, 16(6), 710–722.

Barker, G., & Ricardo, C. (2005). *Young men and the construction of masculinity in sub-Saharan Africa: Implications for HIV/AIDS, conflict, and violence* (p. 27). Washington, DC: World Bank.

Bouton, R. A., Gallaher, P. E., Garlinghouse, P. A., Leal, T., Rosenstein, L. D., & Young, R. K. (1987). Scales for measuring fear of AIDS and homophobia. *Journal of Personality Assessment*, 51(4), 606–614.

Brennan, D. J., Card, K. G., Collict, D., Jollimore, J., & Lachowsky, N. J. (2020). How might social distancing impact gay, bisexual, Queer, trans and two-spirit men in Canada? *AIDS and Behavior*, 24(9), 2480–2482.

Breslow, A. S., & Brewster, M. E. (2020). HIV is not a crime: Exploring dual roles of criminalization and discrimination in HIV/AIDS minority stress. *Stigma and Health*, 5(1), 83.

Cadwell, S. (1991). Twice removed: The stigma suffered by gay men with AIDS. *Smith College Studies in Social Work*, 61(3), 236–246.

Card, K. G., Hawkins, B. W., Mortazavi, L., Gregory, A., Ng, K. H., & Lachowsky, N. J. (2019). Stigma, the media, and pre-exposure prophylaxis for HIV prevention: Observations for enhancing knowledge translation and resisting stigma in the Canadian context. *AIDS and Behavior*, 23(7), 1877–1887.

Carson, E. D. (2010). *The importance of relational communication for effecting social change in HIV/AIDS prevention messages: A content analysis of HIV/AIDS public service announcements*. Athens, OH: Ohio University.

Chalk, S. (2014). *HIV and stigma: The media challenge*. London: International Broadcasting Trust.

Clarke, J. N. (2006). Homophobia out of the closet in the media portrayal of HIV/AIDS 1991, 1996 and 2001: Celebrity, heterosexism and the silent victims. *Critical Public Health*, 16(4), 317–330.

Clift, S., & Memon, A. (1990). Blame and young people's moral judgments. *AIDS: Individual, Cultural, and Policy Dimensions*, 53.

Davies, M. (2004). Correlates of negative attitudes toward gay men: Sexism, male role norms, and male sexuality. *Journal of Sex Research*, 41(3), 259–266.

DeJong, R., Cameron Wolf, S., & Bryn Austin, W. (2001). US federally funded television public service announcements (PSAs) to prevent HIV/AIDS: A content analysis. *Journal of Health Communication*, 6(3), 249–263.

Epprecht, M. (2005). Black skin, 'cowboy' masculinity: A genealogy of homophobia in the African nationalist movement in Zimbabwe to 1983. *Culture, Health & Sexuality*, 7(3), 253–266.

Gates, T. G., & Mitchell, C. G. (2013). Workplace stigma-related experiences among lesbian, gay, and bisexual workers: Implications for social policy and practice. *Journal of Workplace Behavioral Health*, 28(3), 159–171.

Gilad, C., & Stepanova, E. V. (2015). The effect of religious priming on attitudes toward lesbians and gay men. *Psi Chi Journal of Psychological Research*, 20(4), 188–196.

Gillett, J. (2003). Media activism and internet use by people with HIV/AIDS. *Sociology of Health & Illness*, 25(6), 608–624.

Goh, D. (2008). It's the gays' fault: News and HIV as weapons against homosexuality in Singapore. *Journal of Communication Inquiry*, 32(4), 383–399.

Gossett, C., & Hayward, E. (2020). Trans in a time of HIV/AIDS. *Transgender Studies Quarterly*, 7(4), 527–553.

Groves, A. K., Niccolai, L. M., Keene, D. E., Rosenberg, A., Schlesinger, P., & Blankenship, K. M. (2021). Housing instability and HIV risk: Expanding our understanding of the impact of eviction and other landlord-related forced moves. *AIDS and Behavior*, 25(6), 1913–1922.

Herek, G. M., & Capitanio, J. P. (1995). Black heterosexuals' attitudes toward lesbians and gay men in the United States. *Journal of Sex Research*, 32(2), 95–105.

Herek, G. M., Capitanio, J. P., & Widaman, K. F. (2002). HIV-related stigma and knowledge in the United States: Prevalence and trends, 1991–1999. *American Journal of Public Health*, 92(3), 371–377.

Herek, G. M., Capitanio, J. P., & Widaman, K. F. (2003). Stigma, social risk, and health policy: Public attitudes toward HIV surveillance policies and the social construction of illness. *Health Psychology*, 22(5), 533.

Huebner, D. M., Davis, M. C., Nemeroff, C. J., & Aiken, L. S. (2002). The impact of internalized homophobia on HIV preventive interventions. *American Journal of Community Psychology*, 30(3), 327–348.

Jansen van Rensburg, M. S. (2007). A comprehensive programme addressing HIV/AIDS and gender based violence. *SAHARA: Journal of Social Aspects of HIV/AIDS Research Alliance*, 4(3), 695–706.

Jeffries, W. L., Marks, G., Lauby, J., Murrill, C. S., & Millett, G. A. (2013). Homophobia is associated with sexual behavior that increases risk of acquiring and transmitting HIV infection among black men who have sex with men. *AIDS and Behavior*, 17(4), 1442–1453.

Johnson, K. (2005). Globalization, social policy and the state: An analysis of HIV/AIDS in South Africa. *New Political Science*, 27(3), 309–329.

King, R., Barker, J., Nakayiwa, S., Katuntu, D., Lubwama, G., Bagenda, D., . . . Hladik, W. (2013). Men at risk: A qualitative study on HIV risk, gender identity and violence among men who have sex with men who report high risk behavior in Kampala, Uganda. *PloS One*, 8(12), e82937.

Labra, O. (2015). Social representations of HIV/AIDS in mass media: Some important lessons for caregivers. *International Social Work*, 58(2), 238–248.

Lemelle Jr, A. J., & Battle, J. (2004). Black masculinity matters in attitudes toward gay males. *Journal of Homosexuality*, 47(1), 39–51.

Lima, G., Lo Presto, C. T., Sherman, M. F., & Sobelman, S. A. (1993). The relationship between homophobia and self-esteem in gay males with AIDS. *Journal of Homosexuality*, 25(4), 69–76.

Lingiardi, V., & Nardelli, N. (2014). Negative attitudes to lesbians and gay men: Persecutors and victims. *Emotional, Physical and Sexual Abuse: Impact in Children and Social Minorities*, 33–47. Thompson, CT: Springer.

Lingiardi, V., Nardelli, N., Ioverno, S., Falanga, S., Di Chiacchio, C., Tanzilli, A., & Baiocco, R. (2016). Homonegativity in Italy: Cultural issues, personality characteristics, and demographic correlates with negative attitudes toward lesbians and gay men. *Sexuality Research and Social Policy*, 13(2), 95–108.

Lupton, D. (1999). Archetypes of infection: People with HIV/AIDS in the Australian press in the mid 1990s. *Sociology of Health & Illness*, 21(1), 37–53.

Madiba, S. (2013). The impact of fear, secrecy, and stigma on parental disclosure of HIV status to children: A qualitative exploration with HIV positive parents attending an ART clinic in South Africa. *Global Journal of Health Science*, 5(2), 49.

Mann, J. M. (1992). *AIDS in the world*. Cambridge, MA: Harvard University Press.

Mann, J. M. (1996). *AIDS in the world II: Global dimensions, social roots, and responses*. Oxford: University Press on Demand.

Mykhalovskiy, E., & Rosengarten, M. (2009). HIV/AIDS in its third decade: Renewed critique in social and cultural analysis—An introduction. *Social Theory & Health*, 7(3), 187–195. https://doi.org/10.1057/sth.2009.13.

Olatunji, B. O. (2008). Disgust, scrupulosity and conservative attitudes about sex: Evidence for a mediational model of homophobia. *Journal of Research in Personality*, 42(5), 1364–1369.

Parker, R. (2002). The global HIV/AIDS pandemic, structural inequalities, and the politics of international health. *American Journal of Public Health*, 92(3), 343–347.

Petros, G., Airhihenbuwa, C. O., Simbayi, L., Ramlagan, S., & Brown, B. (2006). HIV/AIDS and 'othering' in South Africa: The blame goes on. *Culture, Health & Sexuality*, 8(1), 67–77.

Pratt, G. F. (1992). A decade of AIDS literature. *Bulletin of the Medical Library Association*, 80(4), 380–381.

Purcell, D. W. (2021). Forty years of HIV: The intersection of laws, stigma, and sexual behavior and identity. American Journal of Public Health, 111(7), 1231–1233.

Raimondo, M. (2010). The queer intimacy of global vision: Documentary practice and the AIDS pandemic. *Environment and Planning D: Society and Space*, 28(1), 112–127.

Reddy, V. (2010). The 'queer' politics of homo (sexuality) and matters of identity: Tentative notes in the context of HIV/AIDS. In *Routledge handbook of sexuality, health and rights* (pp. 455–465). London, UK: Routledge.

Robinson, S. (2010). Responding to homophobia: HIV/AIDS, homosexual community formation and identity in Queensland, 1983–1990. *Australian Historical Studies*, 41(2), 181–197.

Rodríguez, M. M., Madera, S. R., & Díaz, N. V. (2013). Stigma and homophobia: Persistent challenges for HIV prevention among young MSM in Puerto Rico. *Revista de ciencias sociales*, 26, 50.

Roggemans, L., Spruyt, B., Droogenbroeck, F. V., & Keppens, G. (2015). Religion and negative attitudes towards homosexuals: An analysis of urban young people and their attitudes towards homosexuality. *Young*, 23(3), 254–276.

Rollins, J. (1996). Secondary effects: AIDS and queer identity. *Law & Sexuality: Review Lesbian & Gay Legal Issues*, 6, 63.

Rosenfeld, D. (2019). *The aids epidemic's lasting impact on gay men*. The British Academy, February 19. Retrieved from www.thebritishacademy.ac.uk/blog/aids-epidemic-lasting-impact-gay-men/.

Ruel, E., & Campbell, R. T. (2006). Homophobia and HIV/AIDS: Attitude change in the face of an epidemic. *Social Forces*, 84(4), 2167–2178.

Saavedra, J., Izazola-Licea, J. A., & Beyrer, C. (2008). Sex between men in the context of HIV: The AIDS 2008 Jonathan Mann memorial lecture in health and human rights. *Journal of the International AIDS Society*, 11(1), 1–7.

Seib, P. (2012). *Real-time diplomacy: Politics and power in the social media era*. New York: Palgrave Macmillan.

Sjöstedt, R. (2010). Health issues and securitization: The construction of HIV/AIDS as a US national security threat. In *Securitization theory* (pp. 164–183). London: Routledge.

Sowell, R., Seals, B., Moneyham, L., Guillory, J., & Mizuno, Y. (1999). Experiences of violence in HIV seropositive women in the south-eastern United States of America. *Journal of Advanced Nursing*, 30(3), 606–615.

Spurlin, W. J. (2019). Queer theory and biomedical practice: The biomedicalization of sexuality/the cultural politics of biomedicine. *Journal of Medical Humanities*, 40(1), 7–20.

Steffens, M. C., Jonas, K. J., & Denger, L. (2015). Male role endorsement explains negative attitudes toward lesbians and gay men among students in Mexico more than in Germany. *The Journal of Sex Research*, 52(8), 898–911.

Stevens, R. C., & Hull, S. J. (2013). The colour of AIDS: An analysis of newspaper coverage of HIV/AIDS in the United States from 1992–2007. *Critical Arts*, 27(3), 352–369.

Strebel, A., Crawford, M., Shefer, T., Cloete, A., Henda, N., Kaufman, M., . . . Kalichman, S. (2006). Social constructions of gender roles, gender-based violence and HIV/AIDS in two communities of the Western Cape, South Africa. *SAHARA: Journal of Social Aspects of HIV/AIDS Research Alliance*, 3(3), 516–528.

Varas-Díaz, N., Malavé-Rivera, S., & Cintrón-Bou, F. (2008). AIDS stigma combinations in a sample of Puerto Rican health professionals: Qualitative and quantitative evidence. *Puerto Rico Health Sciences Journal*, 27(2), 147–157.

Voisin, D. R. (2003). Victims of community violence and HIV sexual risk behaviors among African American adolescent males. *Journal of HIV/AIDS Prevention & Education for Adolescents & Children*, 5(3–4), 87–110.

Wagner, B. K., & Van Volkenburg, M. (2011). HIV/AIDS tests as a proxy for racial discrimination-A preliminary investigation of South Korea's policy of mandatory in-country HIV/AIDS tests for its Foreign English teachers. *Journal of Korean Law*, 11, 179.

Way, P. O., De Lay, K. S., & Stanecki, K. (1994). *The impact of HIV/AIDS on world population* (Vol. 3). Washington, DC: US Department of Commerce, Economics and Statistics Administration, Bureau of the Census.

White, R. C., & Carr, R. (2005). Homosexuality and HIV/AIDS stigma in Jamaica. *Culture, Health & Sexuality*, 7(4), 347–359.

Whitehead, A. L., & Baker, J. O. (2012). Homosexuality, religion, and science: Moral authority and the persistence of negative attitudes. *Sociological Inquiry*, 82(4), 487–509.

Young, R. K., Gallaher, P., Belasco, J., Barr, A., & Webber, A. W. (1991). Changes in fear of AIDS and homophobia in a university population. *Journal of Applied Social Psychology*, 21(22), 1848–1858.

Chapter 17

You Are Entitled to a Strange and Wonderful Queer Future

Vanessa R. Panfil

According to 16-year-old me in 2002, 2:00 am on Sundays could not come fast enough.

That was when a basic cable station would rerun Jerry Springer episodes. My then-girlfriend and I would eagerly watch for gay or trans storylines and, as teens sometimes do, would make out afterwards. I was so pissed the week when the switch to daylight savings time completely evaporated the time slot, and I was left with nothing. These stories were, as can be imagined, often lurid and sensationalized. A man admits to cheating on his girlfriend, and a flamboyant gay man is revealed to be his lover. A woman tells her boyfriend that she is willing to give him the threesome he so desperately desires, but he's angry when her partner of choice is a butch lesbian. A woman wants to confess to her new boyfriend that she was "born a man," after which he insists on fighting her "like a man." I don't know at what point the show introduced this, but after any bombshell disclosures, the show started ringing a boxing bell, as if to tell the guests that it was time to fight out their conflict, or perhaps more accurately, to assault the person who had allegedly wronged or embarrassed them.

The next year, in 2003, I remember watching at least one episode of Maury that featured trans folks on it, mostly trans men, who told their stories. Yes, there were lots of invasive questions about their bodies and physically transitioning. In 2004, I actually started holding small watch parties for the episodes of Maury where he paraded a dozen or so beautiful women onstage, and it was the audience's job to determine whether each woman was really a woman. Some of these women were assigned female at birth, some were drag queens, and once in a while, there were transgender women on the show, although I don't remember the show talking intelligently about their experiences or using the word transgender. Instead, I remember the host asking some women to acknowledge that they were really a man and the women being resistant to that framing.

These were spectacles that were, without a doubt, fucked up. Inviting commentary on and intimate questions about Queer and trans bodies. Stoking deception narratives. Encouraging and supporting violence. And I ate it up! The thought of it now makes me cringe. Oh, to be young and dumb, desperate for LGBTQ+ representation, and thrilled with whatever scraps we could get.

It's not as though I was totally deprived of Queer connection. My high school was nick-named "Fort Gays," and I had dated several girls there. I had attended an "Other Prom" (for LGBTQ+ teens) even before the U.S. Supreme Court struck down all remaining sodomy laws in Lawrence v. Texas. There was an active GLSEN chapter in the area and a drop-in LGBTQ+ youth center a few miles away. My local library had books about LGBTQ+ people, the gay rights movement, and kink culture, all of which I devoured. I had seen plenty of

DOI: 10.4324/9781003400981-20

LGBTQ-themed movies and *But I'm a Cheerleader* was my favorite. (It still is.) But perhaps I wanted to see real (or plausibly real) LGBTQ+ adults, even if the audience was supposed to believe they were leading seemingly strange lives. Real LGBTQ+ adults who, frankly, didn't die young. It's a recurring joke about Queer movies that it's a good one if no one dies or gets arrested at the end. A low bar indeed. And of course, some movies that feature gay, lesbian, bisexual, or transgender characters, like *Gia* and *Boys Don't Cry*, were based on the stories of actual people who experienced extreme physical and sexual violence and met tragic ends. There are scenes from those movies that teenage me did not know how to process and which still play over and over in my head when I'm upset or cannot sleep. And yet, I was still so desperate to consume more, even if it meant a troubling narrative, a shameful lure of guaranteed gawking, and even depictions of violence. I didn't understand the full range of gender expression that was available to me, so I kept seeking. Accessing as many diverse representations of Queer and trans people as I could helped me work through my understanding of my own gender. Truth be told, I am still learning about and exploring how I want to express myself. As a young person, I wanted to belong, even if it meant being part of a spectacle. Even if it meant accepting risk because other people are unreasonable.

I've since learned that I'm not the only one who has sought out highly problematic portrayals just to feel like they were represented. I wanted to see real LGBTQ+ adults, but did I think I was looking into the future? Is that what visibility entailed? Above all, I just wanted a future, even if it was strange. Because to me, even a strange Queer future would be a wonderful one.

The future is actually uncertain for many LGBTQ+ people—or at least, they perceive it to be, and understandably so. In just the last few months, I've heard many instances of this kind of reflection. A trans professor explained her transition and said that she didn't know when she became afraid, but that she was afraid that terrible things would happen to her if she came out, but that her fear was also a wish for someone to notice that she wasn't actually a boy. A Black trans social worker and activist remarked that at 45, she's essentially living on borrowed time, referencing the lower life expectancy for Black trans women. A gay male professor recalled being a teen and not wanting to die of the unusual new cancer plaguing and killing gay men during what became known as the AIDS crisis. A twitter thread delved into how transitioning affects perceptions of time and aging, beyond just making it to being alive in your thirties. Being a potential victim of violence, whether interpersonal or structural, looms large.

It doesn't help that our culture stokes this violence and incites it—the boxing bell encouragement to attack LGBTQ+ people seems to ring in many situations. In my life I have felt fear during incidents where I thought someone else was going to harm me for being Queer or gender nonconforming, where I thought the bell was going to ring for me.

In 2004 when my then-girlfriend and I chose to go to the pumpkin festival in a rural area 45 minutes from my big-city hometown—one that a mentor had referred to as "a hate crime waiting to happen"—was the bell going to ring for me then?

In 2011 when a man aggressively called me a faggot about a block from my apartment, was the bell going to ring for me then? Or maybe that slur was directed at the man walking directly in front of me, but I couldn't be sure—was the bell going to ring for him instead?

In 2015 when a 40-something woman was giving me and my then-girlfriend the death stare on the subway and I asked, looking directly in her face, if I could help her, was the bell going to ring for me then?

In 2017 when a man and his adult son were making jokes at my nonbinary partner's expense outside of a movie theater bathroom and I asked them to stop, and he yelled at me, was the bell going to ring for me then? So as not to escalate the conflict further, my partner and I waited for them to leave the building first. I then spotted a large gun rack on the back of their truck. Was the bell going to ring for us then?

In case it wasn't clear, I am very visibly Queer. It has never appealed to me, in any systematic way, to become less visible to preserve my safety. In the moment, perhaps, but never as a life strategy. While it's not my goal to be a straight person's spectacle, I don't concern myself with whether they will look.

I can think of only one time in my adult life where I was truly shaken from wanting to show out as Queer in public, and it was directly after the Pulse shooting. I tried to take my mind off it that day by going out with a Queer friend for lunch. It was probably the only time ever that I didn't want to eat pepperoni pizza and drink beer. I remember being extremely shaken for days. I had to cancel some work meetings that week. I could not concentrate. I was living several states away from my partner and felt immense sadness and anxiety. My chest feels heavy just thinking about it. In fact, I have avoided looking at this essay because the Pulse anniversary just passed.

Young and dumb me even used to muse that given the choice, I wouldn't have chosen to be gay and genderqueer. I wouldn't have chosen to be a target. I wouldn't have chosen to face those hardships. What the fuck? Why should my identity be predicated on the prejudices and violence of others? Current me thinks this line of thinking is absurd. Even on the anniversary of Pulse.

The work I do also sometimes explores victimization of LGBTQ+ youth and adults. It's not what I focus on overall, but it comes up often, and is an integral part of their experience moving through the world, whether strategically trying to avoid violence, fighting back in the moment, or dealing with the aftermath when violence happens to them. Unsurprisingly, hearing about LGBTQ+ people's victimization comprises my least favorite parts of my job. It can be so terrifying and disturbing to be let into some of the worst moments of someone's life—and of course this person had to endure what they are telling you about. You can't help but wonder if it could have been you. Once, when listening to a young African American lesbian describe being targeted and beaten by several men for her sexuality and her masculine gender presentation, my nostrils and sinuses started burning. It's the closest I've ever been to crying during an interview. (I insisted to myself, it is not a teenager's job to manage your emotions, now pull yourself together.) Of course, it's wrong to only focus on risk. It's inappropriate to make it seem as though LGBTQ+ people—transgender people especially—have no futures: "Unlivable lives," in the words of one social scientist who critiqued the overwhelming focus on risk, violence, and death. We should also be talking about trans resilience, trans accomplishments, trans everyday life, trans joy. Queer potential, Queer aspirations, Queer possibilities, Queer futures.

It would be nice to talk through some feelings with someone, I think to myself. I have been thinking of going to therapy. Two years ago, I mentioned this to a friend. I said maybe I should wait until I really needed it.

She told me that sometimes when rescuers find lost hikers who have died of exposure and dehydration, they find them with a full water bottle. The distressed hikers were saving it and saving it to prolong their life, to sustain them until being found, and got to the point where they were so dehydrated that they hallucinated or passed out, and then they couldn't even draw on the water they had stockpiled to save them.

It's a haunting metaphor.

My partner asks me, every once in a while, if I want to call the psychiatrist, just to get on their schedule because it'll be easier to get help quickly as a current patient than waiting until when I really do want to talk. Maybe this week, I say. Look, I wrote the phone number down on my list. Well, maybe next week, because I'm so busy. If I can just get through this week, I say.

I've been saying that for eight months.

Young and dumb me didn't have a grasp on transphobic and homophobic media representation. Young and dumb me just wanted to have a strange and wonderful Queer future.

Not so dumb after all.

And in fact, I do have that.

There are plenty of things that bring me joy. My cat's soft fur and extremely loud purr bring me joy. Celebrating accomplishments of the students I mentor brings me joy. Snacks and candies from all over the world bring me joy. Fireworks, roller coasters, Halloween. My handsome and charming partner looking immensely good in that T-shirt brings me joy. More than joy. Yeah, actually . . . I need a minute.

. . .

Telling stories of LGBTQ+ resistance and resilience—like building community and meeting their own goals for their lives—brings me joy. Any celebrating of Queer culture, celebrating LGBTQ+ lives, brings me joy. And as for that phone number, yes, I will call it. That will probably also help me manifest some joy.

Aging is a privilege when it should be a right. Do I belong? I'm not sure.

Am I meant for this world?

Absolutely.

Abstract:

Many of today's LGBTQ+ adults saw few positive media representations of LGBTQ+ people during their youth. Portrayals that existed often depicted LGBTQ+ people's victimization and even their deaths, leading many young LGBTQ+ people to doubt whether they would have a meaningful future. In this deeply personal essay, the author reflects on the Queer media representations she saw growing up, how these shaped her identity development and her concerns about being victimized, and her struggles with mental health and wellness as a Queer adult. Although discussing disheartening depictions and experiences, the author advocates for a holistic look at Queer and trans lives that also centers joy, possibilities, and futures, not just pain, loss, and the past. A postscript for the interested reader: since completing this essay, the author has taken significant steps to improve her well-being.

Index